Anacaona

The Amazing Adventures of Cuba's First All-Girl Dance Band

ANACAONA

*The Amazing Adventures of
Cuba's First All-Girl Dance Band*

Alicia Castro

as told to Ingrid Kummels and Manfred Schäfer

Translated by Steven T. Murray

Atlantic Books
London

First published in 2002 in Germany by Econ Verlag,
a subsidiary of Econ Ullstein List Verlag, GmbH & Co. KG, Munich

First published in Great Britain in hardback in 2007 by Atlantic Books,
an imprint of Grove Atlantic Limited.

Original Title © Ullstein Heyne List GmbH & Co.

Copyright © Ingrid Kummels 2002

Translation copyright © Steven T. Murray 2007

Photographs on pages 2, 19, 396 © Ingrid Kummels.
Photographs on pages 9, 390, 391 © Manfred Schäfer.
All other photographs are taken from the personal archives of Ingrid Kummels and Manfred Schäfer.

9 8 7 6 5 4 3 2 1

A CIP catalogue record for this book is available from the British Library.

ISBN 978 1 84354 242 1

Designed by Richard Marston
Printed in Great Britain by MPG Books Ltd, Bodmin, Cornwall

Atlantic Books
An imprint of Grove Atlantic Ltd
Ormond House
26–27 Boswell Street
London WC1N 3JZ

www.groveatlantic.co.uk

Contents

Anacaona, 1934

(from left) Back row: Emma, Bola, Ada, Flora, Ondina. Middle row: Cuchito, Cachita, Alicia.
Front row: Elsa Rigual, Millo

Ada, 1989

Chapter 1
Happy Hour

'Rum is a Cuban's life blood,' says my sister Ada, and she's right. Without rum, how would we cope with life – with the daily grind, with growing older? We three sisters, living here in our parents' house in Lawton, a district in Havana, have reached that happy age at which one may, indeed must, relax and enjoy life. Even skinny Ondina, who hardly eats anything (and at every meal acts as if we're just trying to tease her by giving her an especially large serving), pushes her glass over for a top-up. A little glass or two at lunch-time is a must.

I like my rum with a couple of ice cubes. I leave it just long enough to get nice and cold, then down it quickly before the ice melts in the midday heat and dilutes it. That would be a shame, even with the ordinary rum you can get anywhere now, after years when it was hard to come by. On almost every street there's a family selling it from big plastic containers. Only Ondina protests that it's not up to standard. 'I'll have a dry martini. And don't forget the olive,' she shouts to me in the kitchen. That's her way of bragging about the fact that she used to move in the best circles in Paris.

Ada, unlike Ondina, is not at all particular. Rum, as life, she takes as it comes – with ice or without; a double or, if rum is in short supply, with lime juice and sugar. 'This is as watery as the stuff those stingy Galicians used to serve up in their restaurants,' she complains. 'If you're going to dilute it like that, I'll have three.' She has never paid much attention to reason and moderation. She takes everything in good humour. After all, she's a child of the 1920s, the boom years when Cuba's economy soared and nobody had to worry about the future.

Lawton is the old tobacco workers' district. It's only a quarter of an hour by bus along the Calzada 10 de Octubre (the broad shopping street formerly known as Jesús del Monte) to the heart of Old Havana. From the hill nearby you get a fantastic view of the turquoise sea and the Malecón, the famous ocean-front promenade. The shining white dome of the Capitolio, the former seat of the government, rises up majestically above the weathered roofs and roof terraces of the surrounding buildings. The *aires libres* used to be directly opposite. These open-air cafés were the beating heart of Havana in the 1930s. It was there that my ten sisters and I caused a sensation with our Orquesta Anacaona.

The whole family – eleven sisters, two brothers – used to sit together here at the long mahogany table next to the wall decorated with porcelain plates in the high-ceilinged dining room of our Father and Mother's house. Ada, Ondina and I are the only ones still sitting here. I'm the youngest and I'm over eighty years old now. Ada teases me because I don't hear so well any more. But we all have our ailments: Ada is quite forgetful and Ondina can hardly see a thing because of her cataracts. Never mind – together we make a good team.

By the time I start mixing cocktails in the midday heat, Ada has already done the basic shopping. She sets out before nine with her large linen bag. At the bodega around the corner she buys the special daily ration of rolls and milk that Ondina receives on her ration card, just as children do, because she's underweight.

Ada is usually away for two or three hours. I worry about her being out and about so much – she's eighty-seven after all – but she doesn't let that stop her. She stands in line outside the bodega in her flimsy, loose-fitting dress and comfortable sneakers and passes the time chatting. She is known to be an expert on minor complaints, and is always being asked for advice. 'For a migraine, take three aspirins and dissolve them in camomile tea. And be sure to use genuine Spanish camomile,' she recommends. For loss of appetite she swears by a combination of camomile and penicillin. What she most wants to find out in return is: when will they be distributing the frozen fish? Has anyone seen the ice-cream truck? On what street? This kind of information has been vital ever since Fidel proclaimed the Special Period in Time of Peace after the collapse of the Eastern Bloc at the end of the 1980s, when Cuba suddenly had to fend for herself. Ever since then people have joined forces with their neighbours. Sometimes it's Ada who fetches the bread rations for her neighbours. At other times her friends will return the favour and save her from standing in line for hours to buy sweet potatoes or plantains. Ration cards are passed from hand to hand as if in an endless game of canasta. Interestingly, Ada never forgets when it comes to food. Her stomach has a better memory than her brain.

We're only waiting for Ondina now, so we can clink glasses. She's always doing something around the house, which isn't surprising because ever since the workmen were here some rooms have been utterly devastated.

'We have to knock right through to the steel beams in the ceiling and replaster everything,' said the specialists, forcefully.

'Fine.' What else could I say? They then proceeded to tear down half of the ceiling in the living room, leaving huge piles of rubble behind them. That was months ago and we haven't seen hide nor hair of them since. Now, whenever it rains heavily, huge amounts of water leak into the house. Our beautiful house! But it still manages to look quite elegant, with its many rooms, the double French doors and the ornate ceilings.

Ondina took care to cover the upholstered rocking chairs in the living room with plastic sheeting and had the piano, made by R. Görs & Kallmann of Berlin, shoved into the middle of the room. At least there it can stay dry. She also put the big photograph of us in a safe place. Along with the collection of medals, trophies and pictures of award ceremonies, it had previously been displayed on the big sideboard, like an altar, framed with silk flowers. The large crystal chandelier was moved into the dining room at her command. Ondina can hardly see a thing – or so she claims – but she insists on being responsible for keeping the house clean and tidy. Buckets, bowls and basins cover the floor to catch the rain. When it pours, Ondina is endlessly scurrying back and forth, emptying and replacing the containers.

'*Ave María Purísima*,' I hear her sigh amid all the dripping.

Ondina has always been a little highly strung. I try to comfort her: 'It's still a while before the rainy season starts.' With the rainy season come the hurricanes, which will pound against the heavy shutters with a deafening racket. I hope the workmen show up before then.

When our morning chores arc complete, we have earned a break. I lean back in my rocking chair with a glass of cool rum and enjoy the fresh breeze coming through the open door to the courtyard. I gaze at the fragrant mango and cherimoya trees, and the tall, luxuriant palm trees. So why on earth does the doorbell have to ring now?

Ondina strides resolutely down the long hallway.

'Who's there?'

'Pardon me, my name is Gutiérrez. I'm a journalist and would like to interview you for an article about the all-female band Anacaona.'

'Gutiérrez? Never heard the name.' She inspects the stranger through the narrow bars of the viewing grille in the front door. 'And who sent you here? How do you know where we live?' Somehow the stranger eloquently succeeds in convincing Ondina that he is harmless. One by one she unlocks the three deadbolts. 'Come in, young man.'

So much for our cocktail hour. I tidy myself up while Ada hurries to help Ondina. They quickly remove the plastic sheeting from the rocking chair, and the journalist – a tall, very handsome man – sinks obediently into it. Ondina apologizes for the mess, complaining about the unreliable workmen, then rushes into the dining room and grabs the telephone. As she dials she sighs, '*Ave María Purísima*, I'm not even properly dressed.'

'Then you shouldn't have been in such a rush to get the door,' I tease her.

'Ziomara has to come over right away. I hope she's home,' she says, ignoring my gibe.

Our little sister Ziomara is used to telling our story to the press. She lives with her husband, Enrique, only two blocks away. Fifteen minutes later she steps into our living room, impeccably dressed, made-up and coiffed.

'Quiet please! Recording!' As the tape starts rolling, Ziomara begins.

'It was Cuchito, our second oldest sister, who had the idea of forming the all-women Orquesta Anacaona. That was in the early 1930s, when the dictator Machado was tyrannizing the people with a bloody fist. Gradually all eleven sisters joined the band; most of us were still minors at the time. George Gershwin, Cole Porter and Nat King Cole… all the great musicians who travelled to Cuba would come to our performances in the *aires libres*, the open-air cafés. That's how we were discovered.

'Do you want me to tell you how we girls from Lawton ended up on the Champs-Elysées in Paris? One day, when we were performing in one of the *aires libres*…'

As soon as Ziomara mentions the trip to Europe Ada can no longer keep quiet. '*Señor Reportero*, we travelled to France on a luxury liner. There was every imaginable variety of food on board – vast buffets with eight kinds of ham, beautifully arranged on silver platters. And the cheese! Never in my life had I seen so many different types of cheese…'

'For God's sake, Ada,' Ziomara interrupts her, 'do you really think that Señor Gutiérrez has nothing better to tell his readers than what we had to eat on the ocean liner?'

Ziomara resumes. 'When we started out at the open-air cafés, we were earning a mere pittance. In order to bring more money in for our family, I had to pitch in at the tender age of seven. I would go from table to table and offer the tourists, wealthy Americans, promotional postcards with our picture on it. Those were hard times indeed under the dictator…' And so she carries on for an hour and a half.

Postcard that Ziomara distributed in the aires libres

The reporter is barely out of the door before Ondina protests, 'Ziomara, why do you keep saying that? It's just not true. Nobody ever forced you to work at night in the *aires libres* when you were a child. It was only because you harped on and on so much that we finally brought you along with us and, since you were too small to play an instrument, we sent you around with the postcards.'

~ **Anacaona** ~

Ada, Alicia, Ziomara and Ondina

Ondina, Ziomara and Ada all start talking at once.

'That's not true!'

'Oh, yes, it is!'

'I should know, I was there!'

I leave them to argue among themselves, although I'm the one with the best memory, and may God and San Lázaro preserve it for a long time yet!

I would have told the reporter that, for me, there was nothing I enjoyed more than going every evening from humdrum Lawton to the vibrant nightlife of Old Havana; or that initially Father was dead against us performing in the open-air cafés, saying there was no way his daughters were going to work at night near the sleazy bars and brothels. I would also have mentioned that we stood our ground in the face of male chauvinists, who believed that a woman's place was in the home by the stove or working in a brothel. But unfortunately my sisters won't let me get a word in.

After cocktails and lunch, Ada and Ondina take their siesta. Ondina above all needs the break, because every other day – during the few hours that Lawton is supplied with running water – she gets up before seven and busies herself with our cistern. Everybody fills their tanks, tubs, bathtubs and buckets at the same time. Ondina takes this task especially seriously, ever since the incident a couple of years ago when the cistern suddenly ran dry. There wasn't a drop of water in the house. Our youngest brother worked out that our water had seeped back into the public mains through a defective valve. How Ondina had carried on! 'We ration ourselves, only for the neighbours to take showers day and night. . .'

Now, to prevent the precious water from running out unnoticed, Ondina has turned off all the pipes. She has to run a hose through the whole house each time she wants to fill the cistern. Every ten minutes she checks to see whether everything is in order, and she leans into the tank so far that only her narrow backside sticks up.

'One day she's going to fall in,' Ada jokes. 'And I'm not going to pull her out.'

Ondina has never been afraid of anything. As a child she would race so fast on roller skates along the paths in the park across the street that sparks would fly. And at thirteen she took to the stage. Her teacher Lázaro Herrera,

the great trumpet player, had talked her into it.
He recognized her talent immediately and
knew that she was ambitious, fearless and
self-confident all the qualities you need
to become one of the best. With only
three months of trumpet lessons
under her belt she walked on stage,
unflinching, to join the musicians of
the Septeto Nacional – then the most
successful *son* septet in Cuba – and
let rip. Without exaggeration, Ondina
was soon one of the best trumpet players
in Cuba.

Ondina

Since I have retired, the kitchen has become my domain. For breakfast I serve
café con leche and toast with Canadian salted butter. Our neighbour Alejandra
buys it for us in the dollar store on Calzada 10 de Octubre; anyone in Havana
can go in there now. We get hold of the currency in the exchange office,
when we have the means. It's astounding how many people pay with dollars
now, but many families get money sent regularly from relatives in the States.
These days you can even have greenbacks delivered to your door by messenger;
all you have to do is make a call. Or you can sell off your jewellery for dollars.
Who would have thought that those gifts from our admirers in our youth would
once again bring us such happiness all these years later?

While Ada is out tending to her transactions and Ondina is busy somewhere
in the house, I sit down at the kitchen table, spread out a white sheet and sort

Alicia

rice. The grains to the left and the pebbles to the right. Then I fry onions and garlic in plenty of oil and add the beans I've had soaking since the day before. Later I add a dash of vinegar, ground oregano and a bay leaf and let it simmer until the cocktail hour. Meanwhile, I rummage through the little chest in the dining room where we keep the sheet music. Cuchito transcribed many pieces of music by hand; as our director she was always on the lookout for the newest arrangements. Whenever a musician came back from New York, we would literally assault them. Bringing back the latest tunes from the clubs on Broadway was a point of honour. The little chest with its treasure trove of musical inspirations accompanied us everywhere, from Broadway almost as far as Tierra del Fuego, to Lake Maracaibo in Venezuela, to the Copacabana in Rio and into the snowy mountains of Chile. Just looking at the yellowing pages is enough for me to hear the music again.

After lunch, while my sisters are relaxing, I take out one of the songs. Playing the clarinet or the saxophone, I let the spirit of the music move me. I like playing in the dining room best; there's always a little breeze blowing through the courtyard door. The palm trees outside are my audience. 'Siboney', my favourite piece, was written by Ernesto Lecuona. In my opinion he is the best composer

12

Cuba has given to the world. We worked with the maestro many times, performing in his show for months on end. All artists dream that their work will move people, perhaps for all time, and beyond all boundaries. And I am sure the tunes that popped into Ernesto's head on evenings when he was in love, or feeling melancholy or cheerful, will continue to resound long after his death. I'm the only one of us sisters who still practises regularly. When Ada retired, she gave in to the pleading of younger musicians and sold all her instruments. 'I've been making music for more than fifty years; now I'll give the younger generation a chance,' she said. Ondina gave away her trumpet when Lázaro begged her to help get one of his pupils out of a scrape.

Millo

But there are still plenty of instruments left in the house to be able to have a jam session. Just a few days ago there was a knock at the door. Ondina hurried to get it and let out a yell when she saw Frank Emilio Flynn and his wife standing there. 'We just thought we'd look in on you *muchachas* from Anacaona.' That's what he always says... They live just a few blocks away. We're always happy when Frank visits. He's blind, but refuses to let that stop him, and even today he is *the* greatest jazz pianist in Cuba.

I went straight to the kitchen and fixed him a mango juice with plenty of ice, because Frank doesn't drink alcohol. Before he could even sit down, Ondina simpered, 'Frank, play something for us. I haven't heard you play in so long.' She can be extremely charming.

'Hang on, Ondina. Let him catch his breath.'

It was no use. 'If you don't want to go in the living room, no problem, I'll push the piano in here.' Frank Emilio laughed out loud. He knows that Ondina weighs seventy pounds at most and can barely push a chair, let alone a piano. We all gave in and went into the living room.

As soon as Frank sat down he coaxed perfect melodies from that out-of-tune instrument, as only a great master can. Luckily he couldn't see the pails and bowls placed all over the house. And Ondina? Instead of sitting still and listening, she hurried to the telephone and dialled various numbers until she got Pedrito Soroa on the line, one of our musician friends who was a member of the Orquesta Riverside. Half an hour later he and his brother were at the front door, with their conga drums piled high on a wheelbarrow.

Frank Emilio gave his all to one piece after another: bolero, *son* and jazz. Pedrito and his brother played the drums. At last Ondina

Yolanda

was happy. She ran a wooden spoon up and down a potato grater to accompany the improvisations. All at once it was like the old days: passers-by, parents, children and lovers stopped on the street and peered in at us through the wide-open French doors, as if looking across all the decades we had practised and played in that living room. And so many of those times were with Frank Emilio. Even though he's almost eighty, he still flies to Europe each year and fills huge concert halls in Germany and France. Thinking about the moments of recognition when applause warms the soul makes me a little wistful. That's what we musicians live for: those flashes of total joy.

Every now and then we're invited to award ceremonies, because our Orquesta Anacaona, which played together for more than five decades, was declared part of the 'cultural heritage of Cuba' in 1989. I appreciate the honour, but now I find it too exhausting to travel to Old Havana just to be lauded. Small tributes please me so much more. Recently, Virulo, a popular comedian here, appeared on a TV show. In one sketch he impersonated a singer trying to impress a night-club owner with the words, 'You won't find anyone better. After all, I began my career as a girl singer with Anacaona!' That made me smile. . .

The next morning people kept asking Ada about it as she stood in line at the bodega. And it's true, many big stars started out with us, or accompanied us on tour: Celia Cruz, Omara Portuondo and Graciela Pérez.

The young musicians who played with us at the end of our career continue nowadays with new colleagues, still using the name Anacaona – that was their fervent wish. When our successors, the 'new' Anacaonas, performed not so long ago on Cuban TV, Ondina was quite beside herself.

'Just look at them! They're running around half-naked in shorts, skin-tight

Anacaona in the Havana-Madrid Club on Broadway, New York

leotards and dresses with necklines almost down to their navels,' she commented indignantly. 'I thought it was about playing music!'

'Ondina, times have changed,' I said, trying to mollify her. 'On TV, all the soap operas show lovers lying in bed, stripped to their skin. And young women standing at the bus stop these days look like they just stepped out of the shower. But let's be honest, even we started our career with a scandal.'

In the 1930s, *son* was regarded in Havana's better circles as the vulgar music of the common people. Music for blacks. And certainly only played by men. When, all of a sudden, we young girls began playing these electrifying songs, with their suggestive lyrics, it shocked many an upright citizen.

Even though many of us are now single, or were only married for a short time, we have never lacked for charming companions, even today. It's a blessing that we've been able to count such excellent musicians and wonderful people as our friends all these years. I'm thinking of Lázaro Herrera in particular: the legendary trumpeter visited us every month until only a year ago. Even at the age of ninety-six he would still take the bus, and walk in the midday heat from the bus stop on the Calzada to our house, and back again after a few cocktails and a couple of hours of telling stories. Unfortunately he hasn't been well lately and has had to take to his bed. An interview with him was broadcast on television recently. His mind was still quite lucid, but the words wouldn't come out the way he wanted them to. We who were familiar with him and his incredible experiences knew he had so much he wanted to say – he just wasn't up to it any more.

That made me think. A short time later our niece Ingrid showed up and started pestering me with questions, and it seemed to me like a stroke of fate. Ingrid's mother, Millo, was once the star of the orchestra. She played percussion,

Ada and Lázaro Herrera, 1991

conga and bongos, and she was my favourite sister. We told each other everything and even shared our jewellery. She left the band in 1953, when she got married, and they later moved to live in Germany, but she visited us whenever she could. Millo came to Havana for the last time in 1981, when she was very ill. Three days later we carried her to her grave. After that, Ingrid came to Cuba more and more often. I made sure she knew what an exceptional percussionist Millo had been. And the more I told her, the more she wanted to know.

We would often retreat to one of the rooms upstairs, where no one could bother us. My sisters have a habit of interrupting constantly and they like to think they know best, but upstairs with Ingrid, away from them, I sometimes felt as if

I were confessing to a priest, even though I have never been to confession in my life. And I know why, too: it's not pleasant to stir up painful memories. Some things are better left undisturbed. Everyone has their secrets, large and small. If I don't speak candidly now, how will anyone understand what we did and why we did it? After confession, all is forgiven and forgotten. But I don't want everything my sisters and I experienced to vanish with us. That's why I want to tell our story. I want to talk about how we moved back and forth between simple living and luxury, between moments of heady success and times when it felt impossible to go on. About our daily lives and how each of us had to find her own way, on her own, without any fuss, and prove her mettle. After those long conversations my niece and I always treated ourselves to a glass of rum: Havana Club, the seven-year-old king of rums. You drink it neat. Without ice, lukewarm in the palm.

Chapter 2

Our Family – an *Ajiaco* with Many Ingredients

'How come you sisters look so unusual, like *mulattas* with a touch of Indian blood?' I am often asked. We Cubans pay close attention to skin colours and try to arrange them on a finely graded scale from white to black. My sisters and I stand out because we have a bronze skin tone. *Café con leche*, some say. Others describe it as *apiñonada* – light brown like pine nuts. To top it off we have long, straight, dark hair and slightly almond-shaped eyes. We're living proof of the fact that blood from every part of the world runs in Cuban veins. That's why we like to say, 'We Cubans are an *ajiaco*.'

Ajiaco is the festive dish served up on Christmas Day. We used to keep a piglet in the back yard, and we would feed it scraps in the preceding months; then at Christmas-time we'd slaughter it. On the twenty-fourth we had a fine roast, and on the twenty-fifth an *ajiaco* was prepared from the head and the leftover meat. Truly delicious. To the meat we would add corn, white and yellow malanga, plantains, manioc, squash and sweet potatoes. The base is the *sofrito*, a sauce of olive oil, garlic and green pepper in which the ingredients are sautéed. The trick is to have each ingredient retain its characteristic flavour and yet develop something new in combination. That's why the comparison is apt. We Cubans are not merely the descendants of white Spaniards and black Africans. We're made up of just as many ingredients as a good *ajiaco*.

Alicia, 1989

Our family is an especially rich recipie. On our father's side we have Chinese grandparents and on our mother's side a Basque grandfather. There may have been Africans involved as well, but no one knows for sure. In some of our old family photographs, the faces of certain individuals have been carefully clipped out; I assume someone was embarrassed that we might have had African ancestors. A few of us turned out somewhat dark-skinned, like our sister Yolanda, but Mother would always insist it was because we had Indian ancestors in the family too.

Father's parents' surname was Cuang-Lee. They were poor farm workers from the south of China. In the mid-nineteenth century, when Cuba became the biggest sugar producer in the world, tens of thousands of Chinese were recruited and shipped out. 'You'll make a lot of money. You'll be rich when you return to your homeland.' This promise lured our grandparents here from the other side of the world. The plantation owners and sugar barons came up with the idea of using Chinese rather than black workers after the blacks successfully organized a rebellion on our neighbouring island of Haiti. However, the Chinese were not used to the back-breaking work they faced in the sugar-cane fields. And to make things worse, their white masters had them whipped by black overseers for the slightest misdemeanour. Many Chinese could not stand being publicly debased time and again for no reason, and took their own lives. I had to read about all of this in a book because Father never mentioned it. He probably wanted to spare himself – and us – the memories of the humiliation his parents had endured.

Nevertheless I did find out something about Father's childhood. He was born in 1884, when his parents were living on a haçienda in Guanajay, not far from Havana. They christened their son Matías. Soon afterwards, slavery was abolished in Cuba, but Father still grew up like a slave. His half-brother Bernardo told me about it: 'Matías had a very hard life as a child. By the time he was four he had to help his parents in the fields. He led oxen by a rope tied through their nose rings, while his father ploughed the earth for planting.' Officially the family was 'free', but they did not have the means to leave the haçienda. Father's parents were deeply in debt to the owner, one Señor Castro. Their wages were only just enough to buy food, and on pay day they had to incur new debts to be able to purchase even the most basic necessities in the haçienda's store.

Father always told us that he took his new surname from this Señor Castro, but there is a persistent rumour in the family that he actually lost his Chinese surname in a card game. I suspect Father might once have been a bit of a gambler because, although in general he was never strict with us, he always categorically forbade us from betting. The only exception he made was for the state lottery. Every week he played with a few centavos in the hope he would be able to travel to the land of his forefathers on the winnings. It remained a dream.

We never found out exactly why Father hated gambling so much. The Chinese were known for being keen gamblers. They loved mah-jong, a game played with pieces resembling dominoes. The *charada*, the Chinese lottery, was also extraordinarily popular among whites and *mulattos* alike. There were thirty-six numbers, each corresponding to a Chinese symbol. Number one was a horse, number two a butterfly, number three a sailor, number four a cat... People would play the numbers according to their dreams. 'I dreamed that I was in the cemetery' – that meant the number fourteen. If a nun appeared in your dream, you would bet on number five.

Particularly big prizes were promised in illegal *charadas* organized by rich Chinese who had come to Cuba from California. They used these games to hoodwink their own people. The Cuban Chinese were considered to be extremely gullible, hence the saying 'Someone has cheated you like a Chinaman.' Even today the *charada* is a great passion for many Cubans. It's still forbidden, but one of my neighbours told me that many people play in secret, adapting their game by betting on numbers in the Venezuelan lottery; on Saturday nights they tune in to the Venezuelan radio station to hear the results.

Father grew up in somewhat confusing family circumstances. His parents separated when he was still small; they were forced to do so because Señor Castro sent each of his workers to wherever he needed them most. And so Matías ended up with a foster mother named Toya, a black woman '*de nación*', which means that she was born in Africa and had been brought to Cuba as a slave. She raised little Matías and, naturally, he became very fond of her – she was like a mother to him. All his life he spoke of her with tenderness and affection. He had very little contact with his real father, who was said to be a true *regadera*, a 'watering can'. He apparently wasn't satisfied with just one woman, and Matías had a whole bunch of half-siblings as a result.

Young Matías resolutely saved his earnings and paid off his debts to Señor Castro. Then he moved to Havana, where he got himself a job in a cigar factory. But he had more in mind than simply earning money – the cigar factories were also known as the 'people's universities'. The workers sat close together at long rows of tables, as if in a giant classroom. On a rostrum at the front stood a lector, reading aloud from the daily newspapers, political books or novels in a deep, measured voice, while the workers quietly rolled the tobacco leaves. This special type of education was a privilege for which the workers had fought hard over many years. As a result, Matías and his colleagues were politically well-informed, and were regarded as the 'professors' of the working classes. In those days my father was very much into Marx and Engels and the idea of a society in which all people are equal and are paid equally for their work. But the nineteenth-century novel *Cecilia Valdés* also impressed him. It tells the story of a seductive and stunningly beautiful *mulatta* and her lover, a white law student. Mindful of his social standing, the student abandons Cecilia to marry a white woman – but the *mulatta* gets her revenge in the end.

Matías lived on Calzada de Zanja in El Barrio Chino, the Chinese quarter and the most cosmopolitan area of Havana. The pavements were crowded with Americans and Europeans in elegant suits, Spaniards with embroidered white shirts, *mulattos* and blacks in simple trousers, the women in white dresses with bell-shaped skirts. And among them all mingled the Chinese in their unmistakable blue cotton outfits and sandals, many of them wearing wide, conical straw hats. The Chinese shops lured passers-by with goods that Matías had heard of but never seen before: jade Buddha statues, chests filled with packets of unusual teas, boxes of fireworks and exquisite fine porcelain. From the ceiling hung embroidered silk pyjamas, giant paper butterflies and the pagoda-shaped lamps which no Chinese restaurant could be without. Matías was particularly taken with the theatres – there were two on Calzada de Zanja alone – and by the artists, who were also enchanted by the exotic flair of the quarter.

Matías

But Matías was most attracted to the many musicians who lived in El Barrio Chino. In the store around the corner he got to know a tall, slim man with blond hair in a crew cut. Carlos Alberto Zaldarriaga was a typical Basque, but when it came to music, he was a real Cuban. He played cello, bass and piano and was a superbly gifted interpreter of the *danzón*. He had been a member of the legendary orchestra of Miguel Faílde, the master tailor from Matanzas who invented the *danzón*. The unique thing about his style of music was the way it incorporated classical melodies such as French chamber music or Beethoven's 'Moonlight Sonata' into popular tunes. This inspired dancers to move in a loose embrace, maintaining a genteel distance while also executing lively and coquettish steps. That was something entirely new. Musicians particularly loved the *danzón* because it allowed them to show off their versatility as well as their expert musicianship.

Concepción

Carlos Alberto soon invited Matías to his place for an evening with friends and bohemians. While he was there Matías was struck by Carlos Alberto's daughter Concepción. She had just turned fourteen and was very shy, but seemed amused by Matías's politeness and good manners. Soon afterwards he began courting her in earnest, a campaign that was overshadowed by the serious illness of Concepción's mother, Caridad García, who suffered from tuberculosis. One day, she called Matías to her sickbed. 'Don't abandon my daughter,' she pleaded. 'Concha is still so young. Please marry her.' A short time later Caridad García closed her eyes for ever. She was only thirty-three years old.

Matías fulfilled his promise. On the day before Christmas Eve 1904, he and

The family on Calle Gervasio, 1921: Alicia on her mother's lap

Concepción were married. The newlyweds moved into a large house on Calle Gervasio, between Reina and Estrella, near the Iglesia de la Reina, which they rented from Antonino Rojas, an architect friend of theirs. They in turn rented out a few rooms and gradually saved up enough money to open a store in the Barrio Chino. In addition to groceries, Father sold snacks. He would marinate swordfish in lime, garlic and ginger, and deep-fry it. With this he offered hot, steaming yuca smothered in bitter orange juice and garlic, with chopped onions, parsley and a dash of olive oil. These delicacies attracted a good business and the Spanish grocery store across the street remained almost deserted. Gradually

Father expanded his wares to include wines from France, Italy and Spain, spicy chorizo sausages, pork ribs, shoulder of ham, stockfish and *tasajo*, a type of beef jerky. He even set up a little bar in the corner with the requisite large mirrors on the walls all around. People would meet here for a drink on weekdays; and on weekends, after the dances, the crowd of drinkers would be so big that people hardly had room to shop. Business was booming, although of course Father had his setbacks when customers signed for goods on credit and never showed up again or when friends took advantage of him.

Father may have been a businessman, but his heart belonged to music. He was eager for his wife – who was really still no more than a girl – to learn to play an instrument. Concepción and her older sister Pepa sang romantic songs in duet, but just for themselves and for friends. Matías convinced them to take piano lessons, but by the time Concepción reached the age of sixteen, when she started having children, she gave up music, saying, 'The piano is not for me. My destiny is to raise a family.' She could have been a great musician, but the children were arriving in rapid succession: Cachita in 1905, Cuchito in 1907, Emma in 1909, Otto in 1911, Ada in 1913, Flora in 1914, Bola in 1916 and Ondina in 1917. In 1920 I was added to the list. After me came Millo in 1922, Ziomara in 1925, Yolanda in 1929 and finally Lenin in 1931. Even before I came into the world, Father had taken his two eldest daughters, Cachita and Cuchito, to the district music school of Havana and enrolled them both for piano lessons. In that distinguished building, Cachita and Cuchito studied the method of Fernando Carnicer, a Spanish composer who taught there.

It was never Father's intention to form a band. All he wanted was to make music at home, to entertain family and friends and make everyday life more enjoyable. To him art should not be treated as a luxury; it should be the focal point of life. It was a time of prosperity and expectations were high. The streets were paved with gold, because the world needed sugar and Cuba produced it in abundance. The First World War had sent prices soaring sky-high. Father was doing good business and was particularly pleased that culture was also flourishing on the basis of this new wealth. Operas, theatres, orchestras – all the top-flight artists of the world gathered in Havana to perform. Money was no object; the best bel canto singers, even Caruso, came to Cuba because the Teatro Nacional could offer higher fees than La Scala in Milan.

The price of tickets to the Teatro Nacional was correspondingly high and my parents could not afford them, so they often went to the Shanghai, the Chinese theatre on Zanja. The Havanan Chinese also invested heavily in the arts and opened six theatres. They invited many artists to come from Hong Kong, San Francisco and New York. Mother later told me about the opulent Chinese operas that she loved so much, admitting that, although she never really understood the mysterious plots, the booming vibrations of the huge cymbals and kettledrums, the chime of the lone gong, and the bright sound of the wooden cornets always transported her instantly to the realm of the Chinese mandarins and all their incomprehensible power struggles. The singers took to the stage in long satin robes decorated with curious patterns, while women with carefully coiffed hair gesticulated wildly. A huge dragon with a golden mask would also often appear, along with tigers that danced around it in a circle. The effect of these productions was exotic, dramatic, electrifying – and my mother adored every minute.

My parents found great fulfilment in cultural life and wanted their children to have the best possible schooling so they, too, could enjoy the same opportunities. That wasn't easy; a private school would have been far too expensive with so many offspring. The obvious solution was therefore to send us to the school of the Sociedad de Pilar, a convent where the *Señoras de las Luces* – the 'Ladies of the Lights' – taught classes free of charge. You could barely make out their faces through their veils. Father had no time for Catholicism, but he respected these nuns because they attracted us kids like magnets, giving us sweets and teaching us songs. As soon as each of us was old enough, they would come to the house and ask Mother, 'Give us Ada, give us Flora, give us Bola for the school…' So we all went to the convent, with its huge classrooms with thick stone walls and ceilings so high that we pupils could easily feel small and lost. In the afternoons my elder sisters went to catechism in preparation for their first communion. Years later, when it was my turn, I was the first to rebel. 'What on earth am I supposed to confess? I haven't committed any sins yet.' I knew the priest would have either reproached me for not confessing truthfully or not believed the sins I made up, so I simply didn't go. It just wasn't for me.

Much later I learned from Cuchito that the nuns had even arranged for a church wedding for our parents. One day the Sisters showed up at the house and warned them that, if they wanted their children to remain in the convent school, Mother and Father would have to have a church wedding. Our parents had only had their marriage recorded by a notary, which was the normal procedure. 'Get married in church? We already have as many kids as pipes on an organ!' my father protested. But the nuns refused to let up, and so one Sunday Father and Mother, with all us kids in tow, went to the Iglesia de la Caridad, where the priest married them 'in the eye of the Lord'. Soon afterwards Father complained, 'These nuns have put one over on me!' I wanted to ask what he meant, but all I ever heard from him was, 'Girl, don't you ever forget to go to mass!' As for him, he never set foot in a church again.

Father's religion was Communism. At first he was enthusiastic about Otto von Bismarck, whose single-mindedness and far-sighted foreign policy impressed him enough to name his first son Otto. Then he turned to the teachings of Marx and Engels. Later still he greatly admired Vladimir Lenin, so much so that he named his second son Lenin after him. It was a rather prophetic move; three decades later, under Fidel, our little brother Lenin Castro would enjoy a successful career as an engineer. His name can't have hurt his chances in the new political landscape. Father kept up with current events and bought at least two newspapers every day of his life. He also acquired a Spanish encyclopedia for a hefty sum.

My parents worked hard so that we could enjoy such cultural privileges as music lessons. Mother's older sister Pepa, on the other hand, lived quite comfortably. She had made an excellent match, marrying Julián del Cueto. He was a captain and veterinarian in the military, and his father, José Antolín del Cueto, had been a *Mambí* – that is, he had joined in the struggle of the black plantation workers against the colonial rule of the Spaniards. The situation led to war with Spain. By the time it ended in 1898 with Cuba's independence, José Antolín del Cueto had become one of the rebel leaders and he was richly rewarded. Later they even made him president of the University of Havana. Then one day he married his maid, Flora. People were scandalized – a university president and a maid! A black woman at that! But he did not care, because he loved her above all else. He named one of his extensive properties in the country outside Havana 'La Florita' in her honour. He even had a chapel built there, and decorated it with valuable statues of saints. They had seventeen children, of whom only twelve survived. Almost all of them were sent to school in England, and eventually became doctors, lawyers and engineers. Some of the girls became nuns, a calling that only daughters of well-to-do households could afford to pursue. José was so rich that he was able to buy each of his children a farm. Julián was given a farm with mango, avocado, zapote, mamey, anonna and cherimoya trees.

They always brought an abundance of fruit whenever they visited us, to the delight of us children.

Pepa and Julián had no children of their own, which was one reason they could afford to live a life of luxury. Pepa loved to move every two or three years, just so she could have a new house to decorate; her homes were always furnished in the latest style. She had my elder sisters come and assist her every time she moved. All day long they would help her pack and unpack. Julián was eccentric too, in his own way. He insisted on wearing only English fashions, and he loved to eat pies full of raisins and fruits that were exotic to us Cubans, such as apples, cherries and raspberries. He had brought these passions back with him from his time as a student in England.

Cuchito's friends from the Kuo Min Tang

Father, for his part, upheld Chinese tradition. He and my elder sisters joined the Kuo Min Tang society. There were a number of such societies in Havana, most of which admitted only genuine Chinese as members, but the Kuo Min Tang was not as strict, allowing people who, like Father, were of Chinese descent but had never mastered the language. The society also did a lot for culture; it was the only one that later had a brass band, and it also sponsored weekend dances. Young single girls were strictly chaperoned at the time – it was unthinkable for them to go alone to any of the usual public dances, but in the Kuo Min Tang the dance evenings came into the category of 'culture'. No wonder that Cachita, Cuchito and Emma soon became enthusiastic fans of Chinese culture! Every Saturday they enticed Father, Mother and the whole family to the dance hall. The tables and chairs, where mah-jong was usually played, were cleared away, and a band would set up and play under a huge portrait of Confucius. Couples would circle the dance floor while parents sat at the tables, watching, and young-sters sat on benches. Mother made sure that none of her daughters danced more than three times a night with the same boy. She didn't want others thinking she allowed her offspring too much freedom; the good reputation of our family was at stake. After the dance my parents would take us all to the Pacífico, the best Chinese restaurant in the *barrio*, or we would go to the Cantón.

Father chose Chinese men as godfathers for Ziomara and me. Ziomara's godfather, Luis Yong, whom everybody called Afún, was a real Chinese and spoke Spanish with a funny accent. He showed up for Ziomara's baptism with a huge bag of candy and a box full of rockets. That evening, he put on a huge fire-works display in front of our house, as is the Chinese custom. Ziomara had the loveliest christening of all of us.

Sometimes, however, Father cursed his heritage. Customers would come into his store, sit down at the counter, order a beer and something to eat, and yell, 'Well, *pasana?*' *Pasana* is derived from the Spanish word *paisano*, meaning 'fellow countryman', and people used it to make fun of the grammatical mistakes the Chinese often made. Frequently the Chinese had problems distinguishing between the masculine and feminine form in Spanish, and instead of *paisano* they would say *pasana*. Father hated it when someone called him *pasana* just because of the way he looked. After all, he spoke perfect Spanish – without an accent – and he took great pride in his attire, wearing elegant suits. But people would not give him credit for that and teased him by calling him a *figurín chino* – a Chinese dandy.

'They deal in drugs and they're all doped up with opium.' That's what everyone presumed about the Chinese. But the Spaniards were given just as hard a time. They were reviled as hopelessly stingy, with the Galicians the most hard-bitten skinflints of all. Of course, the Spaniards also aroused a lot of envy, since many of them owned grocery stores. However, a shop owner could not afford to be overly generous: if he let people buy on credit, sooner or later he would go broke.

During the boom years, the Chinese had begun to compete fiercely with the Spaniards. They joined together and purchased rice and beans in large quantities directly from abroad. These import businesses had the best connections with San Francisco, New York, Lima and China. Since they would divide up the bulk orders among themselves, the Chinese were able to sell goods cheaper than the Spaniards. For this reason, many people preferred to go to the Chinese stores.

The drugs and opium are another story. The boom years also brought many shady characters to Havana. Although we were no longer living in the Barrio Chino, my parents were horrified when they heard that some societies there were less interested in culture than in the quick money they could make in the drug, prostitution and gambling trades. People said Chee Kung Tong was such a society, and that's why the members of Kuo Min Tang had declared war on them. Whenever someone died during the shoot-outs between the two groups, the police would clamp down hard, smoking the bandits out and deporting them from the country. Nevertheless, the Chinese never succeeded in shaking off the reputation of being opium dealers.

New Year's Eve party in a club in Havana, 1924

Chapter 3
Sextet with a Black Blonde

Mother never told me about the calamitous events of 1920 until after
I was grown up; it distressed her so much all those years. My parents were still
living in the Chinese quarter when the price of sugar, which had climbed to dizzying heights in recent years, suddenly plummeted. Sugar factories were going
bankrupt one after another, and with them many banks also collapsed. Even the
Banco Asturiano was declared insolvent overnight. In one fell swoop, my parents
had to cope with the loss of their entire life savings. Even the tiny Spanish gold
coins that Mother had collected and put in the bank for safekeeping were gone;
she had intended to use them to pay for our education. Aunt Pepa later told
me, 'Your father wanted to take a rope and hang himself.' My parents had always
worked hard, but all of a sudden they didn't have a single centavo. We were
ruined.

It was at this time that their tenth child came into the world – and that
was me. The year 1920 divides us siblings into two camps of two different temperaments. Ada, whose childhood coincided with a period of prosperity, has
a decidedly cheerful nature. Even when times are hard she remains carefree
and gregarious. She's one of the lucky ones. The younger ones are more level-
headed. I for one learned quite early on that life doesn't hand anything to you
on a plate.

Ada aged twelve

But Father didn't give up. He borrowed money from Aunt Pepa and bought himself a cart. He pulled it through the streets selling fruit, with Cachita and Cuchito helping him. Besides fruit they offered fritters of all kinds – potato, sweet potato, cod… Father also made *tapones de botella*, a kind of spring roll with shrimp and lobster (which were cheaper than meat) and plenty of vegetables. People went crazy over them. After a while Father opened a fruit stand on Calle Reina and slowly worked his way back up again, driven by his concern that all his children should have good food to eat. 'It's better to spend money on food instead of saving and later having to buy expensive medicines,' was his motto. But when Ada came down with the flu and lay in bed with a fever, he immediately called a doctor to the house. 'No way are we going to give her some ridiculous household remedy or boil up some sort of concoction. Someone with medical qualifications has to come.' That was how I came to meet my first Frenchman, Dr Villiers, a stout gentleman, very amiable. I found this unusual, because whenever anyone

mentioned the French they commented on how reserved they were. Dr Villiers had all of us children line up as he took a bottle of tablets out of his leather case and, with a sweeping gesture, produced a bottle of cognac. One by one he put a tablet in our mouths and then gave us a spoonful of cognac with sugar. A very effective combination against the flu, he claimed.

Thanks to the fruit stand, Father was able to pull the family out of lean times quite rapidly. One morning he read in the paper that there were stalls and small shops for sale at the newly built Mercado Único. This market hall was a huge two-storey building that quickly became the favourite among the housewives. There they could find everything their hearts desired: fragrant baskets of mangoes and herbs, rows of brightly coloured, shimmering fish from the morning's catch, cage after cage of crowing roosters piled high to the ceiling. Father acquired a store in one corner of the Mercado Único, at the corner of San Gregorio and Estévez, and it soon became exceptionally popular. Why? Because he would put pulses such as black beans and chickpeas in containers to soak overnight, so that people wouldn't have to boil them for so long the next day. He also sold Biscay-style stockfish, along with dried meat and other delicacies such as smoked pork ribs. And he never missed a day's work. If there was no streetcar running due to a strike or bad weather, he would simply get up earlier and head down there on foot – even during hurricanes when palm trees were being snapped like match-sticks and it was dangerous to be out on the streets.

No sooner was Father's business up and running than he began cultivating friendships with influential people who were members of the Club Atenas, the club for distinguished *mulattos*. One of them was Félix Ayón. Also of Chinese heritage, he was a politician, and a very clever one at that. He ran for office in the city council, as a member of parliament, and later as a senator; and he always won. Well-heeled supporters financed his campaigns. He went far, and later even became an adviser to President Batista.

The architect Antonino Rojas kept pressing Father as his fortunes improved: 'Why don't you build yourself a house? You're spending seventy pesos every month on rent, yet you own that beautiful plot of land you won in the lottery.' Father had unexpectedly been presented with building land while he was still a cigar roller. In those days the tobacco factory raffled off plots of land in Lawton for their workers, back when it still had rural character, with small farms and wonderful gardens, and you could see the Chinese in their wide-brimmed hats cutting grass on their plots with a sickle. They also kept pigs and burned charcoal. Father actually won one of these raffles. Not that he was given the land outright; he merely had the right to acquire the lot at a good price. Many cigar rollers would erect simple wooden houses with rough wooden beams on the ceilings and large verandas. In this way, over the years, the 'tobacco workers' quarter' was built up.

Eventually, Father was persuaded. He commissioned Antonino to build a large house with sturdy walls. It seemed as if he wanted to build a fortress that would stand for ever, one which could be enjoyed by his grandchildren and his grandchildren's grandchilden. The plot was uneven, though, and first had to be levelled off with construction rubble. Truck after truck arrived. 'All this rubble is eating up my money,' Father moaned, as the project grew more and more expensive. The rough construction was not yet complete when he had to take out a

40

Matías's shop at the Mercado Único

mortgage, which hung over our family like the sword of Damocles. But when the house was finally finished, it was magnificent. Father named it 'Villa Concha' after our mother and had the name engraved in the wrought-iron garden gate. Beyond it, after crossing a small front yard, you reached the veranda, framed by two mighty pillars in the neo-Hellenic style which gives Havana its unique character. Father's initials, M.C., were set in a circle on the floor, in a mosaic of black and white stones.

The tall front door opened into the living room. The six ground-floor rooms were connected by a long hallway and had very high ceilings so the air could circulate. The walls and ceilings were elegantly plastered and extravagantly decorated with stucco, even in the bedrooms. English fixtures and fine pastel-coloured tiles were used in the bathroom. A priest came to bless the house when it was finished.

We moved in after the devastating hurricane of 1926, when I was six years old. We children had one large room on the second floor, and slept three to a bed in each of the three beds, which we managed easily because we were still small. Ziomara, offspring number eleven, was a baby and stayed downstairs with Mother. Otto had a room on the ground floor. Any overnight visitors slept in a hammock in the dining room. We quickly got used to our new home, and were even more excited about the beautiful expanse of park across the street. I spent every free minute over there in the labyrinth of trees, paths and stairways, consumed with my first passion: roller-skating. Ondina would go first and test out each path. Naturally, the sloping rain gutters next to the stairways had not been designed for children zooming down them on skates, but that's exactly what Ondina did. She was always looking for ways to make her skates go faster.

In the afternoons we younger sisters delighted in watching a very special performance when young men would come courting Cachita, Cuchito and Emma, who were twenty-one, nineteen and seventeen years old respectively. They needed sturdy shoes, those suitors, for almost every afternoon at the same time we would watch them strolling incessantly back and forth in front of the house. Which of our sisters was each man after? In time, we were able to set the clock by the sight of the parade of suitors. This persistence was the only way each of them could prove his serious intentions, only then would he dare tackle the next hurdle: ringing the doorbell and formally introducing himself. Father, Mother and the sister in question would discuss it, and if there were no objections, the suitor was admitted to the house. Our parents would allow him into the living room to have a chat with the focus of his affections, but only in the presence of others. I was often sent in as a chaperone for the sweethearts! Depending on how interesting or amusing the suitor was, two, three or more sisters would often sit around and listen. How we young brats loved our roles at these important meetings. There weren't many occasions when a child was taken so seriously. When it was my turn, I too had to meet my boyfriends in the company of one of the younger ones, Millo, Ziomara or Yolanda. They would want to prevent us from kissing. That's when I understood why my elder sisters had always been so mad at me.

The elder sisters helped Father and Mother as best they could, selling fruit or taking care of the younger kids. Cachita and Cuchito gave music lessons. The third eldest, Emma, learned typing and stenography and later worked in the Ten Cents, a department store. Child number four, Otto, helped Father at the store. Our parents attached great value to all of us learning a skilled profession. Flora became a seamstress, taught by one of our godmothers; Bola learned to do machine embroidery and repair shoes; Ada had also been taught embroidery by the nuns, and at thirteen she was taught hairdressing by a Señor Pérez. Father put up a glass sign on the house: INSTRUCTION IN MUSIC THEORY, SONG AND PIANO. EMBROIDERY, SEAMSTRESS AND HAIRDRESSING SERVICES OFFERED.

Cuchito chose her own path. 'Bourgeois society wants to force all us women into the same corset,' she protested, 'of staying at home, washing, cooking – not to mention bearing children.' By 1925 she had taken a place at the University of Havana, studying dentistry. That marked her as a complete outsider. '*Mujer que aprende latín no puede tener buen fin*' – 'If a woman studies Latin, she'll come to a bad end,' was a riff she often heard. Her dream was to have her own dental practice, lead an independent life, perhaps even marry and have children later, but only if they didn't limit her too much. And this was in the days when people still looked askance at women who walked down the street alone. In Havana the mores were those of a small village: extremely prudish and rife with double standards. Men enjoyed the flair of city life without restrictions; many of them spent more time in certain houses on Calle Virtudes – the 'street of virtues' – than they did at home. There they could pursue affairs with their mistresses in an informal atmosphere, drinking with them and chatting in convivial groups. In the boom years, the wealth attracted not only the most famous artists, but also certain 'professional ladies' from Paris. Many of them were educated and were able to make a small fortune with their services in only a few years in Havana.

It was a time of radical change. Cuchito began her studies in the year that the handsome Julio Antonio Mella was stirring up the students with his rousing political speeches. He and his followers turned the university upside-down.

Cuchito

Numerous professors who had gained their positions through corruption were fired, and for the first time the working class were allowed to climb the wide steps up to that distinguished university, which stands majestically high on a hill. Mella then joined forces with a tobacco worker, Carlos Baliño, and founded the Communist Party.

The university was Cuchito's world. I think that dentistry was less fascinating to her than the opportunity to be among like-minded people, people who enjoyed the same books, the same music, and shared the same vision. In the evening she was always in a hurry to get out of the house.

My elder sisters took the opportunity to chat with her fellow students while they waited for her on the veranda. The students would complain that since the stock-market crash, Cuba was dependent for better or worse on the financial interests of the United States. And they told my sisters about the *Minoristas*, a group of writers and artists who believed that only by focusing on our own Cuban culture could our country be saved from the Depression. Even in everyday life it was important to shake off the dictates of the United States. They thought it ridiculous that people in Havana who considered themselves to be cut above the rest bought their produce not in Cuban bodegas, but at American grocery stores, and preferred canned American pears to fresh, sweet Cuban mangoes.

Sometimes Cuchito brought along her friend Isolina Carrillo, who, like Cuchito, believed that music was the key to the roots of Cuban culture and lifestyle. They took music lessons together with other fellow students; Cuchito studied guitar, Isolina the piano, and others learned the mandolin. Those were the most popular instruments among women. Isolina became a superb pianist and later composed the wonderful romantic bolero '*Dos Gardenias Para Tí*', which is once again on everyone's lips today thanks to Ibrahim Ferrer. In the evenings they would all go to visit friends, who put on recitals and jam sessions in their homes. Most of all they liked to spend time with Nicolás Guillén, a writer from Camagüey. All three of them were passionate about *son* music as the perfect expression of what was uniquely Cuban. Nicolás summed it up: 'Cubans speak a little like *son* and they walk like *son*; in our everyday life *son* is in our humour, in our women, in compliments – it is our way of life.' He loved Cuchito's candour, her unconventional ideas, and was captivated by her charm.

Sergio Miró

He fell in love with her. Another of Cuchito's admirers was Sergio Miró, who actually wanted to be an actor and learned to play the drums just to impress her. Isolina Carrillo became good friends with Alejandro García Caturla, a celebrated composer. She was black and he was as white as milk. He was attracted to dark-skinned people and made no bones about it. Such relationships were far more effective at making people think than any political manifesto.

But Cuchito also took her studies seriously and she was making progress. In 1930 she had only three more semesters left until her graduation. Events were heating up. The dictator Machado was in power and politicians were lining their pockets, a practice that had already become the norm under their predecessors. There was good reason why Presidents Menocal and Zayas were nicknamed 'the Emperor of Cuba' and 'the Black-Marketeer' and why so many people consequently voted for Machado and his promises to put an end to corruption. But soon everyone had to admit that when he came to power, the mismanagement of the economy plumbed new depths. Machado erected the Capitolio, a huge palatial edifice in the heart of Havana, for the sole purpose of enriching himself and his cronies. There was never enough money in the treasury since the earmarked funds kept disappearing into secret channels. My parents wondered why, despite the many millions spent, the huge building site was mostly deserted. Machado was nicknamed 'the Butcher', because he had his opponents murdered one by one. He even sent his assassins to Mexico to get rid of Mella, the student leader, who had been forced to flee.

Cuchito still attended the university every day, but suddenly her studies were not her primary interest. She was crazy about Raúl Roa, the new spokesman for the resistance. 'Down with corruption! All power to the workers!' The slim man with the gaunt face and dark forelock had the students in the palm of his hand. Later Cuchito told us that Raúl Roa and other activists had persuaded her to take part in militant actions in order to put an end to the dictatorship. They had certainly asked the wrong person. Poor Cuchito, she was much too timid. At one protest march she saw the police beating to the ground anyone who stood in their way. The students had to drag the victims off, drenched in blood. That was more than she could handle. She was gripped with fear, even worse than before exams, and for days she had such severe stomach aches that she couldn't even get out of bed.

Machado ordered the university to be closed indefinitely. Students from well-to-do families went to Mexico to continue their studies. Cuchito made some extra money giving music lessons, but the cost of studying abroad was far beyond the means of our family. Gone was her dream of a dental practice. I have no idea how she coped with this blow. I was ten at the time and didn't understand these matters, but I could see the sadness in her eyes. Cuchito didn't even discuss her feelings with our parents. She, who could win over people in no time with her frankness, withdrew into herself. Because of that, none of us knows exactly when she got the idea to form a *son* septet, the first one composed solely of women – but she did, and it would fundamentally influence the course of our lives.

I'm sure that one of the musical get-togethers at our house inspired her. Those were unsettling times, but my parents still invited musicians over every weekend. One evening they announced: 'María Teresa Vera is coming next Saturday!' She was celebrated all over Havana in those days because of the way she blended romantic tunes and *son*. Columbia Records kept bringing her to New York to make new recordings.

The day before the famous guest was to visit us, Father had a goat slaughtered in order to prepare a modest meal of *chilindrón*. He marinated the goat meat in a lot of chilli peppers, and shortly before María Teresa arrived with her musicians he gleefully put the huge roast into the oven.

~ **Sextet with a Black Blonde** ~

María Teresa and Father were old friends. She came from the same village as he did, Guanajuay, and in addition to a childhood of deprivation, they shared a passion for music. María Teresa's maternal grandparents had also been slaves. She was a modest and simple person with a natural elegance. Nicolás Guillén, the poet, described her this way:

> *They went to hunt guitars under the full moon*
> *and brought back this one:*
> *pale, slender, with the eyes of an inexhaustible mulatta,*
> *her waist of fiery wood.*

Entranced, I watched as she picked up the guitar and began singing. The fragility of love, disillusionment, bittersweet desire and the indomitable hope of fulfilment – these feelings became so tangible to me when I heard her sing:

> *I have a pain in my soul*
> *That I don't want to show*
> *Not only so I won't cry*
> *But because I want to tear out*
> *This love that lives in me.*
>
> *Your kisses were the cause*
> *But I don't blame you*
> *I blame myself who believed*
> *That you felt the same*
> *And then understood*
> *How mistaken I had been.*

I know it will cost me dearly
But I am resigned to it
And to my pride. I say
The same as to my heart
You can't always win
This time it's my turn to lose.

Towards midnight Father invited María Teresa and the other musicians into the dining room and took the *chilindrón* out of the oven. Cool beer flowed and afterwards they drank rum. I was already in bed when the partygoers started to sing: 'The goat that breaks a drum pays with its hide! And what is even worse, she ends as *chilindrón*.'

Even more extravagant were the parties we held on name days. For Mother and Cuchito it was Purísima Concepción, the Immaculate Conception, on 8 December. Cachita, whose complete name was Caridad, was on 8 September, and Emma on 2 January. For Caridad, an especially beautiful altar was constructed in the living room with many flowers and candles. Caridad, the Virgin of Mercy, is the patron saint of Cuba and corresponds to the African goddess of love and joie de vivre, Ochún. I should explain that our religion developed out of the beliefs of the African slaves and those of the Spanish. The slaves had their gods, the Orichas, and the Catholic Church had its saints. Although it was forbidden for the slaves to worship their gods, they did so in secret by disguising them in the raiment of the Spanish saints and giving them Spanish names. This duped the Spaniards into believing that the slaves were now worshipping the saints of the Catholic Church. The Orichas and the saints became one, and this is why Cachita's patron saint is both Caridad *and* Ochún. Ochún is coquettish and has a passion for life and love. When she dances she rotates her hips

sensually, moving her arms fluidly and letting her many little golden bracelets tinkle, so that no man can resist her. That's how she once seduced
Changó, the Saint of Thunder and Lightning, an irresistible ladies' man. In
the Catholic religion he is a woman, St Barbara. According to legend, when
the two lovers met for a secret rendezvous one time, Ochún's husband suddenly appeared in front of the house with a machete. This was no problem for
Changó. He put on women's clothes and strutted unnoticed out the door as
St Barbara.

As I said, Cuchito had to give up her studies, and the political situation was
weighing on all of us. But then her name day arrived, and my parents decided to
ask the Septeto Nacional of Ignacio Piñeiro to play at the dance. The septet was,
and is, the epitome of *son*. One of their famous songs is called '*Échale Salsita*' –
'Put on a Little Salsa'. From this, Cuban musicians in the United States devised
the term 'salsa', because salsa began as Cuban *son*, and then took root in the US.
In 1929 the Septeto Nacional had just returned from the great Ibero-American
Exposition in Seville with the highest award. My parents had been friends with
Ignacio Piñeiro for years. His life had been as eventful as my father's: he had at
various times worked as a cigar roller, cooper, dock worker and mason. Father
called him up and told him, 'It would be a great honour for us if you would play
at my daughter's and wife's name day.'

'Why not? Of course we'll come,' replied Piñeiro, who was then at the peak
of his fame.

A thin sliver of moon shed just enough light to illuminate the contours
of the park as I watched the musicians from the Septeto Nacional set up their
instruments and start to play. Besides Ignacio Piñeiro there were Lázaro Herrera,
Alfredito Valdés, Bienvenido León, Eutimio Constantín, Miguel Angel Portillo
and Francisco González, whom everyone called 'Panchito Chevrolet'. Guests

stood in the living room, talking and drinking aperitifs. My parents had covered a bookcase as tall as a man with white satin and decorated it with candles and a picture of the Virgin of the Conception. Shortly before midnight the guests knelt down one by one before this altar and prayed, making a personal appeal to La Concepción before promising her something in return. At the stroke of midnight the candles were lit and the altar glowed brightly. The Septeto Nacional first played the requisite religious songs, then the party began in earnest. When Ignacio and his band let rip, a storm of music flooded our living room. The songs of the Septeto Nacional were played all the time on the radio, so the whole neighbourhood was crammed onto the veranda; no one wanted to miss the chance to dance to their latest hit. Alfredito Valdés sang:

One night I left the house in search of adventure
Looking for a taste of pleasure and joy
Oh my God, how I had my fun
In a torpor I spent the night
Strolling happily past homes so light
And came upon a bacchanal
In Catalina I ran into the unexpected
The voice of someone shouting like this:
Put on a little salsa!

Even Father lustily sang along to the suggestive lyrics; he pretended not to know that Catalina referred not only to a village east of Havana, but also to a woman: 'Put on a little salsa!'

The very next day Cuchito told Father for the first time about her idea for a *son* septet. A *son* septet made up exclusively of women? Women beating on bongos, playing clave and singing sexy lyrics? He suddenly became disapproving.

But Cuchito refused to give up and smiled mischievously at the way he was contradicting himself. Eventually he caved in, agreeing that perhaps she could succeed in making it work. And it wasn't long before he became the most enthusiastic and ardent advocate of her plan.

Son is very sophisticated music. At first I didn't think much about it, but I have come to realize that its unique quality derives from the many different rhythms, which complement each other and converge to create a rousing harmony. Most of the rhythms have their origins in religious traditions, and ultimately in Africa. The drums are a way of communicating with deities such as Ochún, Changó and others. The different drumbeats form their own language and the musicians bring out the 'words' by beating sharply or slowly, forcefully or gently, either on the rim of the drum or in the middle of the skin. A good player allows the drum to speak with an infinite variety of beats. It's not merely a question of technique; the musician must also be blessed with grace – not only when speaking with the deities but also for *son*.

Son septets developed this music further and gradually added 'modern' instruments such as guitar, double bass and trumpet to the various percussion instruments. In this way they blended the exciting African rhythms with tuneful Spanish elements. Quite unique. This was so new and so complex that until well into the 1950s all the bands in other countries that wanted to play Cuban rhythms such as *son*, cubop, Latin jazz and salsa had no choice but to hire percussionists directly from Cuba. At the time Cuchito had her idea, people thought women were incapable of playing this type of music. In traditional music especially, playing drums was the exclusive domain of men.

In the days that followed, Cuchito got together with several of her girl-friends. Isabel Álvarez, also called 'Beba', owned one of the apartment buildings in which our family had once lived, and was Ziomara's godmother. A powerful, staid woman, she learned to play the bongos. Berta Cabrera, the steady girlfriend of our cousin Rafaelito, took over the double bass without hesitation. Cachita, our eldest sister, joined them, as well as Ada, who had also studied at the music academy and became the first female tres player in Cuba. The tres is a deceptively simple-looking yet extremely difficult instrument. It resembles a guitar, but the strings are arranged in three pairs. It takes great skill to play it well, but the sounds that a talented and inspired musician can produce on a tres are unique. Elia O'Reilly came on board next, an excellent singer with the gift of *inspiración*. She knew how to spontaneously change lyrics or make them up on the spot. And *son* thrives on improvised lyrics.

After a week, the founding members were brooding about a name for the group. Elia O'Reilly had an idea. 'Do you know about Anacaona? Her story still touches everyone's heart.' Anacaona was an Indian princess at the time the Europeans discovered America; she lived on the island of Hispaniola – known today as Haiti and the Dominican Republic. She resisted the Spanish bravely, but was treacherously murdered by the followers of Columbus, and her people were exterminated, just as almost all the native inhabitants of Cuba gradually were. My elder sisters often wore their long dark hair in braids and had that distinctive bronze-coloured skin tone. 'Everyone says you look like Indians. Why don't we name the septet Anacaona?' Cuchito thought it was a brilliant idea.

Cuchito had trouble finding a female musician who could play the trumpet, which wasn't surprising given that hardly any woman in Cuba had attempted this instrument. 'So instead of the planned septet we will have to perform as a sextet,' she decided without more ado.

It wasn't long before her sextet was attracting attention. They were invited to play on a broadcast from the Bellavista radio station in the Hotel Palace in the Vedado district, but the hotel insisted on having a trumpet player, because *son*

Cuchito wth her Indian-style look

with trumpet was the latest craze. In distress Cuchito convinced Félix Chapottín, a virtuoso *son* trumpet player, to help out. What radio listener would notice that there was a man in the 'female septet'? The announcer played along and introduced Anacaona as the first women-only *son* septet. Scarcely had the notes of the first number died away when the radio announcer gushed across the ether, 'Ladies and gentlemen! The musicians of Anacaona do more than lay down a sensational *son*. Before me stand seven radiant beauties. What a shame that you can only hear them and not see them – especially the blonde on trumpet, who simply takes my breath away.' He was saying this about Chapottín – a *negro prieto*, a black man even blacker than his black hair! Everyone had tears running down their cheeks from laughing so hard, and had to struggle to regain their composure.

The problem had to be solved. Ondina, who had just turned thirteen, was not given any choice in this situation. Cuchito and Father decided that she would take trumpet lessons from Lázaro Herrera of the Septeto Nacional. Lázaro was one of the best trumpet players in Cuba, but to us he was always just Lázaro. Ondina agreed at once, which was unusual for someone normally so headstrong. Only later did we work out why she had said yes. She was after the money for the streetcar rides to Lázaro's house, which lay in the middle of El Barrio Chino. Each time Father gave her the ten centavos for the streetcar, he would warn her, 'Don't forget to come back at such-and-such a time on the dot.' And what did Ondina do? She spent the money on ice cream and had to walk all the way home! She was always well prepared with excuses for her lateness by the time she reached the front porch.

I'm fairly sure that Father knew Ondina was cheating, but he ignored it because he wasn't very strict. He never raised his hand to any of us. He didn't need to. If he ever did have cause to yell, as he sometimes did, we all wanted to

Cuba's first female septet, 1932: (from left) Ondina, Bola, Berta Cabrera, Cuchito,
Isabel Álvarez, Ada and Elia O'Reilly

sink into the ground. But that almost never happened. For the most part, our family life proceeded quite harmoniously, and this was in part due to the music, which could be heard emanating from one room or another all day long. While we were practising Father enjoyed walking through the house, listening and making sure that we weren't loafing. One day, however, Father turned serious. He found out that Ondina was losing interest in the trumpet – and ice cream. 'You promised to learn the trumpet. If you don't keep your word, you will never be allowed to learn another instrument again.' It worked. Ondina didn't say anything else and, out of sheer defiance, learned her instrument almost perfectly in a few months.

It was Lázaro Herrera's nuanced style of trumpet playing that shaped the music of the Septeto Nacional, and the *son* in general. Ignacio Piñeiro, the leader of the band, played the double bass. He was not an exceptional interpreter of the music, but he was an incomparable composer. He gave the *son* wonderful declarations of love: '*el son es lo más sublime para el alma divertir*', 'son is the most sublime music to entertain the soul'. But he was unable to put the music down on paper, so Lázaro did this on his behalf – during his time in the military band in his home town of Güines he had learned to read and write music. He also led the septet on the occasions that Ignacio temporarily left the group to work as a skilled mason; he could earn more doing that than performing on stage. That's how things were in 1933. The creator of so many unforgettable *sones* would go to work every day at the never-ending Capitolio building project, making sure that the Italian Carrara marble foundations of the dictator's ostentatious building were perfectly level and straight.

Lázaro became one of our best friends. One Sunday my parents invited him to dinner. While Father and Mother were busy in the kitchen, Cuchito seized the opportunity to cajole him into telling one of his incomparable anecdotes. 'Pecoso,' she asked cautiously, 'how are the music lessons with Isolina progressing?' Everyone called him 'Pecoso', the freckled one, because his face was speckled like the egg of a guinea hen. But that did not diminish his effect on women in any way – on the contrary. Lázaro was a hot favourite among the ladies. Like many musicians, he embraced life with gusto. Indeed, how can a musician sing convincingly about love and women if he doesn't keep falling head-over-heels?

Isolina Carrillo, the pianist, had started studying trumpet with Lázaro. Cuchito noticed that her friend was making no progress at all, yet she was becoming more and more smitten with Lázaro's charm. 'Does she at least know her scales?' Cuchito asked. Lázaro just smiled knowingly. Then she made another attempt: 'Lázaro, haven't any of your girlfriends ever resented your countless infidelities?'

'Well, yes, that does happen once in a while.' Finally his tongue was loosened. He told us for the first time what happened when the Septeto Nacional had been awarded the gold medal at the Ibero-American Exposition in Seville. The newspapers were full of praise, and their photos were being taken everywhere. Lázaro's ex-girlfriend, a black Cuban whom he had left in the lurch and who was living in Spain at the time, learned from the newspaper that her 'beloved' Lázaro was performing in Spain.

'After the show she was lying in wait for me. I saw her run towards me with a knife in her hand. I was barely able to dodge the blade. That woman never gave up. She was a *guapa* – courageous and violent at the same time. At every performance she would stand like a faithful fan right in front of the stage. And every time I saw her, I broke out in a sweat.'

~ **Anacaona** ~

At that moment our parents came out of the kitchen and Lázaro quickly changed the subject.

He praised Ondina, saying that she had a good 'lip', since she could hold any note and be right on key, and she had musical intelligence. In three or four months she learned to play several *son* pieces perfectly. It was probably because all of a sudden she had nothing else on her mind but learning the trumpet, and, unlike other pupils he had, she considered Lázaro as her teacher and nothing more. Soon he organized her debut, but didn't let her in on his plan. He asked her to accompany the Septeto Nacional to a nightclub, presumably just so she could listen to them. The nightclub on the Parque Central was very well known. It was there that the first big neon advertisement in Havana blazed brightly: a huge green frog with big letters next to it that said, 'It's water that frogs are in – so drink La Campana Gin!'

Ondina sat excitedly in the first row and listened hypnotized to the *son* rhythms. After a few tunes, Lázaro suddenly came down from the stage, handed her his trumpet and said, 'Now it's your turn.' Ondina's eyes grew wide and she hesitated for a moment, then took the trumpet and started playing with no inhibitions. And her first tune with the Septeto Nacional was '*Échale Salsita!*' – 'Put on a Little Salsa!'

On the beach at Marianao, 1933: (from left) Cuchito, Alicia and Ondina

Chapter 4
Island in a Sea of Vice

My sisters claim that I began playing music when I was eleven, but that isn't true. By the time I did seriously pick up the clarinet, music was already central to my life. As far back as I can remember, music was in my blood. When I sat in the dining room doing my homework, Cachita and Cuchito were giving lessons in the next room. Song practice, melodies on piano, guitar or clarinet – our house was one huge vibrating box, and I soaked up the sounds like a sponge. By the age of eleven I knew all the lessons by heart.

Rita María Iturralde, my sisters' piano teacher, was the first to notice my talent and tell my father. 'Matías, send Alicia to me for lessons. I won't charge you anything. I don't want a single centavo, but I want her for a pupil. That girl has talent and it would be a sin to ignore it.' But even before my future teacher took me under her wing, I had borrowed a little book from Cuchito and begun to coax notes out of the clarinet and saxophone. With that instruction book on the music stand, I tried fiddling with the keys. I even tried out Ada's double bass this way, just for a change.

At twelve I took part in the rehearsals for Cuchito's septet. And one day they told me, without making a big fuss, 'Tonight you're playing with us in the *aires libres.*' Berta Cabrera, the bass player, had fallen ill, so I had to jump in. It was my first appearance in public. Legally it was forbidden for minors to work as musicians, but my sisters knew how to get around the law. They dressed me up to look like a grown-up, painted with heavy make-up and stuck in a long dress to hide my skinny legs.

The heat of the day had dissipated by the time two cabs drove us and all our instruments down the Calzada, past the harbour to the *aires libres*. The cafés beneath the cool arcades were quite familiar to me, as were the scattered trees in the Parque Central across the road, and the recently finished Capitolio. But on this evening everything seemed magical. The red sunlight climbed faster and faster up the treetops in the park, and for a few minutes the dome of the Capitolio glowed. Then all at once the day was over and the night began. Trams and cars crowded the Prado, the main artery of Havana's pulsing heart.

We went to the café at the Hotel Pasaje. Next to it were the Café El Dorado and the café of the Hotel Saratoga. Those three were the most popular – they offered a magnificent, colourful spectacle. The wide pavement was a sea of tables and chairs adorned with parasols and multi-coloured awnings. The interiors of the cafés were luxurious, their walls covered with hand-painted tiles, their floors made of cold granite.

After we set up on the stage and tuned our instruments, my sisters gave me some high heels. There I stood on the main promenade of Havana, visible from far off, with no idea how to walk in those things. So my main concern at my debut was getting used to my shoes – the music, the notes, all flowed out of me as easily as if I were playing alone in the living room. I didn't have stage fright, in fact I didn't really notice all the people around me. I just concentrated on my sheet music, on what the others were playing, and on my cues. And when a tune was over, I was already studying the next piece and identifying the tricky passages. During the break my sisters took me to the café next door. To celebrate the day they treated me to a sandwich, but they didn't tell me how well it went until we were on our way home in the cab. They showered me with compliments: 'Alicia, you've inherited Grandfather's talent – you know when to come in without even thinking about it.' That felt good. Musicians need praise and recognition like a fish needs water.

That evening was also my initiation as the double bass player in the septet, because Berta didn't want to play any more. For me that meant goodbye to school. Suddenly I found myself receiving sympathy from my elder sisters, and even from Mother, when I had no desire to do my homework and made a sloppy job of it. However, I did manage to finish the sixth grade for the sake of appearances. In the final weeks of my school career the teacher caught me daydreaming more than once during class. I could think only about music, of the arrangements and rhyming song lyrics in my head. As soon as I got home I would grab an instrument. I had resolved to become a good musician.

Millo, child number ten, was the next one we recruited for the septet. At the time she had just turned ten, two years younger than me. She and I were not very close at first, although we slept in the same bed. In school she was a real millstone around my neck; she was often teased by older kids and I would have to run to her rescue. And she was always so serious. Even cheerful Ada complained that it was impossible to entice a smile out of Millo. Only when we played music together at home did she blossom. She would listen to us as we practised, then grab something – a chair or a pot – and drum away: tick, tick, ticketick… Even when we weren't practising, she could produce a rhythm from any object. In the afternoon, right after school, we would all sit silently at the table, longing for lunch. These were the only minutes of the day when we weren't all chattering at once, and the constant noise level in the house would noticeably abate. And that's precisely when Millo would start her drumming, that eternal tick, tick, ticketick. I wasn't the only one she drove crazy.

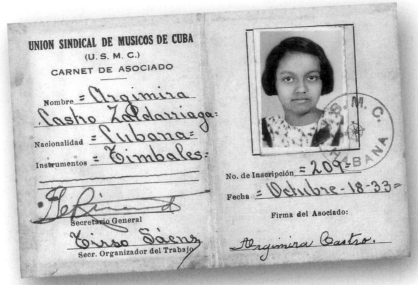

UNION SINDICAL DE MUSICOS DE CUBA
(U. S. M. C.)
CARNET DE ASOCIADO

Nombre = Argimira
Castro Zaldarriaga:

Nacionalidad = Cubana =

Instrumentos = Timbales:

Secretario General

Tirso Sáenz
Secr. Organizador del Trabajo

No. de Inscripción = 209 =

Fecha = Octubre - 18 - 33 =

Firma del Asociado:

Argimira Castro.

Ten-year-old Millo's union card

Father was overjoyed. He was convinced that Millo was a born percussion-ist. He brought Andrés Guerra, a master of percussion whom everyone called *Manzano* – apple tree – home to hear her. He was a black man who had grown up with the rhythms of African music and he now came almost every day to teach Millo the bongos; she was still too small to play the big conga drum. From then on he spent so much time at our house that he became part of the family. Millo looked up to him like a second father. Sometimes Manzano would help Father in his shop at the market, because even though he was a great virtuoso he couldn't make a living from music. Not until many years later were his abili-ties recognized, and he found a steady job as the conga player in the orchestra of Cuba's most important radio station, ICR. As soon as he was earning good money, he gave Mother a gold ring with a big garnet for her name day. Valuable jewellery was an expression of respect and affection.

~ **Anacaona** ~

When Berta Álvarez, nicknamed 'Beba', was still playing the bongos

Millo made such fast progress that one evening we decided to try her out in an appearance at the Dora, a very popular movie theatre only a couple of blocks from our house on Calzada de Luyanó. At the theatres there were usually two screenings, one at seven o'clock and another late at night. In between there were short music shows called *Variedades Musicales*. They would last about a half-hour each. For the first number, Ziomara's godmother, hefty Beba, played the bongos. For the second number we let little Millo play. In her first appearance before an audience she pounded the bongos with such abandon that the theatre went wild. 'That little girl is phenomenal!' Millo was transformed. She beamed with delight at the crowd and they loved her. For the third number Beba took over the bongos, but a chorus of booing and whistling broke out. 'Let the little girl play the bongos!' 'Get rid of the fatty!' the audience cried, with no regard for Beba, who was very talented. When Beba left the stage, all she could say was, 'That's it. I don't want to do this any more.' She never appeared again. Millo was only in fourth grade, but after this show, school was history. She became a musician too.

Our septet now played almost every night in one of the three cafés, taking turns with other groups. Sometimes we would begin in the late afternoon, when members of parliament and senators would still be there. They would just walk over from the Capitolio across the street. Soon enough, journalists from the big newspapers would show up to join the politicians for a cup of coffee and to soak up information and gossip. In the evening, 'lonely' men would start arriving, more often than not married men who had left both wife and wedding ring at home. Couples in love would come too. And in the winter the *aires libres* belonged to the Americans. It wasn't a change in temperature that heralded the start of winter, because when does it ever get cold here? Winter began when the tourists flocked into Cuba from the States by the thousands.

Millo took over as percussionist from Beba; Alicia next to her on saxophone

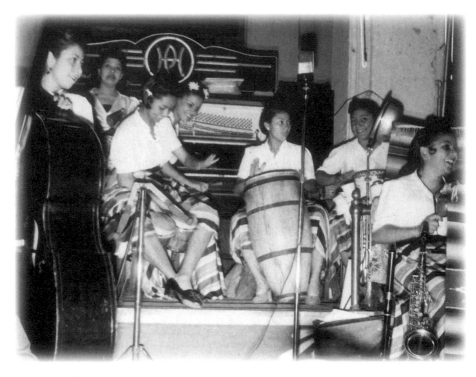

In the Hotel Pasaje

In the *aires libres* a more or less civilized atmosphere prevailed. Even 'decent' women could show up here at night. That was a peculiarity of these cafés; even the side streets off the Prado were regarded as improper – that's where the disreputable demi-monde began. People considered all women decent except for the '*mujeres de mala vida*', the prostitutes. A respectable woman, especially an unmarried one or a young girl, had no business being part of the nightlife of Havana. The men usually enjoyed Cuba's night-time amusements alone, even claiming that they did so out of respect for their wives or girlfriends. Their excuse for not bringing them along was that the reputation of any woman who stepped across the threshold of certain bars would be instantly ruined. In the evening

In front of the Hotel Pasaje

Havana was a world of men, although, of course, everything revolved around women.

We had to pass by some of the more dubious establishments on our way to the *aires libres*. On Calle Monte was the notorious 'dance academy' Marte and Belona, which was only called a dance academy to give it a hint of respectability. Lázaro was the first to explain to us what went on in there. This academy employed female 'dancing instructors'. In order to dance with these ladies, men had to buy tickets costing ten centavos each. It was a gold mine; after a couple of rums some men didn't want to let their instructors go. In the course of an evening they would play sixty or seventy pieces of music – the short versions only. A man could quickly lose track, at least as long as he had any money left. And most of the 'dance instructors' were willing to offer them quite a different sort of dance, for an additional charge, of course. . .

Dens of iniquity and an exciting music scene – that's what the dance academies represented. The old section of the city was full of such places. Like those of us at the *aires libres*, the musicians there also played all the latest hits, and people were wild about them. Many serious musicians also worked at the dance academies, like our teacher Lázaro. Quite a few of them had steady work in the Philharmonic Orchestra, but they were only paid starvation wages, so they also performed late at night in the academies. A person had to earn a living. Eliseo López, for instance, the famous flute player who later formed his own band, financed his law studies with the money he made on the side and finally became an attorney. Others studied to become doctors the same way. For us the dance academies were taboo, although I would have liked to take a look inside, just to see them playing the music that reached the street through their open doors. But there was no way we could have gone in there. Our parents would never have let us go back to the *aires libres*.

We performed mostly at the Café El Dorado, a very civilized place. The Spanish owner, Señor Martino, was extremely considerate. When we arrived at the café in the afternoon, he would be sitting with his illustrious regulars, baseball stars and sports writers, engaged in animated discussions. Martino would politely invite us to their table: 'Girls, could we order you a Manzanilla or a La Ina wine?' Martino knew that we didn't drink anything with a high alcohol content, not even cocktails. Father had told us, 'Order Manzanilla or a wine from Jérez if you're offered something.' And when we girls sat down in a happy circle, everyone treated us with great respect. Nobody could afford to act disrespectfully towards us, because Martino would immediately throw them out. He made sure that only refined, well-brought-up people from the middle and upper classes frequented his café.

We would start playing in El Dorado at eight-thirty and slowly the tables would fill up. Many passers-by would simply stop on the pavement or sit down across the street on park benches to enjoy the music for free. And then there were the men who liked nothing better than to cruise up and down the street in their cars, just to be seen. Pistón, the famous jai alai player, had a brand-new car with gleaming chrome, and he would drive past us slowly, his car packed with friends. They would all shout, '*Adiós! Adiós!*' and wave to us exuberantly. Others that we

In the Café El Dorado

didn't even know did the same thing. And there we stood in the thick of it on the bandstand: me with my double bass, Ondina with trumpet and claves, and Millo on the bongos. Bola played maracas and sang, Ada played the tres, Cachita switched between playing the bass and singing, while Cuchito, the leader, played guitar and sang as well.

Our septet was a sensation. Women and *son*? What a daring combination! In better circles it was the custom to sing about love in the style of the Spanish nobility: 'On the path through my melancholy life I suddenly came upon a flower...' But we sang, 'Kiss me, right here and right now!' The *son* singer, like the man on the street, just blurts out what he wants. In fact, *son* has a lot in common with the *piropos*, the spontaneous poems that men sometimes composed when overwhelmed by the charm of a woman. Unfortunately, these *piropos* are usually not very imaginative. When I turned twelve I was always confronted by men stopping short on the pavement, rolling their eyes in rapture, and shouting, '*Chica! Si cocinas como caminas, me como hasta las raspitas!*' 'Girl, if you cook the way you walk, I'd sure like to scrape out your pan!' I learned as a child to look straight ahead and keep walking without reacting. Usually this indifference did little good: it only seemed to stoke the fire of passion in that type of man.

There were other female bands too, like the Orquesta Ensueño, but they played waltzes, foxtrots and European tunes, mostly slow ballads. We were the only ones who dared give our all to *son* and rumba, the true Cuban music. Millo with her bongos, Bola with the maracas, and Ondina with the claves provided the multi-layered rhythm. The claves are two short sticks of hardwood, turned on a lathe, and they have a bright, metallic tone. This percussion instrument gives the *son* its typical sparkling sound – the melody and rhythm seem slightly displaced and therefore drive each other forward. A fabric of sound is created, chaotic yet cohesive, producing a vibration that grabs the dancers' bodies from within. In 1930 a Cuban *son* was a worldwide hit: '*El Manicero*', 'The Peanut Vendor'. Singer Rita Montaner – who was celebrated in Cuba as '*la única*' – sent the market cry of the Cuban peanut vendor around the globe with her shout of '*maní, maaníííí*'. 'She transformed the sounds of Havana's back yards into a universal genre,' raved Nicolás Guillén, the esteemed poet.

I soon got to know Guillén personally, because in September 1932 the most famous artists in Cuba organized our official debut in the Teatro Principal de la Comedia, on Animas, a side street off the Prado, near the elegant Hotel Sevilla. Newspaper advertisements were very expensive, so debuts were the ideal promotion, because journalists would automatically cover such events. A FEMALE SEPTET CALLED ANACAONA HAS BEEN FORMED. YOU HAVE TO GO SEE THEM! ran a headline in *Diario de la Marina*.

Nicolás Guillén had insisted on being the master of ceremonies for the evening. Other top-notch artists also honoured us with their presence: Rita Montaner, the pianist Ernestina Lecuona, the sister of Ernesto Lecuona, and the Septeto Nacional. The composer Armando Oréfiche was at the piano and later wrote our theme song, 'Anacaona'. At the very end of the evening we played officially for the first time.

It worked. We were immediately booked in clubs, even in 'first-class' clubs. To gain entry to the nightlife of Havana, it made a big difference whether you were male or female, but the shade of your skin was also important, and whether your hair was smooth or wavy, how thick your lips were and how fine your facial features. All these things were taken into consideration, especially if you wanted to become a member of a club.

The Havana Yacht Club, the Miramar Yacht Club, the Country Club and the Jamaica Club were the most prestigious of them all. They stood in a row

along the beach. At the Country Club you could watch horse and dog races and play golf. Only the richest people were guests there, the *'gente de buena sociedad'* ('people of high society'). These clubs all had dining rooms that were kept so cool by air conditioning that even in May the gentlemen had to put on a jacket and the ladies a fur stole. The menu of the Country Club included huge portions of meat, but I lost all appetite at the mere sight of the formal arrangement of plates, various pieces of cutlery, little forks and little spoons, not to mention the flower arrangements, bottles, glasses, champagne buckets and even more flowers. It was also a mystery to me why the rich would set fine tables and chairs on the beach, right in the sand. It seemed such a shame to scratch all the furniture. I thought the marina with all the boats was amazing, and equally impressive, of course, was the swimming pool, surrounded by a long bar, and the dance floor under the open sky. I imagined that I was on a faraway island, not in Havana.

Only those who were white and from the upper class could become members of such a club. Even Fulgencio Batista, who ruled the country after Machado until he was ousted by Fidel Castro, had no luck. With his coffee-coloured skin he was called *El Indio* – 'the Indian' – too dark for the milk-white people of high society. 'The *mulatto* has become president? So what? That's no reason to let him join the Havana Yacht Club.'

We played in all the clubs, even the most exclusive ones, and we thoroughly enjoyed this privilege, more so because hardly any male septet ever achieved such success. Yet as *'mulattas* with Indian blood' we would never have been accepted as guests or members. Every skin colour and social class kept to its own. The middle-class whites would meet at the Club Náutico, the Casino Deportivo and the Club La Playa. The well-to-do *mulattos* had founded the Club Atenas. The

Magnetic Sport Club was exclusively for black chauffeurs. Other blacks could go to the Club Las Aguilas, El Deportivo de la Fe and the Buenavista Social Club. The blacks had the most clubs and, because they liked to party, they were often busy all week long.

Negro de charol, 'patent-leather black', was what people called the darkest skin colour. 'He shines like a patent-leather shoe,' many people would say when they saw a black man, dripping with sweat, lugging a heavy sack through the streets in the blazing heat. Sweat was unacceptable in high society, as was passion – both were considered 'African'. Accordingly, rumba and conga, both the music and the dance, were also despised, as well as the instruments associated with them.

It wasn't so long since the city council had even attempted to ban the playing of bongos in public. African drums, in the opinion of white politicians and even educated blacks of the Club Atenas, were too primitive for a cosmopolitan city like Havana. In spite of all this, we girls stood on stage playing *son*, with passion to boot. The *son* is *sabrosón*, 'pure taste and enjoyment', as a song by Ignacio Piñeiro says. Or as Fernando Ortíz declared, '*Son* is like a musical rum that you drink with your ears.' To this we sang:

> *I want you to tell me why you fear my kisses*
> *When all I do is shower my love and tenderness on you.*
> *I never thought, my love, that you would act this way*
> *And all the more, for you surely know that I love you like a child.*
> *Your kisses do not disturb me, baby, you know that so well,*
> *Though when you kiss me you leave me spinning.*
> *If you want to kiss me, then kiss me more and never stop,*
> *Baby, keep on kissing me, even if it costs me my life.*

And then everyone would sing in chorus:

Bésame aqui ('Kiss me, right here, right now!').

Our fame soon spread through newspaper articles and by word of mouth even outside of Havana. We were now booked in engagements for out-of-town dances – first for smaller towns near Havana, then for bigger cities. I was delighted to get to know my island better.

One dance took us to the vicinity of Madruga, about two hours by car from Havana. We were all pretty excited, because we knew that excellent musicians lived there. José Urfé, who led a renowned orchestra and was a famous composer of *danzónes*, had two talented sons, Orestes and Odilio. We figured that perhaps they'd come to hear us. A few days before the performance, our singer Elia O'Reilly became ill. On the way there, Cuchito broke the news to me, in an offhand way, that I was going to have to replace Elia and sing lead. I felt instantly paralysed. Of course I knew all the songs by heart – I'd always had a good memory – but no one had ever mentioned the possibility that I might take over the lead vocals someday. I protested loudly, but they all talked me into it, praising my singing ability to the skies. When we reached the hall at the crossroads near Madruga, I saw a big placard: SEPTET ANACAONA. VOCALIST: MISS ALICIA CASTRO.

What happened next was inevitable. We had scarcely set up our instruments before the Urfé brothers appeared. Orestes later became my teacher for classical double bass. Years later, at an award ceremony, his brother Odilio told us what he thought of us that first night. For days the news had been going around Madruga that an all-girl *son* septet was going to play for a dance at the crossroads. The young brothers asked their father for permission to rent a car. The entire crème de la crème of *son* musicians in Madruga squeezed into this vehicle. 'What, a female ensemble that's good enough to play the *son* repertoire?' On their way to the dance it was hotly debated. Odilio Urfé recalled:

'I swear, it was overwhelming. I saw them, these stunning girls playing magnificent music. The skill with which they mastered their instruments was first class – I was most amazed by the guitar player. I'm sure that many people went there not only to hear their music. Why try to hide it? Like me, they were entranced by the radiance of all this uncommon, youthful beauty. What a mood of excitement there was! We stayed until one in the morning, and when we got home I talked about nothing but the Septet Anacaona.'

After this event we started out on our first tour to the eastern part of the island. Father absolutely refused to let us travel alone, racking his brain to work out who would be able to take his place at his store. With a heavy heart he decided to ask our brother Otto, who had just turned twenty-one, to mind the store. He was an interesting case, our Otto. As far as I can remember, he almost never slept at home and nobody knew where he was hanging out. At that time my parents had separate bedrooms on the ground floor, either side of the bathroom. Was that perhaps their method of birth control? Otto's bed was in Father's room, but he spent his nights elsewhere. Otto was constantly falling in love. His vice was women, and it even drove him to terminate his studies. But at Father's first store, Otto had often lent him a hand, although he was less concerned about sales than about showering his countless girlfriends with candies, burnt almonds and cookies. No wonder the women liked him. At the Mercado Único too, he was always very generous towards his sweethearts. But Otto managed to stay on good terms with Father, who let him get away with almost anything. He was never that lenient with us girls.

The tour was the fulfilment of a lifelong dream for Father. Packed into two

Nightclub in the basement of the Hotel Pasaje, 1934

large hired cars, we travelled through endless sugar-cane fields, like those Father had worked in as a child. We stayed overnight at comfortable hotels, the promoters invited us to good restaurants, and important people wanted to be seen with us. And how did Father react? He seemed to take it all for granted, and he would do the laundry in the morning for Millo, the baby of the family, whenever she slept in after shows that went late into the night. 'She has to play music, that's more important,' he said with both sympathy and annoyance. Not until we got home did he complain to Mother, 'I even had to wash that kid's underwear.'

Holguín, a city in the far eastern end of Cuba, was known for its thriving cultural life, much like Santiago, the birthplace of *son*. The Avilés family was at the heart of the music scene there. Manuel Avilés had not only fought side by side with Antonio Maceo, the national hero in the war of independence, but had also founded the Orquesta Avilés in 1882. This orchestra was the oldest in Cuba and consisted of fourteen brothers. I was disappointed when Cuchito told us that the planned gig in Holguín had fallen through because the promoter couldn't come up with the money. Posters announcing us were already everywhere, but Cuchito was tough when it came to financial matters. We had passed through the city and were driving back to Havana when all at once our driver noticed that we were being followed by motorcycles. It was the police. They stopped our cars, waved the contract under Cuchito's nose, and claimed that the money had now been deposited. Cuchito had to give in. As we drove back to the city with the police escort, we saw that an enormous crowd had gathered for our appearance in the middle of a park full of huge jungular trees. When we stood on the stage, I saw the fourteen Avilés brothers sitting in the front row. How warmly the audience received us! What applause after each number!

One of the next stops was Cienfuegos, where we played in the Terry Theatre, a breathtakingly luxurious building whose walls were painted with delicate flowers, while the ceiling was adorned with an ornate fresco of angelic figures. The sugar baron Tomás Terry had built it mainly as a monument to himself. He invested some of the millions that he had raked in, on the backs of thousands of slaves, in the arts, and the theatre had been inaugurated with Verdi's opera *Aida*. Our first show was in the afternoon in front of a full house. Afterwards, through a little window in the dressing room, I could see a huge crowd already gathering for our second show at eight o'clock. They were trying to push their way into the theatre. Then I heard shouting. A commotion started and panic seized the crowd. Police cars pulled up and shots were fired. Later they told me that a policeman had fired a warning shot in the air, but it had hit an old man. The poor man died and other people were wounded.

1933 was a violent year, even in Havana. There were various incidents of unrest, sometimes provoked by the dictator's secret police, sometimes by the students from the opposition. The workers called a general strike to demand an end to the dictatorship, whereupon Machado ordered a massacre in the streets of Havana.

After the tour we once again appeared regularly under the arcades of the Hotel Pasaje and in the Café El Dorado, despite the turbulent times. The unrest was coming closer and closer, until one evening the police from the park across the street started beating the demonstrators with brutal force. There was a shootout right in front of the café, and we had to hide behind the piano.

We earned one peso each for playing in one of the open-air cafés from eight-thirty in the evening until one in the morning. That was equivalent to one dollar in those days, a good wage compared to the thirty centavos a farm worker earned in a day. Out of our income Cuchito had to pay for the taxi that took us to work and picked us up again afterwards, and for our cosmetics and clothing. And after we had been playing all evening, we would be terribly hungry, of course. In the *aires libres*, however, everything was very expensive; so on the way home I would always be on the lookout for street vendors offering fresh fried food from their carts. There were croquettes at five centavos apiece, and they came with bread. We had to save our money, but a little snack after work was essential.

The United States had initially supported Machado because it served their economic interests, but now they dropped him because of his murderous conduct. This gave his opponents renewed impetus. The clashes began spreading all the way to our neighbourhood of Lawton. Havana, they say, is built on seven hills like Rome; from our house we could see muzzle flashes on the hills of Mazo and Burro. Gathered on one hill were the military, followers of the future dictator Batista, while Machado's police had dug themselves in on the other. The shots flew right over our house. By August, Machado was on the run, and he took off in a plane for the Bahamas. Terrible riots broke out as people sought revenge on his henchmen. A crowd stormed the presidential palace and plundered it. Soon afterwards a friend who came to visit us presented Mother with a delicate porcelain plate with the Cuban coat of arms on it, straight from Machado's dining room. This plate marked the beginning of Mother's collection. On every tour we kept an eye out for an original plate that we could bring back to her.

Our house was far from paid off. Father had borrowed the money for the mortgage from a Galician, of all people. This Galician and his wife kept dropping by under one pretext or another. 'How lovely this house is. Simply beautiful!' they would sigh. They were utterly in love with our home. And before departing they would always tell my parents, 'Oh, you don't have to hurry with the payments. Take your time.' The Galician was sure that sooner or later the house would belong to him.

Ada kept a sharp eye on the mortgage. She was practically minded and always did the family shopping. She would pay for things with her own money, and carefree as she was, she often forgot to reimburse herself. The result was that she never had a centavo to her name. But as far as the house was concerned, Ada kept meticulous records of everything, because she didn't like the Galician. She kept on admonishing Cuchito, 'Make a budget. How much money do we have left? Let's pay the Galician. He's never going to get our house. Never!' And as she said this her laugh would convey a certainty of victory, which in those days had no basis whatsoever. It was clear that the debts would never be paid off solely from our income at the open-air cafés.

Ondina, 1935

Chapter 5
The *Aires Libres* and Jazz

One thing is certain: our success as the first female septet in Cuba to play *son* encouraged more and more women to form bands and play in the cafés. So in 1933 the era of the female bands began. Within a few months the *aires libres* were firmly in the hands of women musicians. Among our competitors the best bands were Ensueño, Renovación and Ilusión. They performed well but had committed themselves to other genres, namely waltzes, *danzón*, paso doble, everything that was regarded as 'decent' music. Of course, they also had their fans. But all modesty aside, we had the easiest time filling the cafés with our wild, emotional *son* rhythms. Even so it wasn't always easy. There were no amplifiers or microphones, and our singer Elia O'Reilly had to sing at the top of her voice, especially when the wind got up. Elia had a tremendously powerful voice, much stronger than singers today.

We would alternate with the other bands several times a week, because the café owners demanded a new programme every few days. One December evening – in the middle of the American tourist season – we were playing in the Café El Dorado. We saw the musicians from Ensueño walk merrily past, give us an especially friendly greeting, and then set up their instruments at the Hotel Pasaje right next door, only a few metres away. We were just starting to play 'Maleficio', a lively *son* piece about the magic of love, when I suddenly heard an unusual tune: jazz! It was actually jazz!! I held on tight to my double bass, glanced to the side and saw that four brass players had joined Ensueño. They were playing exciting music – and making a hell of a racket. Our patrons were surprised as well, sitting there in the midst of this cacophony of different notes and rhythms. Amused, they let it all wash over them. I was annoyed, but I also admired Guillermina Foyo, the leader of Ensueño, for her coup. You had to hand it to her: she had put together the first female jazz band.

We encountered each other again the next evening. We had hardly begun when Ensueño started playing in the café next door with several trumpets and saxophones. The Americans now preferred to go over there where the music was louder, which is quite understandable. An easy solution would have been for us to agree to take turns playing, a few songs for them and then a few for us. That way the audience would have been able to enjoy both groups, but the musicians in Ensueño played their trump card and blew full blast in the middle of our tunes. Even our most devoted fans were totally perplexed, sitting petrified with their ice creams, cocktails and beers with no idea what was going on.

We had to do something. We sat up until the small hours of the morning talking of only one thing: how could we expand into a jazz band? It was obvious that jazz was the future. Ondina and I were already jazz fans, we loved Louis Armstrong, and Cuchito too felt comfortable in this genre. She had became familiar with jazz while she was at university, because her friend Isolina had dated Alejandro García Caturla, who had started one of Cuba's first jazz bands in Caibarién in the mid-1920s. Even Martino, the owner of the Café El Dorado, began putting pressure on us: 'Girls, you need more horns.'

So the very next day Cuchito brought up the topic with the whole family. Father seemed to have been giving the matter some thought already, because he immediately said, 'What's the problem? We're a big family, and a few of the girls still haven't appeared in public...'

We all turned to look at Emma, the third oldest. 'You've been making good progress on piano, so the trombone wouldn't be that hard for you,' Ada teased her.

'I'll ask Antonio whether he can teach you,' said Father. Antonio Castro was one of the best trombone players and his Hermanos Castro jazz band was celebrated. So Emma said yes right away. Then Father looked at Ziomara. She had just turned nine. 'Your sisters need a second trumpet player, and it's going to be you.'

For a few weeks we obsessively practised jazz, nothing but jazz, for hours on end every day. One evening we played our trump card and ten sisters stepped onto the stage of the Café El Dorado as Anacaona. Next door at the Hotel Pasaje, the women of Ensueño looked on in astonishment and the audience was amazed as well. It was clear that we now had enough horn players to be able to compete. We kicked off with such vigour that the Orquesta Ensueño could hardly be heard. Naturally the guests came back to us. But our renewed popularity wasn't just a result of sheer volume. We had come up with something new to outdo Ensueño. We started off with a paso doble, then introduced ourselves as a jazz band. After a few jazz pieces we suddenly switched to a septet and put our heart and soul into playing *son*. Then we converted into an old-fashioned *orquesta típica* and played *danzón*. We all took turns playing different instruments during the evening. I played saxophone in the jazz band, plucked the double bass for *son* and blew clarinet in the *orquesta típica*. Bola played banjo in the jazz band, shook the maracas for *son* and picked up the wooden flute for the *orquesta típica*. Millo reigned supreme behind the drum kit, bongos and conga drum. The audience also liked it when our horn players swayed back and forth in time with the

89

The aires libres, 1935

music when we played jazz. That was the fashion, after all. And our new singer was a hit too. After Elia O'Reilly had given up her career in favour of married life, we had hired Graciela Pérez. Martino objected to her at first, believing her to be too chubby, but after a few weeks the owner of Café El Dorado was convinced that we – with Graciela – attracted the biggest crowd. He tried to talk us into playing for him exclusively, but we didn't want to tie ourselves down to one venue.

~ **Anacaona** ~

For a perfect show you have to have the right costumes, so we always planned our wardrobe carefully. We were all dressed identically, from our earrings right down to our shoes. All bands did that, but we always tried to come up with the most original outfits. Our sister Flora was a very creative seamstress; she knew all the latest styles from Hollywood and where to get hold of the hard-to-find patterns. One evening she brought home a magazine from the States and asked us to pick something out. We gazed at the movie stars wearing long, skin-tight dresses, dresses with side slits, with plunging necklines, strapless – even in Cuba we used the English word 'strapless', because it *definitely* sounds better than *baja y chupa*, 'pull it down and suck'. The family discussion that evening was like a

parliamentary debate. It was as if the followers of Machado were arguing with the Communists. How long should, ought, must the slit in the dress be? How deep the neckline?

Emma and Ondina, the serious ones, protested in unison: 'We're no floozies. If they want to see flesh, they'll have to go two blocks down. If they want to hear music – and very good music at that – they can come and see us.'

'Emma, believe me,' Ada countered, 'just because someone can see your ankle, they're not going to think you're easy. It takes a bit more than that to be easy. I propose that Flora makes a slit from the ankle to the waist so we don't have to keep arguing about every inch.' I didn't want us to look boring either. It didn't matter to me if some men only clapped because they thought they'd get a glimpse of knee. We weren't appearing in a convent, after all.

Cousin Rafaelito Valdés supported my position. Pepa's son from her first marriage was a caricaturist and journalist, so he acted as a sort of artistic adviser to us. He also designed elegant costumes for us, like the suits he created in the style of satin pyjamas with black pants and white tops with silver buttons. Each of us sported a different embroidered pattern designed by him, all with a marine theme: a seahorse, a shark, a mermaid or a whale. He also had ideas about branding. He was the one who thought up the pennant with the head of the Indian princess Anacaona on it. We always hung it at the back of the stage, and that way people could see from far off which café we were playing in. He also painted the motif on our music stands: Anacaona, with a feather in her hair, armed with a bow and arrow, striding alongside a river through a soft, hilly landscape in the last rays of the sun.

We had so many admirers. The polite, shy ones would discreetly call over the head waiter and tell him to ask us what we would like to order. And it would be for the whole band. Naturally, we would have liked something to eat; one of

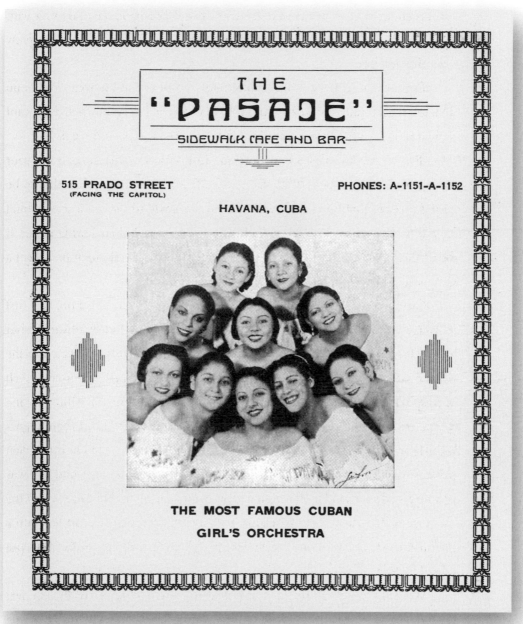

THE "PASAJE"

SIDEWALK CAFE AND BAR

515 PRADO STREET
(FACING THE CAPITOL)

PHONES: A-1151-A-1152

HAVANA, CUBA

**THE MOST FAMOUS CUBAN
GIRL'S ORCHESTRA**

Above and overleaf: Menu and list of drinks at the café of the Hotel Pasaje

DRINK'S LIST

COCKTAILS

Pasaje	.35
Alexander	.40
Bacardí	.30
Daiquirí	.30
Brandy	.40
Bronx	.40
Clover Club	.40
Cabrera	.35
Gin	.40
Ideal	.35
Manhattan	.30
Dry Martini	.30
Mary Pickford	.40
Old Fashion	.40
Pick me Up	.40
Presidente	.30
Sazerac	.40
Whisky	.40
Vermouth	.30

FIZZES

Gin	.35
Silver	.35
Golden	.35
New Orleans	.35
Sloe Gin	.40

RUM

Albuerne White	.20
Albuerne Gold	.25
Bacardí White	.20
Bacardí Gold	.25
Bacardí 1813	.30
Bacardí Elíxir	.30

WHISKIES

Scotch & Rye	.35
Scotch & Rye Highball	.50

PUNCHES

Brandy Egg Nog	.50
Egg Nog	50
Milk	.40
Whisky Egg Nogg	.50
Rum Egg Not	.40
Claret Egg Not	.50

FANCY DRINKS

Absinthe Frappe	.50
Brandy Cobbler	.40
Brandy Flip	.50
Gin Cobbler	.40
Mint Julep	.50
Port Flip	.50
Rum Collins	.40
Sherry Flip	.50
Tom Collins	.50
Whisky Cobbler	.40

RICKEYS

Gin	.40
Brandy	.40
Sloe Gin	.40
Whisky	.40

GINS

Bols	.30
Aromática	.30
Gordon Dry	.30
Sloe Gin	.35

BRANDIES

Domecq	.30
Domecq Tres Cepas	.35

Domecq Fundador	.40
Martell Three Stars	.40
Henne:y Three Stars	.40
Felipe II S. B.	.50
Anticuario S. B.	.50
Tres Copas	.35
Soberanos	.40

VERMOUTHS

Fernet Branca	.35
Nollie Pratts	.30
Ama	.25
Gancia	.25
Torino	.25
Pemartín	.25
Brocchi	.25

LIQUORS

Anisette	.35
Anís Mono	.30
Apricot Brandy	.35
Cherry Brandy	.35
Benedictino	.35
Contreau	.35
Triple Sec	.35
Crema Cacao	.35
Crema Menta White	.35
Crema Menta Verde	.35
Crema Cassis	.35
Curacao	.35
Gran Marnier	.50
Kummel Gilka	.35
Kirsh	.35
Chartreuse Yellow	.35
Maraschino	.35
Raspail	.35
Liquor Berro	.30

BEERS

Tropical	.25
Tropical 50	.30
Cristal	.25
Polar	.25
Hatuey	.25
Pilsner	.50
Beck Beer	.50
Bass Ale	.50
Guinnes Stout	.60

MINERAL WATERS

Poland Water	0.50	0.30
White Rock Water	0.40	0.30
Vichy Water	0.60	0.30
San Francisco Water	0.20	0.15
La Cotorra Water	0.20	0.15
San Antonio Water	0.20	0.15
Canadian Dry	0.25	0.20
Coca Cola		0.15
Quinabeer		0.15
Ginger-Ale "San Antonio"		0.15

SCHERRIES & MOSCATEL

Viña 25.	.30
Moscatel.	.30
Fine Sherry.	.30
Agustín Blázquez.	.30

PORT WINES

Oporto Constantino.	.30
Morgado.	.30
Old Madeira.	.30
Invalid Port Warres.	.30

RHINE & MOSEL

Ruedesheimer.	3.00	1.50
Liebfrauenmilch.	3.00	1.50

HUNGARIAN WINES

Tokaji Furmint.	2.50	1.50
Tokajer Szamorodnes.	2.00	1.15

ICE CREAM

Vanilla.	.25
Chocolate.	.25
Guanabana.	.25
Coconut.	.25
Almond.	.25
Strawverry.	.25
Sugar Apple.	.25

FRUIT JUICES

Grape fruit.	.20
Orange.	.20
Pineaple.	.20
Water melon.	.20
Guanabana.	.20
Lemonade.	.20
Coconut water.	.20
Tomato juice.	.25

PORTUGESE WINES

Verde Basto.	3.00	1.50

FRENCH WINES

Pontet Caned, Red.	3.00	1.50
Saint Julien, Red.	2.25	1.25
Chateau Margaux, Red.	3.00	
Medoc.	3.00	1.50
Chablis Sparklin.	5.00	2.50
Chablis Still.	3.00	1.50
Chambertin, Red.	3.00	1.50
Chambertin Sparklin.	3.00	1.50
Mouxeaus Sparklin.		2.50
Graves White.	2.00	1.15
Sauternes White.	2.00	1.15
Hout Sauternes.	2.25	1.25
Chateau Iquen.	4.00	2.10

RHINE AND MOSEL WINES

Ruedesheimer.	3.00	1.50
Liebfrauenmilch.	3.00	1.50

SPANISH WINES

Marqués del Riscal, Red.	2.00
Castell del Remey, White.	2.00
Castell del Remey, Red.	2.00
Federico Paternini.	2.00
Tres Ríos, White.	2.00
Tres Ríos, Red.	2.00
Cía. Vinícola, White.	2.00
Cía. Vinícola, Red.	2.00
Vino Gallego.	2.00
Champagne of all brands.	6.50

SANDWICHES

American bread combination.	0.30
Cuban „ „	0.35
Club sandwich.	0.50
Swiss cheese.	0.25
Sweet ham.	0.30
Foigrass.	0.40
Caviar.	0.45
Turkey.	0.50
Sardines.	0.35
Chicken salad.	0.60
Assorted meats and crackers.	0.60
„ „ Turkey.	0.70
Rochefort cheese.	0.40
Cream cheese.	0.30
Fruit salads.	0.40
Fruit cocktail.	0.50
Peaches and Pears (can).	0.25
Anchovies.	0.40
Angulas.	0.40
Bonito.	0.60
Atún.	0.40
Merluza.	0.60
Calamares.	0.60
Salmón.	0.40

SPESIALITIES

Hot Chocolate.	0.25
Milk.	0.25
Cocoa.	0.25
Coffe and milk.	0.15
Lipton tea.	0.15
Ice tea.	0.20
Toast and Butter.	0.10
Malted milk.	0.30
Chocolate milk.	0.25
Lady fingers.	0.10

those delicious caviar sandwiches, for instance. But they cost a steep forty-five centavos, and Cuchito had impressed upon us that we should only order beverages. So we would order a milkshake or ask for malt beer. Both are nutritious and filling. Many gentlemen would ask the head waiter in amazement whether we wouldn't prefer champagne. At the Hotel Pasaje the guests drank Vichy water, Chablis, Château Margaux, Liebfraumilch, Beck's beer or a Guinness Stout with their sandwiches. The fans who couldn't afford any of this would stroll along under the arches and try to draw our attention by calling out, 'Chinita, I'm getting palpitations', 'Chinita, you're so beautiful, give me a smile!' I ignored such foolishness, but Ondina didn't; she was fifteen, after all.

In the Hotel Pasaje – at the table the owner, Ramón (second from right)

Millo and Ziomara in Café El Dorado

One Saturday Ondina poked me in the side at the Café El Dorado and asked, 'Why do those guys at the table over there keep staring at me?'

'They sit there almost every night,' I said. 'Maybe they're students.' They didn't drink much and were livelier than the other patrons. Then I too noticed that they kept looking at Ondina and gesticulating. They whispered to one another, seemed to be amused, and kept laughing out loud.

Ondina was steaming. 'Those jerks are making fun of me. I'll show them.'

A couple of days later Ondina was at Lázaro's house for trumpet lessons. Her fury was still making her edgy. She told him about the presumptuous youths and said, 'Teach me "The Mother".' Here I have to explain that there is an old melody that follows the rhythm 'Stick it in your mother's c—!' There's no misunderstanding the meaning of *that* tune. Ondina pestered Lázaro: 'What notes do I have to play if I want to insult the mother of such a lout?'

'But *Chica*! Why do you want to learn something like that? The young men only wanted to pay you compliments, flatter you because you play so well and you're so good-looking.'

'Flatter, my foot! They're making fun of me. I want to get even.' She was so insistent that Lázaro finally revealed it to her: 'La-la-la-do-ti-la-do-fa'.

The following Saturday, the students were sitting at their usual table, and they were already grinning by the first song. The piece was almost over when Ondina suddenly stood up, turned in the direction of the animated group and let her trumpet blare out across the café: 'La-la-la-do-ti-la-do-fa!' Martino, the owner of the premises, and all the rest of us were paralysed with horror. But one of the young men carried on smiling. Despite the insult, he stood up, beaming, came over to Ondina and declared his love – in front of everyone and in all seriousness. His name was Mario Escobedo and he was from Cienfuegos. His mother was Italian and his father Spanish. Days later he came courting Ondina at the house, and she was more gracious towards him. Later, when he became a pilot in the air force, he would fly his plane to follow her on tour. He was often already at the venue even before we arrived by car or bus, welcoming us in his cheerful manner.

Mario and his friends weren't the only ones who were always hanging around when we performed. There was another young man, extremely good-looking, very athletic. I couldn't help staring at him. He was blond, had blue eyes, beautiful teeth like pearls on a necklace, and was six feet tall. Everything about him was perfect! He always came with a friend and one evening the two of them headed towards me and introduced themselves rather formally. My heart was pounding hard. Rogelio Reyes y Gavilán was the name of my heart-throb, but he said to just call him Roly. Reyes y Gavilán – that name made it instantly clear that he belonged to the upper class. His family had lived in Cuba for hundreds of years and were very well known; they were millionaires. Roly told me he was a member of the Miramar Yacht Club. He was the number one backstroke swimmer there and won races constantly. Roly and his friend Fabio invited us all to have a drink. Oddly enough, Roly didn't seem to have much money, but I later learned that his parents kept him on a tight leash.

So now I fell in love for the first time – and in a big way! It quickly became clear that Roly was crazy about me too. One evening he asked, 'What do I have to do for you to invite me to your house and accept me as a true boyfriend?' I evaded the question. At night when I went to bed I couldn't sleep. I was just fourteen, head over heels in love, and it scared me. 'What if this man someday no longer returns my love? I will suffer so much if he leaves me. I won't be able to stand it.' Thoughts like this kept running through my head. 'He loves me, but surely for him this is just an adventure. He would never marry me.' Maybe I was talking myself out of it. I didn't know what to do. These thoughts tormented me even at the café, where I kept running into him.

Suddenly his friend Fabio de Moya started courting me too. A couple of days later he said, 'Alicia, would you permit me to visit you at your house?' Without thinking, I said yes. That's how Fabio, not Roly, became my first boyfriend. Fabio was also from the upper class, light-skinned, with blondish hair. He was almost as good-looking as Roly, but he wasn't quite six feet tall. And I wasn't in love with him. That's an advantage, I thought: I have this relationship well under control. The only problem was that I was officially going out with Fabio, while Roly was always nearby. And I couldn't get him out of my head. The relationship with Fabio didn't last long. When we broke up, Roly's interest was sparked again and he began courting me. But I kept my distance.

In the following weeks I suffered greatly, but luckily I didn't have much time to be sad. There were simply far too many suitors coming to court us at the *aires libres*. I was particularly amused by four brothers, whose last name was Azores. Their father was Lebanese and they were very well educated. They came to our show almost every evening. One Monday, on our day off, all four of them showed up at the house to pay a visit. I especially enjoyed that day. I took a long bath in the morning and then loafed around and relaxed in the hammock upstairs. Around four o'clock Father called up the spiral staircase, 'Alicia, come down, the *Polacos* are here!' He meant the Azores brothers. Father called them *Polacos*, because in Cuba people call everyone from Europe *Polacos*, Polish people. My friend Eladio Secades later offered an explanation for this: 'We Cubans throw all immigrants into one pot as *Polacos* because we're so uninterested in where foreigners come from that we can't even be bothered to look in an atlas.'

The Azores brothers' visit was a great success: Alfredo flirted with Bola, Cheo with Ada, Jorge made a try for Millo, and even I caught one of them: Miguelo. He had the darkest hair of them all. It wasn't any big love affair between us, but we had a lot of fun. The eight of us would play dominoes for hours on end, or someone would suggest we go to the café across the street for a milkshake.

Another suitor was Gustavo de la Vega, a warm-hearted young man, also from a good family. His uncles were all specialist physicians. I liked Gustavo. He was good-looking, even if he didn't quite match up to Roly. He also spoke perfect English. Gustavo worked in the Banco de Nueva Escocia and together with his two friends he followed us everywhere. 'Where are you playing tonight?' they would ask, and then come with us, no matter where we were appearing; or they would take us out to dances. So Gustavo's friends became our friends too. I had no idea whether Gustavo was in love with me or with Millo – or both of us. Sometimes he devoted all his attention to me when we went out and said,

'Alicia, I want to dance with you!' The next moment he would turn his attention to Millo and joke, 'No, now I would rather dance with you, Millo.' It was a game, but our friendship became even closer. By now, Millo and I had no secrets when it came to matters of the heart. We agreed that one of us would marry him. He was tremendously likeable, pleasant and amusing.

Gustavo and his friends had bought a car together. One evening when the three of them were out together they hit a car that was parking on the street. Gustavo, who was driving, was severely injured. Apparently the others got scared and ran off, leaving him behind in the car. When the police discovered the smoking wreck, Gustavo was still alive, but he died on the way to the hospital. All he had on him was our band's business card, so the police called us first. We were shocked. We told his mother the news at once. She almost went out of her mind with grief. Millo and I worried for a long time: why hadn't his friends helped him? If they'd taken care of him at once, his life probably could have been saved. But it was his fate to die young, we told ourselves. We loved him very much – and we always will.

A lot of good-looking young men went in and out of our house. With eleven young women and girls, it was practically like a parade! Of course it inevitably caused jealousy. I didn't have the slightest idea how two-faced some people could be; I was so naïve. 'Oh, I'm so fond of you,' some would say with a smile, then the next moment they'd stab you in the back. The problem was finding out whose intentions were good and whose weren't.

One afternoon Bola was planting lilies in the front yard next to one of the big laurel bushes when she discovered something strange and called for us to come outside. Deep in the ground lay a cross made of wood that was tied together with something, I don't know what. Someone must have buried it there, but why in the world would they do that?

In front of the laurel bushes: (from left) Cuchito, Ziomara, Millo, Alicia,

Ada, Bola, Cachita and Ondina

Ada immediately had an answer: 'It's a *trabajo* for black magic!'

'A *trabajo*?'

'*Trabajos* are objects that bring bad luck. They're meant to make you break up with your sweetheart, to mess up your job, or to ruin your health.'

We puzzled over this for a bit, but then didn't give the matter another thought. However, as we worked in the garden the next day, more strange objects appeared – eggshells, bone splinters, hair, all kinds of things. Mother was now quite worried and ordered us to get rid of the two big laurel bushes. But we loved them, because they formed an arch, a green portal. 'Ay, when one of us gets married, she'll look great posing for pictures beneath the arch.' It made no difference. We dug the bushes up and threw them away, because Mother was too afraid that envious people would keep hiding their evil magic at night underneath the beautiful laurel bushes.

After my piano lesson I talked to Rita María Iturralde, my teacher, about what had happened. According to her, there were not only people who deliberately wanted to harm others with black magic, but also people who didn't wish any harm, yet couldn't help sending out negative vibes. 'They have the evil eye. They praise a plant, a flower, a child, it doesn't matter what, and something bad happens.' There was a woman in our neighbourhood, Rita María explained, who only needed to make a seemingly harmless comment, like 'Look, what a beautiful plant. How lovely it is. . .' and the very next day the plant would wither and die. Was it the evil eye? I didn't want to know about any of these things, but then something happened that convinced me.

It all started when a gentleman from Santiago kept coming to the Prado night after night. He was a big admirer of our band and said he was enchanted by us and our music. He told us about his children, who were also musicians. 'You perform on stage and are very successful. There are certainly many people who envy you for being so popular. Protect yourselves from the evil eye. Wear an amulet!' The next evening he gave each of us a piece of jet, a deep-black semi-precious stone, carved in the shape of a fist with the thumb sticking out like a thorn between the index and middle finger. We followed his advice and always wore the amulet on a necklace underneath our clothes. Months later, Millo's whole body swelled up, and her face too. She was completely disfigured. Then she noticed that her amulet was gone. She had apparently lost it. I worried for a long time about this incident. Why did she swell up like that? It couldn't have been the food, as we had all eaten the same thing.

Millo at once got hold of a new jet pendant. But she lost this one too, soon after she got it. It was because of her power of attraction that this kept happening to her. She lived for music. The audience was enraptured, they went crazy over a young girl who could drum with such passion. And Millo always smiled as she played. When a musician drums hard, his face is usually tense. But Millo would sit there beating her drums and gazing at the audience with a relaxed expression. She radiated joy; she was dreamy and introspective, and evoked in many listeners the feeling that she was communicating with them personally. At the same time she gave the impression of being distant and unapproachable. That was her charm. The man from Santiago consequently bought Millo amulets that were bigger and more powerful. Yet it was always in the *aires libres* that they kept either breaking or disappearing.

Millo became the star of the band and was adored by many men, not just the one from Santiago. She was showered with jewellery. One admirer was a regular visitor to the *aires libres*, though he was more an admirer of her music than a suitor, because he was about forty and Millo still a youngster. They got to talking and found out that they were both born in November. 'I'm going to bring you two topazes; that's our birthstone,' he declared. He gave her two large rectangular yellow stones, which she had made into magnificent earrings. So by the age of twelve Millo was already wearing spectacular jewellery. Another of her admirers, an American, showed up one evening with gold earrings set with tiny rubies and diamonds. Those fantastic works of art glittered mysteriously like oriental lanterns against her dark hair. That's when I learned that jewellery has something magic about it, that some pieces brought me luck and protected me. I didn't want to take my jewellery off even when I went to bed. Father took a sober view of all these gifts. 'Take the jewellery, but don't let yourselves get involved with the men. Gold is gold. Jewellery keeps its value.'

For a brief time there were eleven sisters playing in the jazz band. Two soon left, so in the long run there were only nine of us in the band. Sister number one left us on a beautiful summer's day in La Villa when we went to the Yayabo Club. Almost the whole family and a few friends came with us, including Carlos Bernal, nicknamed 'The Blonde', and Titi Varona. While we were playing, a drunk made a pass at our trombone player, Emma. There he stood, right in front of the stage, which was decorated with betel palm fronds. He was beaming at her, waving and shouting for her to come and dance with him sometime. Emma ignored the embarrassing scene, but the man was obstinate. It wasn't unusual for some guy to be absolutely determined to dance with one of us, but we had all agreed not to get into conversation with people from the audience when we were doing a show. Anyone who wanted to meet us had to think up something clever. In the middle of *El Barrilito* or 'Roll out the Barrel', as the polka is known in English, the drunk insulted Emma in front of everyone: 'Who do you think you are? You've danced with me plenty of times at the dance academy.'

'Me, in a dive like that?' she exclaimed.

Emma aged eighteen

Now it was time for little Ziomara to play her trumpet solo. She positioned herself in front of the drunk and played him the 'La-la-la-do-ti-la-do-fa' – 'Go stick it in your mother's c—!' But to our horror the drunk started singing along: 'In your mother's, your mother's, your mother's!' Burning with fury, Ziomara raised her trumpet to smash him over the head. Two of our friends hurried over and escorted the unpleasant fan off the premises. Mother immediately gave Ziomara a talking-to, pulling on her braids.

Emma had dissolved into tears. 'I've had enough of these bellowing louts!' she announced.

We tried to cajole her: 'You shouldn't take it so seriously. You want to hang up your trombone just because of some boor?'

It did no good. She gave up music. And so we had to talk Ada into playing trombone as well as tres and fiddle. 'Now I'll get to take trombone lessons with Antonio Castro,' she rejoiced. Cuchito also learned to play trombone.

Emma now turned all her attention to her previous occupation. At the age of thirteen she had learned to type and take dictation, and she soon found a job with Don Pepe Serrano, owner of what used to be called the Ten Cents department store but was now named Casa Grande. Don Pepe made import and export deals, and Emma became an apprentice in his office. Then the Casa Grande went bankrupt. The section heads took employment with Felipe Quinsama, owner of the big La Filosofía department store on Calle San Nicolás, and Emma went along with them. A good tactical move, because at La Filosofía she was able to make a career for herself. The associates soon said to her, 'Emma, you've saved up some of your salary; why don't you invest it in this department store? We're an anonymous joint-stock company.' She seized the opportunity, became a stockholder and rose to section manager. From then on she was able to help us out of a jam at many a difficult moment.

~ **Anacaona** ~

The second sister who played in the band for a short time only was Flora. She was also employed at the Casa Grande department store, where she sewed baby undergarments. The clothing was sewn by hand and then embroidered with the most exquisite stitching. When Flora lost her job because of the closure of Casa Grande, Cuchito talked her into joining the band. Cuchito was determined to integrate another original percussion instrument into the orchestra: the marímbula. Flora liked the idea because she wanted to be with Ada. Those two were just as inseparable as Millo and I were. They were always telling impudent jokes, laughing and spreading good cheer. And how they loved to dance! They did an astounding Charleston on the dance floor that could take your breath away. From then on Flora took lessons on the marímbula and played in the septet.

During her time at the department store Flora had met a colleague, Inocencio González, and fallen in love with him. This somewhat older man with a jaunty expression, a roguish smile and slightly wavy hair was born in Asturias in Spain and had come to Cuba as a child. He had instantly taken a liking to Flora, with her cheerful nature and spontaneity. Over time, as things grew more serious, González was firmly against her playing in the band and insisted, 'I don't want you putting yourself on display. You don't need to!' All at once Flora began talking about giving up the marímbula.

When Father heard about this, he summoned her. 'Flora María, what do you mean you don't want to go on playing?' He always called her Flora María.

'I don't want to go on, because González doesn't approve.'

'No, no, no! Tell that Galician to come and see me right away. I have to speak to him urgently.'

He wasn't really from Galicia, but the next day González came to see Father and was told, 'You have no right to order Flora María about. If you marry her, you can order her around as much as you like, but as long as she lives in this house and is single, you don't make the rules.'

Father was quite indignant, and when González finally got a chance to speak, he replied, 'We *are* going to get married, Matías.' Father was speechless. He would have liked to object, but that was no longer possible, since he had been the first one to mention marriage.

González and Flora went to the notary a few days later and signed the marriage contract. From then on he was able to have a say in her life, as her husband. He did so amply, and the first thing he did was to end Flora's brief musical career.

Our brother Otto was an example of how differently men usually reacted to the so-called marriage question. Otto had fallen in love with Felicia, a very beautiful but rather difficult woman. Her family lived in Batabanó, a fishing village on the south coast. Otto worked in Father's store and made a good salary, but I would often hear him asking for his wages early in the middle of the week. In fact, with all his requests he was probably getting more than his actual salary. At any rate we noted with astonishment that Otto was able to afford to move Felicia's whole family from Batabanó to Havana. He took them all under his wing, spending liberally. It wasn't long before Felicia became pregnant by Otto. He, however, had no intention of getting married at all. Our discussions at home grew more and more heated. Father and the elder girls kept trying to persuade him: 'Would it seem right to you if someone did something like this to one of your own sisters?' Otto finally relented, but his marriage to Felicia wasn't happy and lasted only a few years.

The next in line for marriage was our eldest sister, Cachita. She radiated warmth and at the same time was a quiet, modest, almost shy person. All at once she was being courted by Carlos, who was a bit of a daredevil. Mother put up with him because she knew his parents, who came from Matanzas, like her own parents. The family lived in a frame house across from the San Francisco movie theatre. Carlos would walk back and forth in front of our house, as suitors normally did. Sometimes he would stop outside the front door and signal to Cachita through the narrow windows set into the French doors. He would shower her with compliments from the veranda, and of course she was

Cachita aged twenty-seven

flattered. And she didn't seem particularly bothered by the fact that Carlos was known for loafing around in the park across the street, smoking marijuana.

Cachita and Carlos got married – against the wishes of Father and Mother. But they had the blessing of Aunt Pepa. 'I can only advise you not to listen to what people say. If you love him, do what your heart tells you. . .' Pepa sometimes meddled in our family affairs just so she could defy Father. Carlos, however, was an incorrigible ne'er-do-well and had never learned to read and write. But Cachita was sure that she could make something out of him. She tried to find him a job and finally got him a position with Campiña, one of Cuchito's suitors, who had started a bus company called Omnibus Aliados. But Carlos soon abandoned his career as a bus driver because he thought he could make more money as a singer. He joined a trio in the style of Servando Díaz, but that was a financial disaster. He seemed to think that a musician could make money without working.

The young couple moved into the second floor of an apartment building in the neighbourhood. One day Cachita came home and discovered that someone had broken in. The bedclothes, blanket and jewellery were gone, including Cachita's cuff bracelets, the kind made of solid gold, real cañitas. Our Uncle Japón accompanied her to the police station to file a report. The police superintendent told her right to her face, 'Your husband did it.' Carlos and his brother-in-law were notorious for this sort of thing, but Cachita refused to believe it. She didn't report him, but after that she gave the money she made every evening in the *aires libres* to Mother for safekeeping. Carlos was furious and quarrelled with her about the money, but Cachita held firm, until one night Carlos pulled a knife out from under the pillow and threatened her with it.

She came home to us in tears and told Father about it. 'You go to the police station right now and report this,' he told her.

The policeman gave her some good advice: 'Kick him out. We'll go with you to the apartment right now. Pack everything he owns in a box or just hang it on the clothes line in the courtyard.'

She didn't have the courage to follow this advice, but she did finally get a divorce.

I wasn't alone in losing my appetite for marriage after that. None of us paid much attention to the well-meaning advice of friends and admirers who told us to tone down our lifestyle, cut back on our performances and turn to the calmer, more settled life of 'respectable' women. Our favourite dream was to be invited to play abroad, in New York or Europe, in the most exciting metropolis of music and nightlife.

None of us apart from Cuchito had any idea how hard it is for a band to establish itself or for a musician to make a living. Winning popularity with the public was one thing, but getting decent pay and good contracts, especially abroad, was a whole different story. When we played in the *aires libres*, agents often came up to talk to Cuchito. One of them, named Morales, acted very importantly and bragged about his far-reaching contacts with big promoters. He ended by saying how profitable it would be for everyone if we worked with him. 'And how do you envisage dividing the proceeds from these appearances? What percentage would you want?' Cuchito asked without beating about the bush. Morales started to stammer. 'How much would you leave for us: seventy, fifty, thirty per cent?' Cuchito grilled him. He instantly lost interest when he realized that Cuchito knew what she was talking about. She got her business sense from Father. Shrewdly calculating, she would review the offers with a critical eye. Is the partner serious? Does the venue have a good reputation? 'We don't unpack our instruments without an advance,' was her motto. The music business, or rather doing business with musicians, can be a real snake pit.

Up until this time, the year 1935, none of us had travelled beyond the borders of Cuba. The women in the Orquesta Ilusión, on the other hand, had an invitation to Jamaica. I wasn't the only one to envy them. Cuchito was torn, because her colleagues needed a trombone player. Herminia, a musician with Ilusión and a friend of Cuchito's, had asked her to join them. Cuchito agreed, also out of friendship. 'I'm going to go with the girls. We'll see if it brings us luck and we finally get an engagement abroad.'

She was gone two weeks when an offer for a tour of Puerto Rico came sailing through the door. Our first foreign engagement – and Cuchito wasn't here! Should we accept the offer anyway? She was the only one who knew about contracts. And on top of that our singer, Graciela Pérez, had fallen ill.

'You'd be nuts not to go to Puerto Rico. Who knows when another chance like this will come along,' Emma told us. That convinced us. We negotiated with the promoter, who had some quite unusual ideas: 'I need Anacaona to be as complete as possible and then I need the same number of musicians again to assemble a big band.' Our job was to play in huge dance halls, like the one in Hotel Condado in San Juan, during Carnival and get the crowds in party mood. The promoter therefore also drew up a contract with the female orchestra Orbe. At that time the group and their director, Esther Lines, were in the process of breaking up. There were arguments in almost every band and as a result of the tensions there was a big turnover in artists; they would sometimes form new groups together. Even in our band temperaments sometimes clashed. But because we were sisters, we had no choice but to make up.

The promoter kept coming up with new demands. For one thing, he needed at least three violinists. Even with both bands together there were only two. We immediately thought of our cousin Ninón, who had studied violin but didn't play music professionally. This beautiful Chinese girl, very sporty and with a perfect figure, had caused a furore in Havana because she was the first woman to appear on the beach in a two-piece bathing suit. She practised judo and popularized it among women.

A week later we were sitting together on the train – twenty women and girls – on our way to Santiago at the other end of Cuba, from where we took the ship. Cuchito must have travelled through Santiago at the same time accompanying Ilusión on their way home from Jamaica. Only when she got home did she find out that we had just missed each other. She was inconsolable.

We had hardly boarded the ship, which for some reason was nicknamed the *Dictator*, when each of us, according to the old custom, tossed a centavo into the sea. The coins were for the black Virgin of Regla – or Yemayá, as she is called by her African name – the owner of the sea. All travellers who wish to cross the sea unharmed have to throw a centavo into the sea. But you can't give her any of those shiny aluminium centavos, they have to be dark like the American pennies, made of copper, because Yemayá has dark skin.

I was excited about the sea voyage. We crossed the *Paso de los Vientos*, the Windward Passage, between Cuba and Haiti, and the *Paso de la Mona*, the Mona Passage, between the Dominican Republic and Puerto Rico. The crew explained to me that the sea is just as varied as the mainland, with its own valleys and mountains. When we hit a storm, most of us were immediately seasick. Only Ada, Bola and Cachita discovered a new talent. They never got sick at sea, no matter how high the waves.

We had barely arrived in Puerto Rico when the friction began. The husband of Esther Lines, the director of Orbe, suddenly started acting like he was our manager. On the third day he mentioned casually at breakfast that the orchestra on this tour would be called 'Orbe-Anacaona', and he showed us the poster that was going to be put up all over

Ondina with admirer on board the Dictator

Getting things swinging at the Carnival parties

town. We choked on our coffee. This self-appointed director had slyly printed all the promotional material behind our backs. It was bad enough that Orbe got first billing. Now we realized that we were being exploited because Cuchito wasn't with us. And Cachita, our substitute director, was far too reticent to say anything. Ada was the first one to speak up.

~ Anacaona ~

'What you're doing here is in breach of contract. We are Anacaona and remain Anacaona, and not Orbe-Anacaona,' she told him.

Without thinking I too piped up, adding to the tension: 'Either you change the posters or we go home today.' We were determined to abandon the tour if the name wasn't changed. But he wouldn't give in. Without another word we went to our rooms. Only when he discovered that instead of coming to rehearsal we were at the hotel packing our bags did he whimper, 'All right, the band will be called Anacaona.' In the programmes, flyers and posters the name 'Orbe' was obliterated with a thick black line. Only the name 'Anacaona' was left visible. After this incident the name 'Orbe' was never mentioned again, and we even had a lot of fun working with the other women.

The masked balls in Puerto Rico amused me, because the people came up with the most outrageous costumes, just like in Cuba. On our second evening, despite all our principles, I briefly leapt into the fray and had a little dance. After all, Cuchito, who had always kept a strict eye on us before, wasn't there. The guests were so dressed up they were unrecognizable, and that gave the dance its special appeal. There was no way of knowing what or whom you were dealing with. I noticed that in Puerto Rico the girls were carefully supervised by their mother or a chaperone, who made sure that no young man got too close – just like in Cuba. Now, however, the girls formed groups to buttonhole the men. 'Come on, let's dance, come over here!'

'Which one do you want? Which one do you prefer?' they asked impudently. If a boy decided on a partner dressed in a sugar sack with only two slits left for the eyes, he could expect to find an old lady concealed underneath. And if a man embraced a girl with beautiful long hair and huge breasts, he might come to discover that he was holding an attractive young man in his arms. Our opportunity to join in the fun was limited, because we were being paid for our performances, after all. Ninón and I constantly had to run back on stage, and the later it got, the more I saw how the teasing sometimes resulted in dicey situations. From a safe distance I saw more than once how petty jealousies would escalate into full-blown brawls.

During our two months in Puerto Rico I naturally missed Father, Mother and Cuchito, but otherwise I hardly suffered from homesickness because we sisters formed a family all on our own. It gave me self-confidence to know that we had successfully prevailed over Orbe's manager. At the age of fifteen I could reassure myself that in the end, bad times also have their up-side. To be honest, homesickness didn't really grip me until we were just about to arrive home. After making a wide turn into the Bay of Havana our ship moved slowly towards the harbour entrance, towards Morro Castle, the noble fortress that is the symbol of the city. I gazed at the ocean-front promenade, the Malecón, and at the tall buildings with their façades bleached by the salty wind. How surreal and lovely Havana looked all of a sudden. Ondina and I stood next to the first engineer and the radio operator, who were also enjoying the view from the deck. We had become friends, since this was now our second journey with them. Suddenly the radio operator said, 'Ondina, quick, get your trumpet and play the national anthem. You have permission to climb the mainmast.'

Ondina dashed off and without the slightest hesitation climbed all the way up the mainmast. From that dizzying height she played our anthem, 'La Bayamesa'. We sailed through the narrow passage past El Morro. The harbour district looked close enough to touch. Cars stopped on the streets and the passers-by stood still. The sailors from the Cuban navy who were working on the deck of a ship clicked their heels together and saluted. No one moved a muscle as the anthem was played; it was just like a photograph. 'That is the most beautiful island the human eye has ever seen,' I thought. That's what Columbus once said, when he saw our land for the first time.

With make-up on they looked like young ladies: (from back left) Concha Giral, Bola, Cachita, Elsa Rigual, Ada, Ondina, Millo and Alicia

Chapter 6

In the Paris of the New World

The following year we received a letter from Mérida, Mexico. Adolfo Rosado, manager of the biggest theatre there, the Péon Contreras, was inquiring whether we would like to appear during Carnival. An interesting offer, yet we wondered how he had come to hear about us. Later we found out that a friend of his had heard us at the *aires libres* and had raved about us: 'These girls are fantastic. Having them here for Carnival would be a sensation.' So Rosado's curiosity was aroused. He promptly asked his friend to send him a picture of us, which he then passed around the table to his friends. His Argentine partner who ran the theatre with him exclaimed, 'That's the girl for me!' Another said, 'No, I prefer this one!' And Adolfo too joined in: 'Leave this one to me!' In next to no time they had divided us up and had decided to invite us to perform.

They came to the harbour to meet us at the ship, full of anticipation. Adolfo later told us what his first impression had been: 'It was a huge surprise when we saw our chosen ones for the first time. Coming down the gangway of the ship were not the young women we had imagined from the photo, but a bunch of kids!' Millo, Ziomara and I were wearing checked cotton dresses, scarves on our heads, striped socks and white sandals with buckles. In the photograph in question, on the other hand, we were posing in elegant evening gowns, made up like real ladies.

Ondina aged eighteen

Adolfo Rosado was very solicitous. He booked rooms for us at a hotel in Mérida that belonged to one of the foremost families in the city, the Gamboas. The 'Paris of the New World' was what people called Mérida during the sisal boom at the end of the nineteenth century. The hotel belonging to the Gamboas still possessed an opulent splendour and the extensive grounds spread out over an area the size of a cattle ranch in the midst of the city. The owner of the hotel, Mireya Gamboa, treated us like daughters.

After only a few performances we became well known in the city, and this had unexpected results. Ondina, who was about to celebrate her eighteenth birthday, was besieged with admirers. She looked fantastic; she was slim, yet curvaceous in all the right places, and, most importantly, she wasn't as aloof as before. With her cool, witty charm she drove the men crazy. Which is exactly what happened to a very well-known singer named Carlos. He presented a daily radio show in Mérida that everyone listened to. One afternoon he started raving about his 'Princess Yokoito', meaning Ondina. The whole city heard his undisguised declarations of love. 'Princess Yokoito, with your eyes so clear and cool like the pond in a Japanese garden, my tortured soul goes up in flames at the sight of you. You relentless pulse that drives my heart wild, to you I dedicate the next song...' And Ondina? She acted as if this had nothing to do with her.

On our day off we would sit on the terrace of the hotel overlooking the swimming pool and the huge hibiscus trees. One day when we were waiting for our lunch we heard faint music coming from the street. Ada crept over to the balustrade to look. In the middle of the street in front of our hotel stood a whole band playing merrily away. We didn't think much about it, but that evening, just as we were going to bed, Millo and I heard soft, romantic music outside. Excited, we lurked behind the windows and saw the same band playing on the street.

Mireya said, 'They're giving you an evening serenade, to lull you to sleep.' A lanky young man with a dark mane of hair combed straight back stepped forward and sang:

> *Estrellita, little star of the distant sky*
> *You know my longing*
> *You see my pain*
> *Come down and tell me if you like me a little*
> *Because without your love I cannot live*
>
> *You are my star, my beacon of love*
> *You know that I soon will die*
> *Come down and tell me that you like me a little*
> *Because without your love I can no longer live*

How were we supposed to get any sleep after that? Mireya knew what to do; she dashed down to the street and invited the musicians in, saying, 'The Orquesta Anacaona would like to express their thanks with a tequila.' We slipped into our clothes and darted down to the terrace. There the leader of the group introduced himself, Raymundo Montoya, a first-class trombone player. The other musicians simply called him 'Papa'. *La papa* means 'potato', and *el Papa* means 'the Pope'. The double meaning of potato and Pope was a way of teasing Raymundo, because he had once wanted to become a priest. His band was known all over Mexico as Orquesta del Cura, the 'orchestra of the priest'.

Our guests hadn't even finished their drinks before it was clear to everybody that Raymundo's musical performance had been intended for Ondina. He only had eyes for her. But Ondina showed no sign of interest. One day he gave her a phonograph and a record by Louis Armstrong, whom they both greatly admired,

Ondina with an admirer

and with this he finally won her attention. Ondina sat relaxing in her hotel room and listened to the tunes. Then Cuchito turned serious and urged Ondina to return the present. 'If you keep that record player, Raymundo will think that you're considering a long-term relationship with him and might even think of marriage.' Ondina just stared mutely at the wall. She knew Cuchito feared that the band might break up because of this love affair. The next time she went out with Raymundo, Ondina gave back the record player and told him that she couldn't accept the gift, but she wanted them to remain friends. What a blow for Raymundo!

From then on Cuchito tried to keep admirers at an even greater distance, but it wasn't easy – the Mexican suitors were charming and so well mannered. With delightful gestures and an air of romance, they overwhelmed us with compliments. After our performances we would spend time with Raymundo and his musicians, as well as with Adolfo Rosado and his friends. They arranged excursions to the pyramids at Chichén Itzá, to the Indian markets in the countryside, and they showed us all of Yucatán. Despite all precautions, two months later Cuchito realized that Ondina, quite unnoticed, had found a new lover – namely Adolfo Rosado, our business partner. We all got along well with him and he always claimed that I was his little sister, because with my round face I looked like a Mayan Indian from Yucatán, but Adolfo had been fascinated by Ondina from the very first moment. She was the woman he had picked out in the photo. One day at dinner Adolfo and Ondina announced to everyone that they were going to get married. Cuchito was speechless. Even more so the next day, when Ondina ordered a bridal gown to be made. She wanted to prove that she was serious and wasn't going to let herself be talked out of marriage a second time.

The news spread through Mérida like wildfire. Ondina's friend spoke on the radio in a tearful voice about his unrequited love for Princess Yokoito. Our hosts, the Gamboas, hurried to give Ondina a hammock, a double one for married couples, and Adolfo himself gave her two breathtaking gifts: an expensive bracelet set with jade and a silver rosary. The wedding preparations were in full swing. There was nothing else for Cuchito to do but inform Mother and Father in Havana. Three days later at breakfast, Millo and I were imagining how the Yucatecans might celebrate a wedding, when Ondina suddenly dashed across the terrace, a big bag in her hand, and announced as she rushed by, 'I'm giving the presents back. I'm not marrying that Mexican, not on your life! *Basta!*'

Ondina said no more about her change of mind. We had no idea what had happened. We were all sure that she was in love with Adolfo, very much so in fact. I think it had something to do with her inferiority complex. She was always finding fault with something about herself. She felt like the ugly duckling, although she had a curvy figure, great legs and a full face – there was nothing wrong with her. On the contrary, Ondina had the best figure in the whole family. But because of her lack of self-confidence, she had already managed to offend her first admirer and his mother too. Ada thought there must have been a misunderstanding between Ondina and Adolfo; they had only known each other a few months, after all. Maybe a strange gesture or a funny tone of voice had prompted doubts which had now overcome her.

Our next engagement took us away from all this personal turbulence to the capital, Mexico City. We breathed a big sigh of relief. But then Ada announced that she had to leave for Havana. Her fiancé, Roberto del Cueto, had been bombarding her with telegrams, insisting that she return home immediately. Ada had been going steady for two years with Roberto, the younger brother of Julián, who was married to mother's sister Pepa. Roberto was a brilliant catch, an attorney

Overleaf: At a party given by the State of Veracruz Band in honour of Anacaona.
Right front with bottle, Adolfo Rosado.

Jalapa. Ver.
4-18-36.

by profession, and, like all his brothers, he owned a farm. When he and Ada got engaged, he gave her a ring with a cross made of exquisite diamonds and he was still showering her with gifts. He always brought her those lovely tin boxes of Huntley and Palmer's crackers – the best biscuits in the world. And naturally the rest of us benefited from his gifts. He only had one fault. Every time Ada had to travel or be away for more than two days, he would get mad and they would argue. Ada decided to give in one more time. She left the tour and took the first ship back to Havana. A short time later they broke up. I no longer know which of them had finally had enough. At any rate, Ada didn't want to look at that diamond ring any more and gave it to Mother. She kept it along with all her other valuables in her closet. Mother's closet became a regular museum for our love affairs, musical experiences and travels over the years!

To me, marriage seemed fundamentally difficult for a musician, because most suitors wanted to take us away from our audience so they could have us to themselves. Jealous men simply couldn't understand that in a sense a musician has to be shared. They just couldn't grasp that the show is one thing, but life's quite another. On stage we danced, joked and amused ourselves with the audience; but when we were done working, it was something else entirely. This kind of male possessiveness was the reason why almost all the female bands dissolved over the years. Soon Ensueño, Renovación, Ilusión and countless others no longer existed, because many musicians gave in to their partners, got married and vanished from the stage.

Besides the official performances, after two weeks in Mexico City we were invited to do a guest appearance of a special kind. We entered a modest private residence through a back courtyard in the city centre. Our hosts, who greeted us effusively, were prominent exile Cubans, friends of Cuchito and her former university colleagues. They didn't want to show their faces in public because they

Ada

*(From left rear) Ada, Alicia, Millo, Cuchito, Concha Giral,
Ondina, Cachita and Elsa Rigual*

belonged to the left-wing movement 'Joven Cuba', which was fighting for Cuba's economic independence from the United States. The regime's opponents had fled to Mexico and built up an operational base there, hence the secrecy. This is how I met Raúl Roa, the intellectual leader of the group. At a second private soirée we met the future president of Cuba, Carlos Prío Socarrás. Cuchito had no inhibitions about joining in discussions with the intellectual circle, but I contented myself with listening. I was impressed by the eloquence of the politicians and the candour with which they talked, yet at the same time I didn't feel at ease in their company. It seemed important to them that we support their ideas, but I was a musician and didn't feel qualified to do so.

After this second trip abroad, which lasted more than five months, we finally did it: Ada, who administered the cashbox, was able to pay the Galician back his loan. What a triumph after all those years of uncertainty! The mortgage was paid off. Until then all of us received only pocket money, because Cuchito had been putting our earnings into the household funds. For this reason, Father felt indebted to us for the rest of his life. Right up to the end, he insisted on paying all the associated costs of running the household. I always protested, because we often earned more than he did, but we didn't want to hurt his feelings, so instead we often bought other things, such as new furniture for the living room. Only the dining room survived our zeal to modernize, because Mother managed to stop us in time: 'Are you crazy, girls? The furniture in the dining room stays. It's made of mahagony.'

Chapter 7
'Who Here is Working with an Indian Woman?'

In the early days of our septet we used a waltz for our theme song. On a trip to the Dominican Republic – the homeland of Anacaona – our friend Armando Oréfiche, the famous pianist, felt inspired to dedicate a song to the Indian princess. When he played it for us on his return, we were so enthusiastic that we asked him if we could use it as our theme song. From then on we would sing it at the beginning of every show:

> *By the blooming river*
> *Walks sad Anacaona*
> *With a wounded heart*
> *For the one who will not return.*
> *Hear the tender* areíto
> *That she sang yesterday*
> *In the green palm forest*
> *With her love of sweet illusion.*
> *Anacaona, your song*
> *Was the lament of a grieving heart.*
> *Anacaona, queen of the tribe,*
> *Your fate carried a curse inside.*

~ Anacaona ~

Anacaona, that song awakenened
Your harsh struggle to survive
Anacaona, your life was so cruel.
Anacaona, unhappy Indian queen.

Everyone in Cuba knew the name Anacaona, but most people only knew that she was cruelly murdered by the Spaniards. To my shame I must admit that even we didn't know any more than that. Graciela Pérez, our vocalist, pored over magazines and books and one day told us at rehearsal:

'At the time of Columbus, when the Spaniards were subjugating our land, Anacaona's husband, Caonabo, was the ruler of one of five kingdoms on the island of Hispaniola. Using some false pretext, the Spaniards made accusations against Caonabo, claiming that he wouldn't acknowledge the King of Spain and the Pope. They took him prisoner and carried him off on a ship heading back to Spain. On the voyage, in the middle of the Atlantic, Caonabo died. I believe many people died during the crossing in those days. His wife, Anacaona, took over the regency.

'She was an unusual woman, a great beauty but also an excellent poet and composer of areítos. And she was also a diplomatic politician. She realized that she could not defeat the Spaniards, so she put aside her pain over her husband's death and came to an arrangement with her enemies. One day the Spanish governor, Ovando, announced that he would pay her a visit. Anacaona prepared an overwhelming reception for him where the most beautiful women in the kingdom danced and the areítos composed by Anacaona were played. But Governor Ovando suspected some sort of conspiracy. He gave his soldiers a secret sign and they butchered all the guests. Anacaona was thrown in chains and brought to the governor's residence. There, under some flimsy pretext, she was sentenced to death by hanging and subsequently executed.'

Cuchito had registered the name 'Anacaona' shortly after the band was formed, so we had the exclusive right to use it. Naturally we had nothing against Father naming his market stall at the Mercado Único 'Anacaona' after our first successful performances at the *aires libres*. On the contrary, we felt proud to see it displayed on a big sign. It turned out that in Camagüey there was a certain Señor Álvarez, who was a doctor and also the owner of a food-processing factory. He called his products 'Anacaona', and therefore asked Cuchito for permission to keep using the name. Cuchito agreed and didn't ask for one centavo. Señor Álvarez was so pleased that from then on he would send a package of his products to our house every month. So we regularly ate butter, cheese and chocolate packaged under the 'Anacaona' brand.

This wasn't the end of the difficulties arising out of our name, however. One day Graciela came to rehearsal looking depressed. Hesitantly, she told us about a seance that had been held at her house. Being a spiritualist, she believed that a person's spirit lived on after death and intervened in the world of the living. At this seance several departed spirits had spoken.

'Who here is working with an Indian woman?' one of them asked.

Graciela at first sat quietly, but suddenly the band came to her mind and she stammered out, 'I am.'

Then the spirit came out into the open as Anacaona. The princess spoke via the medium who was leading the seance and ordered Graciela to tell us the following: we should be present at the next seance, and that meant all of us. What Graciela told us sounded more than mysterious. Cuchito didn't take it very seriously and hoped that the matter would simply be forgotten. But a few days later Graciela took us by surprise: 'I've called a spiritualistic mass in honour of the Indian woman Anacaona for tomorrow. You have to come. It's our night off.'

It was evening in Havana as we set off in two taxis to Graciela's apartment, one of those mild summer evenings with lots of hustle and bustle on the streets. But I was thinking only of what this night had in store for us, and gazed indifferently at the traffic. Graciela greeted us warmly, as always. Soon we were sitting in her living room by candlelight, the windows wide open. Traffic noise and radio music seeped into the room, but we felt far removed from all that, as if we were on a lonely island.

A slim young woman from the district of Regla acted as medium. Tense silence filled the room as she slowly sank into a trance; in the candlelight her face took on unreal features. Suddenly it wasn't the woman from Regla who was sitting there, but a stranger. A shiver ran down my spine. Is that Anacaona? Absolutely! It had to be her, because she spat out the words furiously: 'Why have you taken my name? Who let you have this name? Whom did you ask for permission to use it?' She shouted, What right do you have to assume my name? If you do not respect me, you'd better watch out.'

We were all left paralysed, staring at the candle. Nobody dared say a word. The medium relaxed. I looked over at our sister Bola, who had sat down on the sofa to rest. All of a sudden she slumped down, instantly asleep. *Dios mío!* It was as if she'd had a fit. We were frightened. Nothing like this had ever happened to Bola before. Then, just seconds later, Anacaona's husband, Caonabo, spoke through the medium. His voice was that of a strong warrior: 'I have only put your sister to sleep to prove my power to you.'

With frantic gestures the medium tossed a white cloth over Bola so that the spirit would go away. 'See that, Caonabo, the sister will no longer allow you through her body,' she said. And at that the spirit gave in and vanished. Bola woke up completely unaware of what had occurred. The rest of us didn't know what had happened either.

For a couple of days I walked around in a daze. Cuchito's nerves couldn't take any more; she felt guilty and swore to give Anacaona her due in the future. She bought a porcelain figurine and a picture of the princess and put both on the dresser in her room. She regularly put fresh sunflowers in a vase, and set out several glasses of water. Immediately after the seance, Graciela visited a painter and commissioned a portrait of Caonabo. I got to see the picture at the next seance: he looked very manly, a splendid example of an Indian.

From now on Cuchito regularly attended spiritualistic mass, as demanded by Anacaona. And every time she would hear, 'Now the Indian woman is coming.' Anacaona became her guardian angel and after several seances Cuchito noticed that she had the ability to contact the spirits directly. There are people who have this gift, who can hear the departed spirits, while others can even see them. They aren't put to sleep like Bola, and they don't channel the spirits through their bodies, but they have the ability to enter into a relationship with the spirit in a conscious state, even when they don't invite it. It's important to develop this ability under the guidance of experienced mentors. Then the spirit can be very helpful in daily life, and you can ask for specific help in an emergency. I hesitated to get involved in earnest with spiritualism, because the departed spirits can also cause you problems. Sometimes they force you to turn to them by making you ill. They get so close, cling to you so tightly, that your entire body suffers. You get bad headaches or feel dizzy.

That's exactly what happened to Cuchito. She felt sick, and Anacaona, her guardian angel, told her what she had to do. Not until she had followed her instructions did she get back on her feet again. So Cuchito, like so many in Cuba, developed a special relationship with a departed spirit, in this case our patron saint. It was Anacaona who protected her from then on, and I believe it was she who also guided our fortunes.

~ **Anacaona** ~

KONINKLIJKE NEDERLANDSCHE
STOOMBOOT-MAATSCHAPPIJ N.V.
(Royal Netherlands Steamship Company)
(Compañía Real Holandesa de Vapores)
AMSTERDAM

On our way to Panama

In November, once the hurricane season was over, we set sail for Panama. An influential entrepreneur from Colombia, Enrique Pascual, had booked us on a tour of Panama and Colombia. Our group consisted of eight sisters, the vocalist Anita Permuy and the pianist Delia Valdés. Delia was the wife of Alfredito Valdés, the singer in the Septeto Nacional. Our first engagement was in a nightclub in Colón, the vibrant city at the entrance to the Panama Canal. Right after we arrived, the manager asked us, 'How about two of you dancing the rumba and performing as a couple?' His proposal took us by surprise. There are different types of rumba, the most popular one being *guaguancó*, a sensual dance in which the man tries to seduce the woman and she resists, a provocative courtship in which the couple stops just short of touching. It's a kind of

On board the ship

mating ritual, very erotic, but none of us would ever dream of dancing rumba on stage.

Delia and Anita told the manager, more as a joke than anything else. 'If you keep the audience under control and guarantee that they won't storm the stage, we'll do it. What's the problem? It's only a show.' Anita wanted to take the role of the man. The manager opened the nightclub's storeroom and she picked out a magnificent costume: white trousers and a white shirt, both made of muslin. The shirt, a *guarachera*, had a cascade of ruffles on the sleeves, trimmed with bright red piping – a traditional man's costume from Cuba. Around her hips Anita tied a red silk scarf. Delia selected an extravagantly designed, colonial-style dress. It was a pink, fitted gown with flounces set off with black ribbons and a small train. Without much practice, they decided to attempt it that same evening.

The audience fell silent when the two stepped out of the wings. It was only after careful scrutiny that anybody could tell that Anita was a woman in drag. Quite gallantly she led Delia to the front of the stage and moved up close to her from behind – as is traditionally done in the rumba. The two of them rolled their hips close to each other until their bodies were quivering in unison. The audience went wild. Spurred on by cheers, whistles and suggestive shouts ,the unusual dance couple put even more vigour into their display of courtship. The two of them put on a phenomenal rumba show to go with our hot rhythms. And then, as Anita smiled seductively at the audience, she inadvertently stepped on Delia's train. We all held our breath. For a moment both danced carefree until Anita noticed that she was caught and couldn't get loose from Delia. Without moving from the spot, both of them swayed their hips violently. We repeated the musical passage over and over, the audience was roaring, flowers and paper napkins flew onto the stage, everyone was going wild. A female orchestra – the first that the city of Colón had ever seen – and to top it off a show like this: it was a sensation!

Millo and admirers

On the second evening there was a huge crowd. Celina Reinoso, a professional Cuban rumba dancer and actress who was appearing in town at the same time, came to our dressing room in a state of high excitement. 'Girls, you've emptied all the joints in town! The other nightclubs and restaurants might as well shut down. Everybody wants to see you.' Celina told us that even the extensive red-light district, with its innumerable bars and easy women, was totally dead.

Instantly, the bosses of these establishments took counter-measures. On the third evening, a representative of the musicians' union delivered orders for us to pack our bags immediately and leave the city. The manager of our nightclub was told, 'Pay off the girls. It's over! They're not allowed to play here any more.' We had actually been hired for a two-week engagement, but they wanted to get rid of us at all costs and paid our full wages. So it wasn't too hard for us to leave.

Delia and Anita's improvised show demonstrated that giving a sensual and provocative performance on stage was like walking a tightrope. As dancers and musicians we were simply using rumba and *son* to parody love and eroticism with a wink and a bit of banter. In reality we were making fun of the bad reputation of Cuban women. Everyone thought that Cuban women were easy to get into bed. When I was introduced to a man he would say, 'Aaah, so you're a Cuban, eh?' and shamelessly look me up and down in a lewd way. 'Why is it that Cuban women are all so good at shaking their hips?' was the next question.

If I was in a good mood I would tell him, 'Well, dancing is an art. You shouldn't get it mixed up with the blatant flirtation of women who are only out to get money out of their suitors' pockets.' Unfortunately there were Cuban women who had become dancers or singers just so they could go looking for men in the cabarets. They had no conception of serious art.

With the rumba dancers Alberto and Clara

Our next stop was the big Colombian port of Barranquilla. On our third morning there, the waiters at the café where we ate breakfast thought up something
special. They knew that in Cuba, and especially in Havana, one Spanish word
is strickly taboo; it would never pass our lips, although it is common in every
other Spanish-speaking country: 'papaya'. For every Cuban this fruit represents
a woman's private parts. Instead, call it *fruta bomba*. That morning the waiters
shouted the orders out in a loud voice when they were ready. 'Miss Ondina's *café
con leche*!', 'Mrs X's omelette!', 'Mr Y's huevos.' Everyone smiled indulgently
and even we couldn't quite suppress our giggles. And then, ringing out clear as

a bell, came the cry, 'Miss Cuchito's papaya!' Loud laughter erupted all around. We wished the floor would swallow us up, Cuchito above all. That was the end of our breakfast.

An appearance at the national trade fair was the prelude to this concert tour. We were to be the main attraction at a performance in honour of the president of Colombia. We went to see the Cuban consul straight away because we needed a work permit. There, to our astonishment, we found a Colombian in charge, Enrique Buitrago. Apparently they couldn't find a Cuban in a position to take on the post of consul. Buitrago owned a clothing business and was obviously a wealthy man. A special affection soon developed between him and Cuchito. With his far-reaching connections Enrique was able to relieve us of many worries, and he even arranged additional engagements for a small tour to Venezuela. Thanks to Cuchito's winning personality we found a friend and patron in almost every place we went.

At the end of the tour, we bade the consul a warm farewell and stood with our bags at the pier, waiting for *Los Santos*, the American cruiseliner. But the weather was so stormy that the ship couldn't dock and continued on to Cartagena. We were left behind and would have to wait two weeks for the next ship. It was especially annoying that we would have to pay for our own board and lodging, since we had no more engagements, but Enrique spontaneously invited us to stay at his beach house. A true friend. We were even happier about his offer when he assured us that he would visit us as often as he could. He came almost every day and even took us out to eat, so we didn't have to spend all the money we had earned. Twelve-year-old Ziomara loved him like a father, but Enrique naturally liked to spend most of his time with Cuchito.

We were soon able to pay our friend back, because he kept his promise and visited us in Cuba. He called us from the Hotel Nacional, the elegant building with the two towers right by the sea, where he was staying. Father protested, 'No, sir. You helped my daughters so much. We insist that you come stay with us.' We put him up in Cuchito's bedroom on the ground floor and Cuchito moved up to our rooms on the second floor. I think Enrique had actually fallen in love with her in the meantime, and she was not averse to him either. From then on he came to visit every year and stayed several days each time. He assured us that he much preferred the comforts of our big family home to the luxury of the Hotel Nacional.

~

With the 'magician', Alberto Socarrás

Chapter 8
From Broadway to the Champs-Elysées

In the spring of 1937 the record company RCA Victor expressed interest in signing us up and Cuchito negotiated the contract. The anticipated call from them came in June to go to the studio to start recording *son* numbers. Full of awe, we entered the building on Calle Galiano. With one step we left our familiar world behind, the noise, the busy life on the narrow street. We crept along dark corridors to the studio carrying our instrument cases. There stood a row of silent men all wearing serious expressions. All I thought was: how can anyone play music in this kind of atmosphere? We began. After the first piece, one of the men finally managed to open his mouth. 'Please enunciate more clearly,' he said to Graciela. Another commented that Ondina's trumpet was too loud, and a third asked Millo not to come in so early with her solo. Obviously they were keeping track of every tenth of every second.

The first day was long, very long, but despite all the critical remarks, after two days we had recorded six pieces: 'Maleficio' ('The Spell'), 'Algo Bueno' ('Something Good'), 'Bésame Aquí', ('Kiss Me, Right Here'), 'Oh, Marambé Maramba', 'Amor Inviolado' ('Love Inviolate') and 'Después que Sufras' ('After You've Suffered').

During a break on the first day Alberto Socarrás, a slim dark-skinned man in an elegant suit, came over to us. He and Cuchito knew each other. He just

149

sat there for hours, listening intently to our music. From that day on, he and Cuchito were inseparable. The spark had been ignited. When it came to passion for music and a love of experimentation, they were soul-mates. As Cuchito told us after the session, Socarrás was a celebrated and extremely innovative musician who was better known in the States than in Cuba. A flautist, he was one of the first Cubans to make it on the New York music scene. In Cuba, Socarrás had played classical music and had been quite well known, but he had hardly made a centavo. Jazz, his passion, drew him to the United States. In New York he made it into the legendary Cotton Club; for years he had a steady gig there and continued to appear with Duke Ellington, Louis Armstrong and Cab Calloway. His act was known as 'Socarrás and his Magic Flute'. He was the first ever to play a jazz solo on the transverse flute, and he paved the way for a number of Cuban musicians who, side by side with American greats, developed Latin jazz. But he kept being drawn back to Cuba. A Cuban can't just forget his *arroz con pollo*. He came here regularly to visit his mother, but as an asthmatic he found it hard to breathe each time he set foot outside the aeroplane. He often had to be taken directly from the airport to the hospital because he couldn't tolerate the hot, humid climate in Cuba. The drier air in New York suited him better.

Socarrás later told us that from that afternoon in the RCA Victor studio, he couldn't stop thinking about bringing us to New York. And sure enough, a few weeks later he called up Cuchito and said he had an offer for us. A dream engagement! We would play for the opening of the Havana-Madrid nightclub on Broadway, and then perform in their show for another six months. New York! I could think about nothing else but that city, the city we'd dreamed of for so long. I'd pored over magazine pictures of Broadway, Central Park, display windows at Tiffany's and plush interiors of big hotels. I felt like I already knew them intimately. What would it be like to see it all with my own eyes?

Socarrás reserved cabins for us with the Ward Line on a steamer named *El Oriente*. Maybe it was the excitement, but a few days before our departure Cuchito came down with a terrible stomach ache. A doctor was called to the house and diagnosed a serious illness. He forbade her from setting foot on the ship, saying she was too weak to travel. So we had to leave without her – Ada, Bola, Ondina, Millo, Graciela and I. Cuchito was devastated by this turn of events, poor thing. Was fate again going to deny her an

On the Ward Line

opportunity to be with us when we finally reaped the rewards of all our efforts?

An icy wind greeted us in New York. It was November and was far colder than anything I had imagined. Socarrás picked us up at the dock and took us to an apartment. We immediately went shopping for food, as there was a small kitchen; we were off to a good start. Graciela gazed out of the window and called our attention to the building across the street, where good-looking young men kept going in and out. It was a music academy which specialized in vocal training. We spent ages staring out of the window and making comments.

A few days later, while out walking, we got into a tricky situation. Suddenly there was a frantic commotion; people were running back and forth and bumping into us. A group of men were obviously on the run, and were being chased

Ondina with Graciela in New York

. . . with Mario Bauzá

by another group. Shots were fired. 'That isn't so unusual,' people explained to us. 'This is the Bronx, after all.'

Appalled, Socarrás responded, 'No, no, no! You girls can't stay here.'

The next day we moved into another apartment on the corner of West 68th Street and Columbus Avenue, almost right next to Central Park and very close to Broadway. It was a first-class residential neighbourhood, which meant that the rent was high – but the promoter was paying for it. From there both a streetcar and a bus went directly to the Havana-Madrid. On days that weren't so cold we would stroll along Broadway, with its unique mixture of delis, hotels, theatres and shops of every description.

~ Anacaona ~

Socarrás was incredibly considerate to us, perhaps because Cuchito wasn't there to take care of us. He felt quite at home in New York after all the years he had lived there, but he could still remember the little things that could confuse a new arrival from the tropics. He and a friend, an elegant young man with dark blond hair, visited us every day. They wanted to bring the city and the jazz scene to life for us, so they took us along to the Cotton Club to see Cab Calloway, and to the Paramount to hear Benny Goodman. And they had plenty of useful advice. With regard to the notorious cold they suggested, 'Take your baths at night before you go to bed, never early in the morning. If necessary, wash first with hot water and then shower with cold. Then your pores will close up and you won't catch pneumonia.' They also warned us, 'You have to cover up every inch as warmly

. . . with Machito

Graciela and Ondina

as possible. If there's any spot uncovered, that's exactly where the cold will catch you.' We all laughed, but it was a joke that had to be taken seriously. It's no surprise that many women in New York wear woollen underwear in the winter.

We had just settled one night when the doorbell woke me. I went to the door and heard, 'What are you all doing here? I thought you were out playing music!' It was Cuchito. I stared at her and couldn't get a word out; she looked so thin and changed because of her illness. She hadn't been able to keep any food down for such a long time that she was completely emaciated. In the meantime the others had got out of bed to greet her. Although she looked frail, it was a great joy that she was now with us in New York and she soon made a complete recovery, largely due to the excellent American tap water. They said it came from the mountains and was very pure.

We were extremely anxious to see how an American audience would react to our first performance on Broadway. The Havana-Madrid was an exquisite nightclub with a unique ambience, a blend of feudal Spain and fiery Cuba. The guests sat under palm trees at tables draped with white tablecloths and gazed at huge frescos of Mediterranean landscapes and medieval city views, as if they were in the dining room of an Andalusian castle. At the circular bar across from the dance floor, Cuban bartenders served drinks with typical Havanan flair.

The fourteen-piece house orchestra under the direction of Nilo Menéndez played first to warm up the crowd. The dance pair César Tapia, a dark-haired Mexican, and Dorée, a blonde American, then performed the first number of the musical show. The next acts were Alberto and Clara, rumba dancers from Cuba, the Spanish singer Mercedita Zaya Bayán and Alfredito Valdés, our friend from the Septeto Nacional. On this first evening the crowd exceeded all expectations. It turned out that musicians, actors and artists alike were drawn to the Havana-Madrid to hear *son*. While playing we kept a watchful eye on the audience. One

154

night, we recognized Tommy and Jimmy Dorsey in the crowd, their drummer Buddy Rich, Gene Krupa – Benny Goodman's drummer – and the future mambo king Xavier Cugat! Socarrás introduced us during the break. After our performance we sat and chatted with our new friends, or rather, Socarrás told them about us, because our English was very poor. But language was soon no longer a problem, because all these great musicians just wanted to hear us play, and some of them could even make themselves understood fairly well in Spanish. After gigs, they enjoyed our company as much as we did theirs.

Millo wanted to buy a new drum kit, and Buddy Rich insisted on accompanying her to the music store run by a certain Manny. 'I'll help you find the best one,' he said. 'My own isn't very good, because I signed a promotional deal with the manufacturer and can't change.' That's how Millo wound up with a drum kit that Buddy Rich would have liked for himself.

Menu of the Havana-Madrid

To understand what attracted these jazz greats to our *son*, it is important to know that since the early 1930s Cuban songs such as Ernesto Lecuona's '*Para Vigo Me Voy*' ('Say Sí Sí') and Nilo Menéndez's '*Aquellos Ojos Verdes*' ('Green Eyes') had conquered the USA. The world was impressed by the way that *son*, with its unmistakable rhythm, emanated from the very soul of the Cuban

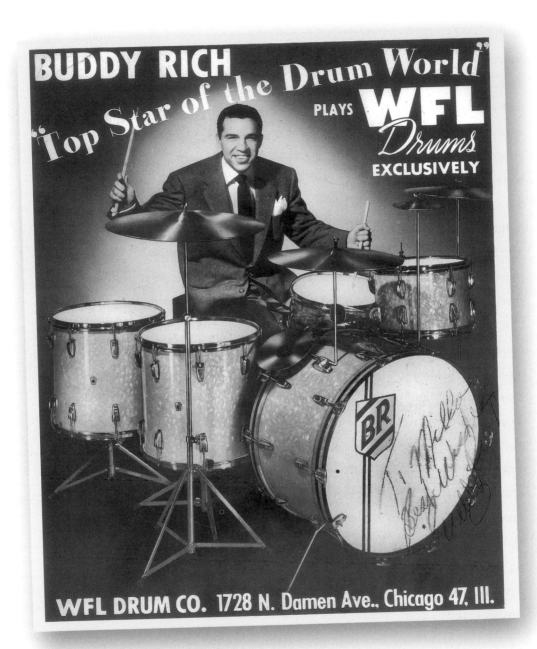

Autographed card from Buddy Rich with a dedication to Millo

musicians. The foreigners trying to imitate us had a hard time. We, on the other hand, were amazed at the wonderful new sounds the Americans were creating in jazz. We all looked up to each other, and there was a sense of competition that was mutually beneficial. Each musician went to a great deal of trouble to master the other's music at least as well as his own. In this way, Cuban music got jazzier, and American jazz picked up Afro-Cuban rhythms. All of this was brewed together on the New York music scene. In January, Benny Goodman and drummer Gene Krupa were the first jazz musicians to give a guest performance in the venerable Carnegie Hall. The bands of Jimmy Dorsey and Harry James, who also regularly came to our performances, recorded Cuban songs.

We would have loved to give the experts a taste of our jazz too. But in the Havana-Madrid we were expected to play only *son*, and always the same pieces. One day it became too much for us, and Cuchito complained to the management. 'No, you can't change any of the music, the whole show is based on those tunes,' she was always told. But these restrictions also had a lot to do with the American musicians' union. We were strictly forbidden to play American dance music. The union had pushed through this rule out of fear that we might take work away from American musicians. Just picture this: almost every night a mysterious gentleman made his rounds of the Havana-Madrid; he was an official with the immigration service, checking to see whether we might be playing dance music. I think he really only came because he liked our style. But even so, if one of the patrons had started dancing, then the official would have been legally obliged to intervene. It made Cuchito nervous, because sometimes it was almost impossible to stop people from dancing. You could see them already jiggling their feet and it was clear that the urge to shake a leg had grabbed them.

Overleaf: At the Havana-Madrid with the dance duo Clara and Alberto, the Spanish singer Mercedita Zaya Bazán and Alfredito Valdés, the vocalist of the Septeto Nacional (far right)

A couple would step onto the parquet floor and instantly someone from the night-club would grab the microphone: 'Ladies and gentlemen, either you sit down or the septet will have to stop playing. If you dance, the musicians will lose their work permits.'

After a few months, playing the same songs over and over was getting on our nerves. We hatched plans with Socarrás. He wanted to market us internationally and he taught us all about jazz. We would practise at two o'clock in the morning, after the last show. That was more convenient for us than getting up at nine in the morning. So we practised with this celebrated musical magician sometimes until dawn, trying to emulate the correct sounds and phrasings. 'You have to feel jazz, just like *son*. You can't think: What am I playing? You have to feel the music as if it were a part of yourself.' One morning, after several weeks of this, Socarrás finally looked pleased with us. I sensed that we had done it at last. The jazz rhythms were coming of their own accord, from deep inside.

Next Socarrás set up an appointment with Mr Carl Fischer. His firm was one of the most important artists' agencies, with branches in Argentina, Brazil, Uruguay, Chile, England and many other countries worldwide. Socarrás knew that Mr Fischer and the head of the International Casino of New York in Paris wanted to mount a gigantic show, and they were still looking for a band. César Tapia and Dorée, the dance duo from the Havana-Madrid, had already been hired and had told the promoter about us. Socarrás also succeeded in arousing Mr Fischer's curiosity by explaining to him that we were not only capable of performing as a septet, but were actually part of a larger orchestra of international stature. They set a date and Mr Fischer rented a studio especially for our audition.

Cuchito, of all people, who was always so conscientious about everything, forgot to tell us about the audition. Mr Fischer and Socarrás waited in vain in the rented studio. What must Mr Fischer have thought of us? The next day he showed up at the Havana-Madrid with the head of the International Casino. They listened for a while. Then Mr Fischer inquired about Millo and about 'that slim girl', meaning Ondina. He knew from Socarrás that she had rehearsed an extra two songs: 'That Old Feeling' and 'Once in a While'. He invited Ondina over to his table and asked in a fatherly tone, 'Please sing the songs in English.' Ondina nodded, went up on stage, and sang them in a very cheeky way. Fortunately no one knew that those two songs made up her entire English vocabulary. Mr Fischer was silent for a while. Then he said that we had convinced him. It was only in the American pieces that he was apparently able to evaluate the quality of our playing. The Cuban *son* was too foreign to him. To everyone's surprise Mr Fischer offered us a contract on the spot. He insisted, however, that Socarrás rehearse the new jazz numbers with us before we left; he would also be joining us as musical director and doing the arrangements.

We felt extremely flattered, but we wanted to discuss it before we accepted. We had had another offer from Hollywood. Paris or Los Angeles? But even our American friends said, 'You should go to France. There's no better gig than one in Paris, and especially at Les Ambassadeurs!' We accepted Mr Fischer's offer.

It wasn't until the end of our New York stay that we had the opportunity to experience different venues. We were invited to give guest performances at NBC Radio, the Hotel Commodore, the Hotel Pierre and finally the Waldorf-Astoria. The Art Deco skyscraper, which had been built only a few years earlier, was the pinnacle of luxury. We had the great honour of being invited to the show on the occasion of Franklin D. Roosevelt's birthday. We shared the stage with an

Guest performance at the Hotel Commodore with Enric Madriguera's orchestra

overwhelming array of artists: the Marx Brothers, Lee Robinson, Duke Ellington, Cab Calloway and many others.

After a dance number by the Norwegian Sonja Henie, internationally celebrated as the 'queen of ice skating', we were next on the programme. We stood on a stage that was normally used for dances. On the upper floor, the house orchestra that had accompanied the other artists remained motionless. Millo, with her bongos, took up position in front of us and we let rip. Unimpressed by the high-society audience, she started her solo in the middle of the number. It was as if she wanted to say, 'What do I care if I'm in the company of important folk? I'm going to play the drums the same as always.' She was totally engrossed in her music and was having so much fun. When the audience applauded thunderously she woke up, saw all the people, including Eleanor Roosevelt, up in the box seats, and realized where she was. 'Thank you, thank you, thank you. . .' Millo repeated as everyone continued applauding. After the performance, actors and other celebrities came up to her, congratulated her and autographed her bongos. They couldn't believe that our sister, only fifteen, had already created her own signature drumming style. Afterwards, we all headed for the banquet, which was opened by Eleanor Roosevelt.

Before we set off on the tour to Paris, we made a stopover in Havana with Socarrás. For two weeks straight we practised at home every day. And what discipline we had! From nine in the morning until noon, from two in the afternoon until six, and from nine in the evening until midnight we practised, practised and practised some more. Finally, Socarrás invited over his former colleagues from the Philharmonic to get their opinion. There, in our living room, stood the foremost musicians in Cuba, listening to us with rapt attention. We didn't even dare to say hello, we were concentrating so hard on not making the slightest mistake. At the first break the tension finally eased. 'Your playing is flawless and you

164

sound as powerful as a large orchestra, even though there are only ten of you! It's the energy of youth,' said one of them. Our line-up for Paris was now set: eight of us sisters – Cachita, stayed home with her husband – the pianist Hortensia Palacios, and the vocalists Anita Permuy and Graciela Pérez.

The trip to Europe was a great personal triumph for Cuchito. She had succeeded in putting together a female orchestra that had a broad repertoire from *son* to jazz and was in international demand. Bourgeois Havana was astounded. The reporter Raúl Suárez Mendoza interviewed Cuchito a mere hour before our departure. The next day this article appeared in the paper:

'The director, Señorita Concepción Castro, is certain of their artistic success and is taking along a rich repertoire of their musical hits. Travelling with her is a wonderful Cuban flautist who has been celebrated in both Europe and the United States. Today at noon they board their ship at the Ward Line dock.

'Equipped with a new self-awareness, the woman of today is setting out to demolish old stereotypes. She finally wants to attain equality with men. The prejudice that for centuries condemned her to restrict herself to the domestic sphere is unimaginably powerful. To overcome these limitations, the modern woman of today is engaged in a fierce struggle for survival.

'She is beginning to contest male dominance in the factories and workshops, as well as in the field of music and other disciplines. She executes these different tasks with a relatively high degree of competence. Destiny has given her the opportunity to make herself useful, while men sacrifice their lives in the trenches, in the fight between brothers, in order to satisfy the vanity and desire for territorial expansion that irresponsible politicians cultivate.

'Today we encounter an extremely interesting woman. She possesses great courage and is an enchanting beauty. She is one of those young women whom our tropical sun lights up with the lovliest shimmer. We are talking about Concepción Castro Zaldarriaga, affectionately called 'Cuchito' in her family circle, the director of the popular and lovable band Anacaona, which has more than once celebrated triumphs with our native rhythms in the most important cities of Central and South America... We were only able to gather some fleeting information as we requested this interview at the last moment.

CUCHITO: *Hello, Señor Journalist. We're leaving Havana today to spend six weeks in Paris, the capital of joie de vivre, where we have been invited to perform.*

— *Are you going straight to Paris?*

CUCHITO: *No, Señor. First the steamer will take us to New York, where we will transfer to the Ile-de-France.*

— *What is your itinerary?*

CUCHITO: *First we're going to perform at Les Ambassadeurs, then we go to London, and perhaps after that to Nice. If our music is well received and they want to extend our contract, we would be more than happy to oblige.*

Cuchito

— *Is there anything you'd like to add?*

CUCHITO: *There is one important thing. We will be doing this European tour under the artistic direction of the fantastic flautist Alberto Socarrás*

Estacho. He has been wowing the crowds for eleven years with his melodies at the most important music venues in the US and the Old World. We have him to thank for the excellent contract we have in our pocket today.

'We saved a rather personal question to conclude our interview and inquired whether she was in love. And 'Cuchi', both intelligent and discreet, simply cast a glance at the flautist Socarrás, as she granted us one more charming smile.'

I was used to travelling by ship, but the *Ile-de-France* was something else. I was overwhelmed. This was no ordinary ship; it was a palace on the high seas. The luxury liner had four stacks, numerous decks, shops, cinemas, restaurants, ballrooms… Two bands had been engaged to entertain the guests. They invited us to play at a benefit concert for a seamen's welfare association. From then on, everyone on board knew who we

Socarrás

were. The captain was so taken with us that for the rest of the voyage we were allowed free access to the first-class deck as well as the second, although we continued to sleep in our third-class cabins. What appealed to us most in first class was the princely buffet. The food was magnificent. I liked the hors d'œuvres best. That was the first French phrase I deliberately committed to memory.

One evening, the younger girls, including Ziomara, who was twelve, tried champagne for the first time. The Cuban consul in France had invited us to join him and, before Cuchito could object, he ordered champagne. There stood a

On the floating palace the Ile-de-France

fine bottle embedded in ice cubes on our table. We were instantly tipsy. It did no good that Cuchito had always drummed into our heads that we shouldn't drink too much. But soon our strict director announced that we were rather tired from the long day and all the practising and were ready to go to our cabins. She had to be kidding! I could have stayed there the entire evening, sipping champagne in that splendid dining room among all the elegant people.

When the head waiter heard that we were leaving, he asked, 'What time would you like your bath to be drawn?' They always solicitously asked this question in French, English or Spanish. 'Would you like bath salts in your bath?'

I say! Unimaginable luxury. He was clearly unaware that we weren't travelling in first class, but had our cabins below in third.

One afternoon the sea turned rough. At supper-time hardly any passengers were in the mood to eat. Ada and Bola stood almost alone at the buffet, because they never got seasick. They began trying out all the delicacies one by one. Several times the waiter hurried to bring fresh plates: 'What would you like? What may I serve for you?' The staff were obviously happy that despite the bad weather there were still some grateful takers for their artfully arranged food. Ada and Bola were in seventh heaven.

We travelled the last stage of the journey by train. It was midnight when I gazed upon Paris for the first time. 'And this is supposed to be the City of Light?' I was disappointed. 'Why are all the façades grey and not painted?' In Havana the houses of the wealthy were always freshly painted, and I had expected something more of wealthy Europe. Later someone explained to me that they didn't paint the stone façades because they valued the patina of age.

Arrangements had been made for us to stay in a luxury hotel right on the Champs-Elysées. We glanced inside the foyer and realized that we didn't have the necessary clothing for such an elegant place. We asked if they could find us an apartment, and they promptly gave us a suite that took up an entire floor. We were instantly at home there. Graciela took over the kitchen and on the ground floor there was a bakery where we could buy eggs, delicious French pastries and all sorts of other provisions.

Paris had been completely under the spell of Afro-Cuban rhythms ever since the late 1920s, when Cuban musicians conquered Montmartre. The Europeans would very much have liked to imitate our rhythms, but they were too refined.

Paris, 1938: (from left) Ada, Cuchito, Alicia, Ondina, Millo, Bola and Graciela Pérez

The music critic Vuillermoz gushed effusively in the magazine *Candide* about the Cuban conga:

'No matter what object they use, the Cubans manage to produce unexpected sounds with their long, withered-looking fingers, sometimes hesitant, sometimes powerful; sometimes loud, sometimes soft; sometimes gentle, sometimes violent. With wood, metal, baked clay or tanned hides, they produce an inexhaustible range of delicious tonal colours, a veritable symphony of sound, creating universal harmony in the rhythm of the dance. Having heard the Cuban percussionists, I can safely forget all our percussion instruments, even the Basque tambour. Cuban rhythms are so enchanting, so full of

nuance, so poetic; the calabash filled with little pebbles sounds like silk being stroked with a rough hand, the sound of the clave is like a hammer falling on a silver anvil.'

Les Ambassadeurs was a cabaret and restaurant all in one, located right on the Champs-Elysées. We played during tea-time as well as in the evenings. But before work, even before the customers showed up, we took tea there. At a long counter we picked out the most tempting titbits from the abundant offerings: petits fours, éclairs, mille-feuilles, tarte St Honoré, and all sorts of other treats that I can't even name. French pastries are the best in the world. Tea was served by the maître d'hôtel. The head waiter was a penniless baron, but he had style.

The way he moved was very elegant. And what perfume he wore! I'll never forget him, simply because of his scent: 'Scandale' by Lanvin. I went crazy for those French perfumes: 'Rumeur', 'Arpège', 'Prétexte'. A friend of mine, the sportswriter Eladio Secades, later explained to me that while married women thought bathing and perfume were merely functional, a hygienic necessity, only true lovers really enjoyed the powers of attraction that those scents could conjure.

At three o'clock, we began playing. Our repertoire was international; we played tangos, waltz, jazz, simply everything. The audience didn't make a sound. There was not a knife or fork or voice to be heard. Utter silence. We nudged each other. 'Ay, it's as if there is no audience here at all,' whispered Graciela, 'but the hall is full of people.'

Cuchito explained: 'Actually, this shows good breeding.' She may have been right. We Cubans are very lively, we talk loudly and usually all at the same time.

In the evening during the nine o'clock show we were in our element. We played only Cuban music – *son*, conga and rumba. That was when the aristocratic crowd of Les Ambassadeurs begain to relax. The beautiful revue girls from the International Casino of New York danced to the rhythms. They strutted down a sweeping staircase in skimpy sequinned bathing suits, one of them with a tiny monkey perched on her shoulder. People were crazy about this tropical revue. The climax of the show was a typical Cuban conga. In the folk conga in Cuba, a group of musicians slowly meanders down the street to the hypnotic blend of the various drums and percussion instruments. Residents, passers-by, everyone gets swept along; they suddenly drop everything and join the line. Electrified, they raise their arms in the air as they follow the musicians, taking broad strides and wiggling their hips. The crowd sways to the rhythmic sounds like a mighty swell through the streets, gathering strength, and no one can escape this musical undertow. The conga in Havana was originally subjected to strong repressive measures, but then, ironically, in 1937, the city council, which for decades had outlawed it as 'primitive' and 'vulgar', officially permitted the conga at Carnival as a reaction to its acceptance among European high society. The Cuban composer Eliseo Grenet had invented a 'civilized' form of the conga for the European nightclubs. The dancers would line up in an orderly fashion and simultaneously do their steps, first left, then right, putting the rhythmic accent on the fourth beat. That's how it was in our show too, which each evening enraptured even the most reserved Europeans. They would jump up from their seats and dance the conga enthusiastically throughout the hall, as best they could.

After the show, at around eleven o'clock, we would shift to Chez Florence, a small, extremely exclusive *boîte* on the Rue Blanche in Montmartre. Many of the guests from Les Ambassadeurs would follow us there. Chez Florence was the hot spot for movie stars, celebrities and others who could afford champagne for 150 francs. There we were on the programme with the Quintette du Hot Club de France, the extraordinary jazz combo consisting of three guitarists, a bass player and a violinist. The guitar player caught my eye at once. He played fantastically, even though he was missing two fingers on his left hand. I became immediately addicted to the improvisations of this Django Reinhardt. He was about thirty years old, and because of his dark hair I thought at once that he was

Tous les
SOIRS
à MINUIT
CHEZ FLORENCE
61, Rue Blanche, 61
•
DJANGO REINHARDT - STEPHANE GRAPPELLY
et leur QUINTETTE
et
THE 10 ANACAONA SISTERS
direct from Cuba
•
Champagne à partir de 150 francs
❀
Directeur : **ALBERT**
des Ambassadeurs
Téléphone :
TRinité 13.90

'Every night at midnight at Chez Florence...'

~ **From Broadway to the Champs-Elysées** ~

a gypsy. Socarrás told me that he was indeed, and that he had lost both fingers in a caravan fire when he was eighteen. His brother also played in the quintet. I especially liked the Frenchman on the violin, Stéphane Grappelli. He was very friendly and had fine facial features and a great physique! And he played like a magician. His refined, swinging violin solos and Django's unique capers through gypsy music and jazz were a breathtaking combination. Although the quintet was at the peak of its fame, the musicians were as unassuming as their colleagues in Havana and New York. We would often sit together after work and have splendid conversations – but only with our hands and feet, because we didn't know any French and they didn't know a word of Spanish. How did we make ourselves understood? With each other's instruments. I often seized Django's guitar or Stéphane's violin and imitated certain musical passages that I found particularly interesting and inspiring.

Marlene Dietrich showed up several times at Chez Florence. After one performance she came up to us on stage, chatted briefly with Cuchito, and shook hands with all of us. I found it hard to retain my composure in the presence of such a star. I couldn't help staring at her, because she looked just like she did in the movies. Her figure, her skin, her complexion, her blonde hair. . . Everything about her was perfect. At Chez Florence we also got to meet the Duke of Windsor. We had read in the newspapers only a year before how this man had abdicated the English throne so he could marry his great love, an American divorcée. Ada had at once remarked, 'That woman made the catch of her life.' The Duke enjoyed the Paris nightlife even more because the burden of protocol had been lifted from him. He even invited us to a banquet that was given in his honour.

Whereas I was crazy about French perfume, Ondina yearned for French couture. She bought herself a stunningly elegant dress that was, of course, sinfully expensive. It fitted her like a glove. When she put it on and strolled along the boulevard past the cafés, the European men almost turned into Cubans. Hardly anyone could resist the urge to watch her walk by.

So we had our fun. We especially enjoyed the parties with the artists belonging to a small Cuban colony in Paris. We felt at home when we sat together with the singers Oscar López and Joaquina Riestra. Graciela Pérez, our vocalist, would prepare a Cuban national dish: black beans and rice, called 'Moors and Christians'. And we would wash it down with champagne. I would have liked to continue enjoying this European life to the full, especially since we had a contract for a subsequent engagement at the London Casino in England. However, a member of the British royal family, the Queen Mother, had just died, so our engagement was postponed. In the meantime, it was suggested that we could go to Spain, but the Civil War was raging there. And in Paris the shadow of the Second World War was already looming. The streets were filled with parades of troops, trucks full of soldiers, and immigrants who had fled from Germany. People were talking a lot about a possible war. The singer and dancer Josephine Baker, the undisputed star of Paris, was being treated with hostility by newspapers in Italy and Germany. There were so many things I couldn't make sense of. But Cuchito sensed that Europe was poised on the edge of an abyss, and she was adamant that we should leave. After we finished our contract, we took the German steamer *Iberia* back to Cuba. Soon afterwards we read in the paper that the *Ile-de-France*, our floating palace, as well as her sister ship, the *Queen Mary*, had been converted to aircraft carriers.

Millo and Cachita, 1940

Chapter 9
A Macho Guy is Always Tempting

After our return from Paris I decided to walk to the *aires libres* for our first performance. My saxophone case in hand, I strolled down the shady Calle San Nicolás, which cuts through the Barrio Chino of Havana like a fire-break. At the intersection with Calle Reina, a cacophony of noise enveloped me, with cars honking, the cries of the peanut vendors and the risqué remarks of the men who lavished a compliment on every passing skirt. I thought about the aristocratic silence of Les Ambassadeurs and the soft clinking of the silverware. Finally, I stood on Paseo del Prado in front of the Capitolio, with its wide staircase of Carrara marble. To my right were the awnings of the Hotel Pasaje.

Our colleagues from the other all-female bands gave us a decidedly cool reception. It was as if they didn't have the slightest interest in how we had fared in Europe. I would have liked to share our stories with them and tell them about the buffet with the Duke of Windsor, about Marlene Dietrich, Django Reinhardt and all the others. But our relationship with them suddenly cooled so much that it led to the following episode.

One afternoon as we were practising in the living room, the telephone rang. Carlos Alberto, our grandfather, had passed away. The news hit us like a bolt from the blue. For as long as I could remember, Grandfather had spent every Sunday with us, eliciting the exquisite tunes of the *danzón* from the piano as if by magic. Now he was dead and his body had already been laid out. That evening we had a gig at the Hotel Saratoga, and the owners of the cafés only allowed musicians to cancel if they could line up a replacement. Cuchito grabbed the phone at once and tried to arrange for a replacement band; it was normal practice for groups to step in for each other in an emergency.

'What a shame, but we really won't be able to help you out...' said the first bandleader.

'Aaah, I'm so sorry, but...' the second one answered. And so it went on. Everyone had an excuse. They all left us in the lurch, and we had no choice but to go and perform. While friends and relatives of Grandfather were saying their farewells, we stood full of sadness and pain on the stage of the Saratoga, playing cheerful rumbas and *sones*. Our audience wanted to be entertained, not knowing that we felt more like crying.

That's how it was with our success. On the one hand we enjoyed fame and prosperity, but on the other hand it made some things more difficult. As far as work was concerned, we had nothing to worry about. We received so many offers that we could pick and choose the best. The gigs at the *aires libres* were no longer interesting to us in terms of wages, but our presence there was excellent advertising. Stars such as Nat King Cole and Cole Porter liked to turn up at the cafés to hear us, or even to be seen with us. The gossip columnists reported it all, always mentioning us being with the celebrities and contributing to our popularity. But we could no longer fulfil the huge demand and appear at the *aires libres* every day, so Cuchito formed an *orquesta típica* that stood in for us when necessary. This 'second Anacaona', as we called the replacement band, played mainly *danzón* and was made up of musicians who had left other female orchestras or whose ensembles had dissolved. Cuchito made sure that this band, sometimes led by Bola, sometimes by Ziomara, had complete command of our repertoire.

We were now able to afford a hint of luxury: our own car and driver. The neighbours were flabbergasted when one day our brother Otto – our chauffeur – drove up in the unusually big black Packard complete with shining chrome. The limousine was armoured and seated seven. It had belonged to a prominent politician under Machado. It took some getting used to, as we had to speak to Otto over an intercom from the rear seats because a thick sheet of glass separated the chauffeur from the passengers. With the rest of our savings we bought Mother a house on Calle Armas. Sure, it was only a frame house, but it had a covered veranda and was in good condition. It was Father's idea. He was thinking of the day when he wouldn't be around any more and he wanted to provide security for Mother. We rented out the house and the payments went to her.

But money alone couldn't solve every problem. For some reason Yolanda had a much darker complexion than the rest of us. Father's pet name for her was *la negra* – the black one. Sometimes he would quip, 'Negra, do you know that I'm not really your father? Your father is the black man who rings the doorbell every day.' By that he meant the postman, a man as black as a Bakelite telephone. Yolanda would immediately start crying.

Mother, who normally didn't get mixed up much in matters of our upbringing, put her foot down: 'Matías, you can't treat the girl that way. Don't ever say anything like that again.'

But if it wasn't Father, then someone else would tease my sister. 'Yolanda is so dark because as the last daughter in Mother's belly she swept out all the dirt!' This was Ada's explanation for Yolanda's complexion.

While we, with our lighter skin colour, were never forced to deal with racism, Yolanda had been confronted with it since she was a child. Emma earned

Back from Paris with the new Packard

a good salary as a section head in La Filosofía department store and, as a staunch Catholic, she insisted on sending Ziomara, Yolanda and Lenin to a distinguished private school. She had already saved up the tuition money. But when she wanted to register Ziomara and Yolanda, complications arose. The nuns refused to take Yolanda, telling Emma that it was impossible that Yolanda, with her dark skin, could have the same father as her sisters. Of course, they knew this wasn't really true, but private schools were rather snobbish and attached great importance to pupils having pale skin. Emma had no other choice than to place Yolanda in a state-run school that accepted all skin colours.

Father too was occasionally confronted with racism. After we had told him so much about New York, he wanted to see it for himself, and in 1939 he set off with Emma and Bola to visit the World's Fair. They had barely stepped off the gangway of the steamer when a border official stopped him and denied him entry, explaining that there was an immigration prohibition for Chinese up to the fifth or sixth generation. Father didn't understand what was going on. He had a Cuban passport and a Spanish name and, as anyone could read, he was born in Cuba. He just wanted to visit the fair. The official insisted that Father was Chinese and intended to immigrate.

Finally Father blurted out, 'Do you know that I am actually African?' With his Chinese face he dared to claim he was African.

'What? You're African? Don't pull my leg.' The official had no idea that this was actually not a joke. Father's foster mother, Toya, had indeed been African, and he had grown up with blacks, and thus did in fact have an African family background. But such subtleties were of no interest in New York. The immigration official had my defiant father confined to what we call 'Las Islitas', Ellis Island. There they detained him in a camp for immigrants of dubious status. Emma and Bola searched feverishly for a way to get him out and called up

Socarrás, who quickly had documents dispatched from Cuba. After a week on Ellis Island, Father was finally able to go to the World's Fair.

That same year we decided to take a booking in Varadero. In my view, it's the most splendid beach resort in the world, with sand so fine and white that it's like pure silver! It took only three hours by car from Havana to reach this incomparable section of coastline, which stretches for twenty kilometres along the narrow peninsula. Scattered along this natural paradise were opulent beach villas owned by rich Cubans and Americans. A small cabaret, El Casino, had just opened. It wasn't particularly luxurious, but the contract for the winter and summer seasons offered us the chance to enjoy beach life day after day. It was the engagement I had been looking forward to most. Memories of earlier trips came flooding back, like the tiny crabs that darted across the fine-grained sand. The view of the hinterland was lovely, with willows, coconut palms, and a thicket of cacti and acacias entwined with vines. And then the sea! The lukewarm water made me forget time; I let my body be carried by the waves for hours on end, weightlessly drifting, while my toes just barely touched the ocean floor. What was the point of learning to swim?

Alicia

We took care of our own fun in Varadero. Admirers and friends promised to visit us, among them Pistón and Guillermo, the two

On the beach at Varadero, 1940

athletes. I was nineteen years old, and I couldn't decide which of them I liked
better. Pistón, it seemed, was interested in me, but Guillermo Amuchastegui also
enjoyed my company. He was considered to be the best jai alai player in Cuba.
The crowd would go wild when, with lightning speed, he caught the ball rocket-
ing towards the granite wall – a feat that was virtually impossible and was quite
dangerous despite the face protector he wore. His fans affectionately called him
El Buey, the Ox, or sometimes, more respectfully, *El Monarca de la Cancha*,
'The Monarch of the Court'. I liked him because of his perpetual good humour
and his uncomplicated nature. Only a few weeks earlier, he had celebrated with
us in one of the open-air cafés after his team had won the championship. He had

brought the trophy with him and placed it in the centre of the table at the Café El Dorado. It was in the shape of a basket, solid gold – eighteen carats of it – and quite big. Guillermo announced in the course of the evening that he was going to dedicate the trophy to his saint, Pilar, because he had prayed to her for help and promised the trophy to her if they won. The next day he actually did take the gold basket to the Church of Pilar and set it in a niche high up on the altar. But now Guillermo had money troubles. 'Alicia, I'm going to ask the saint to lend me the trophy temporarily, because I'm in dire need of cash,' he declared to me with a wink. He took the trophy down from the altar and took it to the pawn shop.

Shortly before we set off for Varadero for the winter season, Captain Tremizo of the Cabaña, a grand restaurant, invited us to dinner. He arranged for military horses to be available to us so that we could go riding after the meal. It was a wonderful country outing, which I thoroughly enjoyed, although I had never been on a horse before. On dismounting, however, I suddenly felt a pain like I'd never felt before. Worried, Cuchito telephoned a doctor friend, Fernández, who suspected appendicitis and arranged for me to be taken to his clinic. I had to lie down in the car on plenty of pillows so that I wouldn't feel all the potholes. In the clinic his suspicions were confirmed. Fernández operated immediately, and with only a local anaesthetic. He made a long incision in my belly, and rooted around inside for two hours – and all the while I was fully conscious. But that wasn't the end of the ordeal. An infection developed in the wound and, as penicillin was not yet available in Cuba, they had to keep reopening the wound to clean it.

Naturally this meant I would have to give up the gig in Varadero. I was the one who had been so keen on living the beach life there, and now I had to resign myself to the fact that I'd be spending the entire season in the hospital, and in quite a bit of pain too. But there was a consolation prize. A nice male nurse called Joaquín was taking care of me. He was literally my biggest admirer, all six foot two of him! He was a member of the rowing crew at the exclusive Vedado Tennis Club. He had been allowed to join the club because of his outstanding athletic achievements, even though his family was of modest means. His father was 'only' a policeman. Joaquín was pale-skinned and his hair was deep black. Quite a unique combination. I also liked the fact that he always sang while working. It wasn't long until he declared his love for me, right there in the hospital room. He certainly was a kind-hearted and sincere person. I liked him a lot, but I wasn't in love with him. I found myself trapped in a tricky situation with no escape, confined as I was to bed. Although I didn't give him any false hopes, Joaquín refused to stop courting me. He brought his mother and sister to my sickbed to introduce them to me. Both of them were named Alicia too. Soon I began to notice that this Joaquín, who was so full of zest for life, was actually deeply unhappy. He told me that his fiancée had died not so long before. She had been a swimmer at the same Vedado Tennis Club. Many people claimed that her fate was sealed when, despite having her period, she jumped into the swimming pool. In any case, she suffered a thrombosis and died. Joaquín confided to me that he wept for her almost every day at the cemetery in Colón. It didn't matter if it was raining or lightning was striking, he had to be close to her to mourn. That's how much he had loved her.

My convalescence was also livened up by visits from Roly, my very first, unrequited love. I believe that it was precisely because we never officially became a couple that he always lavished so much attention on me and kept showering me with little gifts. Of course, he made sure that his current girlfriend never found out. He visited me almost every day, even though, due to a car accident, he had to walk on crutches – and officially he was going steady with Manón Toñarelly. She came from one of the richest families in Cuba and lived in one of the magnificent villas in the Vedado district. Her parents' house took up an entire block.

Alicia with Eladio

The clinic where I was convalescing was quite close by, so she couldn't help noticing that Roly was going to the hospital every day. 'What's he doing over there all the time? Why does he go there every day?' she badgered her friends.

'Oh, he's visiting some buddy of his,' they would say evasively; they never told her that he still had feelings for me.

Another visitor appeared at my sickbed: Eladio Secades, the well-known sportswriter. I had known him for quite a while; he was one of the regulars at the El Dorado and would sometimes buy me an Alexander, a deliciously sweet cocktail of rum, whipped cream and cinnamon. The short, stocky man with dark, curly hair really wasn't my type at all. Besides, he was in his late thirties, old as the hills for me at nineteen, but he was tremendously witty and his dark eyes were gentle and dreamy. He liked to tease Martino, the owner of the El Dorado, who had set his sights on me and made no secret of it. One time Eladio had spontaneously remarked, 'Well, Martino, I don't own a café, but maybe Alicia prefers a fiery reporter.' That was the first time I noticed him. Another time, I saw him sitting in a corner of the café until the end of our show at one in the morning. He would watch until I was done 'coaxing sixty-fourth notes from the belly of the bass', as he put it. I didn't pay much heed to his attentions, but I was fascinated at how brilliantly observant he was of his fellow men. He was the head of the sports section at the *Diario de la Marina*, the newspaper whose building was located around the corner from the Café El Dorado. He also wrote for *Alerta!* in Havana as well as for *El Nacional* in Venezuela and the *Excelsior* in Mexico City. All first-class newspapers. Eladio didn't just report on sporting events, he also wrote commentaries that appeared in many Latin American countries, because he was one of the best in his field and gave everything a touch of humour. The most popular was his weekly column, '*Las Estampas*', depictions of daily life in Havana that were full of fine irony. I soon began reading them with great curiosity, because he captured more or less everything that mattered to him, writing about personal experiences in a coded form.

Eladio had driven to Varadero to see me, and there he learned from my sisters that I was in the clinic. He looked me up at once and tried his best to raise my spirits. He joked about everything. Despite the pain in my belly I couldn't help laughing. When I told him how I often thought about asking departed spirits for good health, he only averted his eyes and gazed piously at the ceiling light, as if he wanted to ask the spirits not to take me seriously. A week later I read this in his column:

'Believing in spiritualism involves spending countless hours at seances in the hope of being able to speak to a dead relative. And then, when someone finally reveals himself,

it's not the relative, but some Belgian fiddle player. Or an English doctor. Can you really cure the most dreadful illnesses merely by setting a water glass on a dresser? If so, spiritualism ought to be legally recognized as hydrotherapy. In reality it's a true theatre of mysteries shot through with a good portion of comedy.'

Sometimes Eladio and Roly would meet at my bedside. When Roly was alone with me later, he would grill me: 'What in the world has he got that I haven't got?' when what he really meant was: I'm superior to him in every way.

I only said, 'Oh, Roly – I have no idea what it is, but with him I always get a belly ache. From sheer laughter. That's what I like about him.'

When I fell in love with Eladio I didn't have the faintest idea that he was already married. I found out about that much later. Men are true artists at pulling the wool over a girl's eyes when she falls for them. *'Por el pico te endormecen'*, 'With their smooth talk they lull you to sleep', goes an old saying. Sooner or later, of course, you wake up and become aware of what kind of game they are playing.

Although the doctor had sternly advised me to take a year off from playing music, I didn't let it stop me from going on stage now and then with my sisters in Varadero. I didn't touch the saxophone, because with my abdominal wound I couldn't breathe deeply enough. Instead I would take up the maracas, or play the bass or the guitar.

Eladio often took me out, although he had to cover all the important sporting events and hardly had any free time. But when he did, he was always coming up with fun ideas. We once drove to Villa Mina, a big hacienda in Marianao on the outskirts of Havana which was later transformed into the Tropicana nightclub. We ate under the crowns of the jagüeyes with their aerial roots, in the midst of the tropical forest. We would go for long walks in Marianao, the diplomatic district with its nouveau-riche villas and chalets. A little further out lay the Sans Souci, a country inn with excellent food, including *lechón asado* – grilled suckling pig. The Cacolota, on Calle Colonela, was another restaurant we liked. Or the Restaurant Madrid. In all these places the cuisine was first class.

'Let's go to Matanzas and eat at the hotel so-and-so. They make wonderful chicken and rice,' Eladio would entice me. We thought it was fun to drive on impulse to Matanzas, Varadero or Pinar del Río. We would go walking in the valley of Viñales, a surreal, otherworldy landscape of fertile plains covered with tobacco fields and limestone hillocks jutting upwards, as if huge marbles had fallen from the sky.

Of course we were never alone on these excursions. My parents insisted that Millo, who had just turned seventeen, always go with us. Oscar accompanied us too, Millo's chosen friend. He was an American but spoke fairly good Spanish. Still, we would always burst out laughing when he stumbled on certain words. Oscar was a friend of Eladio and Horacio Roqueta, another very well-known journalist. The American was crazy about Millo and often told the story of how, when he saw her for the first time in the *aires libres*, he jumped out of his car and ran up to her as if in a trance. It seemed to him that he already knew Millo, because a long time before he had seen her clearly in a dream. Oscar was middle-aged and although he didn't have any wrinkles, he did have some grey hairs. Still, Millo felt attracted to him. Everyone advised her against it: 'You're still so young...', but he became her steady boyfriend, for a time anyway, because he worked as a croupier and dealer in the Casino Nacional and only stayed in Cuba during the season for American gamblers. They didn't start going out right away. Oscar first came to the house and introduced himself to Father. He explained that he wanted to build Millo a house, marry her and settle down in Cuba permanently. Father didn't give his consent. He refused to allow any of those things. The gifts were permitted, and taking walks here and there, but no more than that. The neighbours, however, gossiped and whispered that Millo was going out with him just because he had a lot of money. But the fact of the matter was Millo had fallen in love.

Despite all of our work commitments, Eladio and I found a way to enjoy the nightlife of Havana together as well. Eladio usually had to work in the news-room late into the night. After midnight he would come over and sit through our last set. Cuchito took the instruments home with Otto in the Packard while the rest of us went to have some fun. One in the morning was the hour of the musicians and artists. Along with all the other night-owls, we plunged into the nightlife that was now flourishing once again. The tavern owners rubbed their hands; they knew how hungry and thirsty musicians were after their perform-ances. Many went first to one of the cheap Chinese cafés in the Mercado Único. Eladio and I preferred to go with the others to the OK Bar, a joint with mir-rors on all the walls and a Wurlitzer jukebox. You could get the thickest Cuban sandwiches in that bar: thin slices of pickle, tomato, avocado, Swiss cheese, chor-izo, pigs' knuckles and sweet honey-baked ham were heated up, piled carefully on top of one another and placed inside crunchy toasted baguettes. On enter-ing, you could smell the irresistible aroma of crisp, spicy meat, because the pigs' knuckles were grilled right there in the middle of the place. And if we still felt hungry after that, we would go for an ice cream at La Josefita, which stayed open until the small hours. You could choose from a menu of the most delicious fla-vours: fresh pineapple, custard apple, cherimoya, mamey, annona... I preferred the speciality of the house: vanilla. Nowhere else in Havana could you get such terrific ice cream.

We celebrated Mother's and Cuchito's name day that year in a particularly festive manner – with plenty of candles on the altar. The Septeto Nacional came to our house with many musician friends in tow. One of them I noticed right away, a man who had come with the guitarist Eutimio Constantin. An athletic type, tall, with broad shoulders, a chiselled face and milky complexion. He was extremely handsome, although he looked slightly older. I saw the two men come down the hall to the dining room, stop, and look up at the terrace. There stood Ada, who had just taken a bath, combing her long, wet hair and letting it dry in the afternoon sun.

'Ada, how lovely you look,' Eutimio greeted her. He poked his friend in the side. 'Isn't that a captivating sight?'

When the septet started to play, the stranger made a beeline for Ada. 'May I have this dance? I must tell you frankly, I usually dance on a brick.' What men mean by this is they like to dance as closely as if they only had one brick available for a dance floor. The woman is not supposed to move from this imaginary brick, and cling to him.

Ada only laughed and said, 'What a coincidence, that's just my style!' During the break, Eutimio introduced his friend as José Echarri, but everyone just called him Echarri.

After this evening, Echarri became a permanent fixture among our admirers. The man with the macho words turned out to be most considerate. He set up a regular shuttle service from Lawton to Varadero for us. Sometimes he would bring Ada, sometimes one of the other sisters from Havana to the beach resort, sometimes he would take Millo or someone else back with him. He could have been mistaken for our chauffeur, except that Echarri, like all people who took pride in themselves and could afford it, left the driving to his own chauffeur. Ada

Ada and Echarri

Echarri

Ada's dedication to Echarri:
'To my only, great little love…
for my Saint Pepe'

liked his audacious, direct manner. The polite, shy admirers weren't her cup of tea. And then there was Echarri's love of music. Ada was quite enchanted by the ballads and boleros that he played for her on the guitar, the way he sang with warmth in his voice. Yet even when we got to know Echarri better, one question remained. How did the man make his living? He always had plenty of time, day or night; we never saw him work. Then Eutimio told us what almost every sports fan in Cuba already knew, that Echarri occupied an important spot in Cuban sports history. It was in 1926 at the Central American Games in Mexico City, at the first appearance of a Cuban baseball team in international competition. and Echarri was one of the sluggers on the team. Cuba made it to the final round. In the final inning of the deciding game, Echarri stepped up and with tremendous power and a lot of luck hit a home run! Cuba won the championship and everyone treated Echarri as a national hero. That one home run opened every door to him for decades. That's why, for example, he was in favour with his brother-in law, Señor López Serrano.

Legally, Echarri was married. He had a fifteen-year-old son, whom he often brought along. In the circles in which Echarri moved, it wasn't unusual for married men to be courting and starting relationships with other women, even starting other families 'on the side' – and it wasn't just back then that this was common.

A well-respected Cuban artist – I won't mention his name – had relationships not only with his cook, but also with her sister at the same time. And he had children with both of them. A scandal! His parents, however, who had long feared that their son was gay, were quite relieved to hear that he had devoted himself to two women at the same time. Even in the most humble of relationships, women had to be prepared for such 'machos'. For that reason, it didn't mean much who was officially married to whom. The crucial thing was to which woman the man paid the most attention. Many a time Cuchito would say how ridiculous it was that in Cuba most women had to make it alone, holding the family together while the men orbited like satellites around whomever they felt most attracted to.

Echarri's dedication to Ada: 'To my only darling… my Ada, your macho, Pepe'

Echarri's brother-in-law, Lopez Serrano, really liked Ada. He was extraordinarily wealthy. He owned the Café Tupi coffee company, a slaughterhouse, a high-rise in the up-market district of Vedado, a hacienda, cattle ranches, several beach houses and, naturally, a yacht. Through his brother-in-law, Echarri associated with politicians such as Fernández (who was known as 'Macho'), and Paco, the brother of the future president, Carlos Prío Socarrás. They were both to be mayors of Havana, one after the other. Some of the politicians were involved in illegal businesses, including the brother of the future president who was a large-scale marijuana dealer. They all belonged to the rumbantela set. Rumbantela was the name Mother gave to the party-gang lifestyle that revolved around the rumba. Echarri felt comfortable with these kinds of people, who admired each other because they could throw their money around. Through his brother-in-law, he had access to the exclusive clubs where 'people who in fact have nothing to do relax', as Eladio put it. Ada also found out that Echarri had a permanent position in his brother-in-law's coffee company, but he never did any work. Later his politician friends made him chief of customs inspection at the airport. Not even there did he ever pick up a piece of paper. He merely collected his salary. The customs post was just like the position in the coffee company, what Cubans call a *botella*, a 'bottle'; a source from which money flows without having to do anything to earn it. All Echarri had to do was show up once in a while, act important, spread good cheer, and pick up his earnings. The 'bottle' at customs was particularly lucrative. Everyone knew what went on there. How many times had we been detained for some spurious reason and had our baggage rummaged through until we voluntarily produced a small banknote to resolve the 'problem'?

Echarri and Ada soon got 'married'. At least that's what we told the neighbours, because legally Echarri remained married to his first wife. But he moved into a house in the old part of Havana with Ada. There Echarri played husband and spoiled my sister. He would always bring her the best cuts of meat from his brother-in-law's slaughterhouse. Ada was delighted and at the same time close to despair, because she didn't know how to cook. She could do little more than fry an egg. Almost daily she would call up Mother or Aunt Pepa. 'What ingredients do I need to marinate the steak? How long should it fry in the pan?'

'*Dios mío*, don't tell me you don't know that steak needs to be marinated in bitter orange juice and pressed garlic?' Mother replied, horrified.

'I don't understand a thing about cooking. The only thing I do know is how to play the violin. One thing is for sure: Echarri isn't living with me because of my culinary skills!'

Their happiness didn't last long. After a few months Ada fell pregnant. Echarri didn't want her to have the baby, but Ada held her ground. 'I want this child.' Echarri wasn't used to being defied and so he packed his possessions and went back to his legitimate wife. Ada came back to our parents' house in Lawton, where she brought her son, Reinaldo, into the world. Here the boy wouldn't have time to miss his father. He had ten aunts, two uncles and his grandparents.

Two years later Ada ran into Echarri on the street. She had little Reinaldo with her, a sweet boy with pitch-black eyes, dark hair, and his father's light skin. When Echarri saw his son for the first time, he was thrilled. He turned right around and came back to Ada, and they moved back into their old house. But still there was no trace of a regular family life. Ever the party animal, Echarri would rush around the place with or without Ada. Sometimes she didn't know where he was for a whole week at a stretch. Once it turned out that he had flown to Miami.

'What the hell is he doing there?' Ada asked me in despair.

'Well, Echarri didn't fly to Miami so he could attend church, that's for sure,' I told her.

Even today it's incredible to me how she could put up with him. What's more, she let him run on a very long leash. He was always in the mood to party, and Ada kept up with him as best she could. They would cruise from one get-together to another, often bringing their son along. And Echarri would blatantly flirt with other women. He would court them right under Ada's nose! He liked to act the mystery man. He would gaze deep into the eyes of some beauty, lower his eyelids modestly, and direct his next look dreamily into the distance. It was his way of suggesting that he was the custodian of a profound secret, the secret of the ecstasy of love. My God, he looked ridiculous! This ploy didn't really suit him. But for some reason, Ada liked this type of man. And she wasn't without her own resources. When Echarri started playing the lady-killer at a party, she would soon have the rest of the men dancing around her. Jealousy was the only thing that could penetrate his thick skull. In this way Ada gradually bound him to her, until one day she gave him an ultimatum. 'Whatever you do all day is your own business. But at night you have to be back here. If you ever stay away another night again, don't bother coming back. There won't be anything more for you here.' The threat was effective. From then on, Echarri always found his way back to his nest.

It was now 1940. Fulgencio Batista, who later revealed himself to be an intolerable tyrant, was president. At the beginning of his administration he was still cooperating with the Communist Party, the URC. His party and the Communists put together a progressive and democratic programme. The right to work, the principle of equal wages for equal work, the forty-four-hour week, and women's suffrage were all established. Soon, however, it turned out that the government was doing absolutely nothing to implement the laws. Father was baffled at how the Communists had been able to make a deal with Batista. According to Father, politics was a dirty business. Every politician, whether Communist or conservative, was corrupt through and through. 'One day they attack each other, tossing around the nastiest accusations and suspicions. And the next day you see a picture in the paper and they're cheerfully eating dinner together, the best of friends.' But even then he remained idealistic. He firmly believed that there were statesmen who had character and backbone and took things seriously, but he imagined them to be far away, in Europe or China.

~ **Anacaona** ~

But we lived in Cuba and as artists we were among the personalities with whom politicians liked to be seen in public. This inevitably meant that we ended up meeting Batista. His people had arranged a big party for 4 September and asked whether we could play for the dance. It was the anniversary of the day Batista came to power by staging a coup d'état. The celebration was to take place at the Casino in the city of Columbia, referred to today as Ciudad Libertad. All the colonels and generals resided there, and they had their own clubs too, of course. Columbia basically consisted of nothing but barracks. Cuchito merely said, 'We can't afford to be choosy about our employers. If I played solely for people whose politics were similar to mine, the only place I could appear would be prison or abroad.' We took the gig. In Columbia we filed past Batista with all the guests, shook hands with him, and played *son*, rumba and *danzón* for the military personnel.

Part of our obligation that year was to participate in the Workers' Day parade on 1 May. We marched along the Malecón to the presidential palace. Up on the balcony stood Batista and his entourage. Beside us marched José María Arriete y Bambitelli, the general secretary of the musicians' union. We, the 'Chinitas of Anacaona', were allowed to carry the huge Cuban flag. Because of his skin colour and his smooth hair, people liked to call Batista *El Indio* or *El Chino*. When we finally stood before him, José María Arriete y Bambitelli called out, 'Chino, here are your daughters!' and pointed at us. I felt like sinking into the ground. Arriete y Bambitelli was really quite uncouth. But I let it pass, because he was a union leader who had done a lot for us musicians. Trade unions had previously only granted admittance to musicians who had been formally trained at an academy. In 1932 Arriete founded his union, which was the first to accept musicians from the populace, including those who played *son*. Cuchito had joined his union at once, even though it had the reputation of being Communist. Dealing with

Arriete was very informal, because for years he couldn't afford an office and received all members at his home. One of the things he did for us artists was to secure a pay raise: each musician at the *aires libres* received, instead of one peso, one peso thirty centavos. Thirty centavos – that was enough for a sandwich!

As far as most of my sisters and I were concerned, anything to do with politics gave us the creeps. We made an exception and got involved only when it was a matter of friends or neighbours whose jobs were in danger. Millo decided to give her support to Oropeza, a man from our neighbourhood who was a head waiter at the Hotel Pasaje. He actually had a secondary school teaching certificate, but he had never been able to work in that field. Employment was at the centre of election campaigns. All those employed in the civil service were obliged by their superiors to secure a certain number of votes in their district. That was normal practice. They had to help the party win at least twenty or twenty-five *células*, or voting precincts. This was how they tried to hold on to their jobs, because with each change in the government, the administrative heads were sent packing and entire departments with them.

Oropeza was motivated by the idea of finally being able to get a teaching job in the event of an election victory. He therefore supported the candidacy of a certain Castellano, who wanted to become mayor, and he was active in the Auténticos, the party of Grau San Martín, the esteemed professor of medicine. Oropeza had asked Millo to write and send out campaign letters for Castellano, promising in exchange to secure her a good position if he won. When Father heard this, he asked Oropeza to explain himself. 'A political post? No one in this family wants to have anything to do with such wheeling and dealing. We help everyone we can if it's in our power to do so. Millo will continue to support you, but only because you're a neighbour and a good friend. But we won't get involved in favouritism.'

Millo, Ondina and Ziomara arranged an original conga as part of Oropeza's campaign on behalf of Castellano. They drove through Havana in a streetcar he had hired for the occasion, drumming and trumpeting for all they were worth. For reinforcement, Millo took her pupil Pedrito along on the tour. The fourteen-year-old was one of the boys in the neighbourhood who would stand in front of our house and listen to us practising. His uncle, the guitarist Manuel Soroa, had approached Cuchito and both agreed upon Millo giving the boy two hours a week of bongo and percussion lessons. Later Pedrito became a member of the famous Orquesta Riverside.

I joined them all on the day that Grau San Martín became president. We drove along the Paseo del Prado with Oropeza and his team celebrating the victory of the Auténticos with a conga. All hell had broken loose. A huge crowd jammed the Prado. People were hanging to the sides of the streetcar like leeches. Fireworks were going off everywhere. It was incredible. Even the trams were stopped. I watched the crowd bring a coffin to the Capitolio and place it solemnly in front of the steps, as a symbol of taking the old government to its grave. Eladio later wrote in his column about how we Cubans can't live without our conga. 'There are only two occasions when we all unite spontaneously: when the umpire makes a bad call in baseball and in the conga. Skilful politicians first seek out conga musicians. Only then do they develop their campaign plan.'

Our conga worked: Castellano won the election. Oropeza, however, didn't get his job as a teacher: he and the many eager helpers were quickly forgotten. Poor Oropeza remained a head waiter at the Hotel Pasaje for the rest of his life.

Grau San Martín won the elections because he promised to advance the cause of social legislation in favour of the workers. Times weren't good for us musicians either; cinemas and theatres had abolished live music shows between the features because of the expense. Artists, musicians and dancers had little

Before the trip to Mexico, 1944

work. Arriete y Bambitelli, the general secretary of the musicians' union, fought to have the shows reintroduced. As soon as Grau sat in the president's office, he proved to be a chameleon. He did enact a law that took up Arriete's demands, but he did everything possible to make sure that it wouldn't be implemented.

It quickly became apparent that things weren't going to improve under Grau. During his administration there was also a great deal of repression; everything was in chaos; gangsters ruled the streets, warring with one another and committing murder; and the government didn't dare take any strong measures against them. The climax was an incident at the home of Major Morín Dopico. A group of gangsters used to meet there, among them the gang leader Emilio Tró. A fierce shoot-out erupted between them and their rivals, and there were dead bodies by the time the police arrived. They stormed the house of Morín Dopico and ordered the men to surrender. When the gangsters hesitated, the police took out their machine guns and mowed down anyone who moved. Dopico's wife finally came out of the house and died in a hail of bullets. She was pregnant, but they shot her without mercy. As always, Grau did nothing. The people were firmly convinced that it was his sister-in-law, Paulina, who was secretly pulling the strings, not him. A monumental fountain acts as a poignant reminder. Paulina had used her influence to help her son get the contract to build it. Since she was quite a stout woman, the joke quickly went around, 'That's Paulina's bidet!' And everyone still knows the fountain by that name today.

For our band too, it was a time of change. Our vocalist, Graciela Pérez, left us to move north to the USA. I couldn't imagine our band without her – Graciela was such a great pal and an outstanding singer, besides being cheerful and high-spirited. Her brother Machito, her sister Estela and her brother-in-law Mario Bauzá lived in New York. The two men had formed their own band in 1940, Machito and His Afro-Cubans. Alongside Socarrás, they were the ones who definitively fostered the fusion of Afro-Cuban music and jazz into Latin jazz. Mario and Machito took American musicians into the ensemble, hired arrangers from the States and blended the Cuban rhythms perfectly with the sound of the big bands. Graciela joined this band, which was described as 'exciting with a touch of flamboyance in the Hollywood style' by the music critic Pedro Rojas. For decades, she, Machito and Mario Bauzá greatly influenced the music scene in the States, and in Cuba as well. We had been close friends with all three of them for a long time. In fact, Mario had sold Father one of the first trumpets for Ondina. Both of them had learned under the same teacher, Lázaro. Naturally, we stayed in contact and in that way kept our ear close to the music scene in New York.

In 1944 we were offered a tour through Mexico. It was to last a year. As this concert tour promised to be very lucrative, we decided to terminate our obligations at the *aires libres*. Using the replacement band wouldn't have been good in the long run, either for the audience or for the café owners. When the various husbands and boyfriends of my sisters heard about our travel plans, a few tried to revolt. Echarri in particular threw a fit. He didn't want to come along or to take care of his two-year-old son, and he wouldn't allow Ada to bring the boy along on the trip either. Ada gave in. Fortunately Eladio was not so tough. He didn't mind me being away for such a long time and appearing before large audiences in Mexico. On the contrary: 'Go to Mexico, because that's where your good luck began on your first trip. Take the offer.' Eladio had planned a trip to Mexico City at the same time to coincide with some sporting events, so we knew that we would see each other there.

In terms of my relationship with Eladio, the tour came at a good time.

I wanted to put some distance between us. On the one hand, I couldn't imagine separating; I enjoyed our companionship too much. On the other hand, I was burdened by the fact that Eladio still hadn't divorced his wife. They had no children, so why was it so hard for him to make a decision? He had long promised me that he would get a divorce and marry me. 'I have to take the final step, because there is nothing more between my wife and me,' he claimed, but he kept postponing it. A few weeks before our trip to Mexico he announced that he would now make good on his intentions. Then his mother suddenly fell ill, and he told me that he couldn't burden her with it. How much power does his mother have over him, I wondered. Unfortunately for me, she sided unconditionally with his wife. So the tightrope act continued. Good friends like Miguelito Valdés and his wife tried to encourage me: 'Eladio is totally crazy about you, Alicia! We're sure he will free himself from his wife.' All our friends were of the same opinion. So I exercised patience. I knew that Eladio was very attached to me. In 1943 he had published his sketches of the Havana milieu in book form and won a prize. He gave me the thousand dollars in prize money for safekeeping, because money seemed to slip right through his fingers. As a star reporter he made an incredible amount of money, but he spent it just as fast. He was a gambler. Everywhere he worked there were opportunities for betting. He simply couldn't resist the temptation. He was always betting on a baseball team, a boxer or a racehorse. Mostly in vain.

We had scarcely arrived in Mexico when the turmoil continued. After Graciela had left us, we hired a new vocalist, a fifteen-year-old girl named Georgina. Her talent was average, but she was young, attractive and likeable. Her agent had thought up the stage name 'Rubí' for her. We soon noticed that singing wasn't

'Rubi' at fifteen

all she had on her mind. Her interest was mainly directed at any eligible man. In Mérida she snared a percussionist who was wild about everything Cuban. Even the atmosphere we created made him swoon. The Mexican was a good deal older than she was, around forty. Rubí caught him effortlessly in her net and soon began pressuring him to marry her – and for that they would need documents from Cuba. Cuchito was not happy about it, but let matters take their own course. She acquired the papers for Rubí's marriage via Emma in Havana. In the meantime, Rubí's intended was getting on our nerves with his fast talk. He claimed that he would be the ideal manager for our band, that if only we would submit to his professional guidance we could make a lot more money. We let him talk. As soon as the papers arrived he and Rubí were married, and straight after they returned from their honeymoon Cuchito laid down the law. She was sure that Rubí was only after a residence visa in Mexico. 'Anyone who gets married ceases to be part of the band,' she informed her. 'You may have finalized the marriage with the Cuban consul and all the formalities, but with that you cut yourself out of the band. That's how it is with us.' Rubí handled the dismissal with composure. She stayed in Mexico, but was soon divorced and got married again – this time to a wealthy engineer from Mérida. Meanwhile, Cuchito sent a telegram to Ana María García in Cuba; she already had a reputation as a vocalist and kindly jumped into the breach left by Rubí.

That wasn't the only upheaval. Ariela, who had come along as a pianist and bass player, was always flirting. Without a doubt she was a daughter of the love goddess Ochún. She didn't seem to care whether she stole a man from a woman, a woman from a woman, or a woman from a man. When another all-female Cuban group came to Mérida, a trio called Hermanas Márquez, Ariela became distracted by one of their musicians. She skipped rehearsals more and more often, and one day she even left us in the lurch at a performance. By this time Cuchito had got wind that she was having an affair. Hortensia, our pianist, had told her and warned, 'Watch out. You have to call Ariela to order; or I'll do it myself.' The rest of us hadn't noticed a thing, because we were utterly naïve when it came to lesbian relationships. And Ariela was friendly and flirtatious with both men and women alike. Cuchito at once called a meeting with the two love-birds and asked them about their affair. Ariela at first denied everything, and her girlfriend didn't say a word. But it was instantly clear to us that Ariela had fallen in love. Without batting an eyelid, Cuchito fired her. She took over the bass her-self and the show went on. She could be really tough when it came to discipline within the band. She would fire musicians very quickly, even if they were good. She also demanded that we sisters keep our private lives separate from our pro-fessional lives. She felt that the intrusion of feelings into the job showed a lack of respect for her personally. Ariela and her lover broke up soon after that, but Cuchito wasn't the only one responsible. Ariela's sweetheart was the exact oppo-site of Ariela, very withdrawn, and in the end she liked men better.

After being contracted to the theatre owner Daniel Herrera, whom everyone called 'El Chino', we appeared together with the Trio Hermanas Márquez, the dancer América Imperio and many other artists at the Circo Teatro in Mérida. The programme was quite varied; besides music it included short plays in which the musicians also assumed roles. El Chino, a short, portly, impertinent man, often took the lead role, and that's what brought in the crowds. As an outstanding comedian and dancer, he had already appeared in many Mexican movies with long-legged vamps such as Meche Barba. After a season in Mérida, El Chino went on tour with our entire troupe. For four or five months we travelled all over the Yucatán peninsula, together journeying through vast fields of agave by bus and train, all the way to the steamy lowlands, where impenetrable tropical plants towered as tall as houses. Everything went smoothly until we boarded the train, when chaos ensued, with everyone pushing and shoving to find seats. But we had a trick. Millo and Ziomara pushed their way onto the train and yelled, 'Give me the bongos! Give me the conga drum!' The rest of us quickly passed the instruments through the windows and they spread them out across the surrounding seats, saving them until we could push our way through the crowd to claim them.

When El Chino fell in love with one of the musicians from the Trio Hermanas Márquez, Cuchito immediately decided not to renew our contract. Instead she turned to the agent De la Rosa, who offered us appearances in several large theatres in Mexico City. We wanted to fly from Yucatán to the capital, but because of Mexico's participation in the fight against the Axis powers in the Second World War, there was scarcely an aeroplane left in the country for civilian use. So we had to take a ship to Veracruz and travel from there by train. At the harbour of Progreso we boarded the ship, which in reality was nothing more than a large yacht. On the last leg of the voyage in the middle of the Gulf of Mexico a huge storm blew up. The yacht was tossed around on the choppy seas like a nutshell and had to be navigated back to Campeche, where we went ashore feeling quite bedraggled.

Luckily our good friends the Arceos lived there. The five brothers were all successful businessmen. Mario dealt in medical supplies and pharmaceuticals. Enrique produced the popular Arceo line of beverages, sweet soft drinks flavoured with peach or aniseed. None of us were in love with any of the brothers – they were true friends. We rested for three days in their spacious beach villa and then took the train back to Mérida. In the harbour of Progreso we gave it another try with the first freighter out to Veracruz, because the starting date for our contract was rapidly approaching. There were no vacant cabins on the freighter, so all we could do was sleep on deck. Cuchito insisted on daily rehearsals here too, so on the very first day we set up our instruments on deck. When we started playing the Mexican standard 'Cielito Lindo', the entire crew came to listen. They were overwhelmed. The captain and the first officer suddenly transformed into gentlemen and offered us the use of their cabins. We didn't wait for them to offer twice. There wasn't room for all of us, so we took turns. The first night I was among those who had to sleep in the hammocks on deck. Once again a storm blew up, and I got a sea-water shower. But the next night I slept comfortably in the captain's bed and my sisters got the salt water. In this

211

In the floating gardens of Xochimilco near Mexico City

On the Mexico tour in 1945: (from left) Millo, Ondina, Cuchito, Yolanda, Alicia, Ziomara and Bola

way the sea voyage turned out to be quite acceptable. In the harbour of Veracruz we were greeted by Oscar López and our agent, De la Rosa. Oscar, a popular Cuban singer, had helped us in Paris. In Mexico he knew the audience and atmosphere of each theatre and he sought out the right bookings for us.

After our arrival in Mexico City, as we strolled across the Zócalo, the central plaza downtown, suddenly people began to shout: 'The war is over! The war is over!' A happy, carefree mood spread everywhere with the news of the end of the Second World War. After being separated for months, Eladio and I were finally together again. He greeted me with presents: a wonderful silver bracelet and a silver fox stole. Ondina chose Eladio's colleague, the sportswriter Guillermo Lozano, as an escort. In the evening the four of us went out. We decided to look up one of the best cabarets in the city, El Patio, because we had read that our good friend, and Ondina's ex-boyfriend, the trombonist Raymundo Montoya – alias 'Papa', the Potato or the Pope – was playing there. Only now he was directing his own band. Arriving at the club, we headed straight for the dance floor, although Ondina needed some encouragement. And not only because of Raymundo. Her dance partner, Lozano, was pretty tall and Ondina was worried about looking like his walking stick when dancing with him. We waved to Raymundo from the floor. He put down his baton immediately and grabbed a trombone from one of his musicians. We stopped short in astonishment. Then he raised the trombone and played 'Estrellita del Lejano Cielo', 'Little Star from Heaven Afar'. That was the song he had dedicated to Ondina eight years earlier in his serenade. Ondina was speechless with emotion. She was still very fond of him, I think. When we sat down after the show, she had clearly regained her composure. She was extremely charming, but reserved.

At work, however, Ondina was rather difficult. This is what happened when we played in Mexico City at one of the most renowned venues, the Teatro Lírico:

213
≈

we had just finished the first set, the break was over and the second set was just about to begin, opening with the septet. We routinely took up our positions behind the velvet curtain, where a circle had been drawn on the floor for each musician so that the lighting would be right. Suddenly I heard a heated argument. Millo and Ondina began quarrelling about some silly detail.

'That really puts me off playing any more. Believe it or not, I'm not performing tonight. I won't go on with this!' said Ondina, refusing to take her place. Furiously Millo stood up, raising the bongos high, as if she wanted to hit Ondina on the head with them.

I tried to calm Millo down. 'Don't pay any attention to her, just ignore her. She's only trying to to provoke you.'

Yolanda gave Ondina a good talking-to: 'Of course, there's no problem finding another trumpet player here. There are probably dozens of them in the audience. We'll just get a replacement from the house and then we'll be done with all this fuss.'

The curtain was already drawing back when Ondina took her place at lightning speed. *Ave Maria!*

Things were much more relaxed when we went out the next evening. The Mexican actors Jorge Negrete and Luis Aguilar had invited us. They were the current heart-throbs of all the Mexican ladies, and we would come across pictures of these idols on movie posters and in magazines all over town.

Something more than affection began developing between Millo and Luis. We all went together to the Plaza Garibaldi to hear the mariachis. The musicians there recognized our famous escorts and gave them a spontaneous serenade. Before a crowd of people could form, we retreated into the Tenampa, a popular tavern and a temple to music and tequila. How they all stared, especially the women. But we had been good friends with the actors for years; we had met

Hortensia Palacios at the piano and Millo

Jorge Negrete long before he was famous as 'El Negrete', appearing in movies in the typical outfit of the *charro*, the Mexican cowboy. I had noticed this man with his narrow face, expressive eyebrows and thin moustache for the first time years earlier, when he would regularly come to the *aires libres* with the Cuban composer Eliseo Grenet to hear us. Even after he became famous, he continued to be one of our most loyal fans and would come to our shows whenever he was in Havana. But now, the moment he stepped out of his car he was swamped by so many fans that we hardly got a chance to talk to him.

Shortly after arriving in Mexico City we had called Negrete. His first reaction was to threaten us: 'If you don't come to visit me at once I'll have to tell the general secretary of the musicians' and artists' union to bar you from playing any shows.' This was a flattering joke, of course, but one with a serious undertone.

As the secretary of the union, Jorge Negrete was the man in charge of deciding which Cuban artists could appear in Mexico and which ones couldn't. The competition between our two countries in musical matters was great, both greedily soaked up every musical trend. Plots were constantly being hatched. One had to do with the great Rita Montaner, who was treated with hostility by her Mexican colleague Toña la Negra, Black Toña. Rita had told me that at a concert in the Peón Contreras in Mérida she had been greeted with a deafening chorus of booing and whistling. It was clear that Toña had instigated this, but Rita just remained on stage, put her hands on her hips, and out-stared the audience until the whistlers lost all enthusiasm.

Then she announced, 'So, now it's my turn. Now you have to listen to me the whole evening, whether you want to or not.' Whereupon she went through her entire repertoire. For her part, Toña claimed that the musicians' unions in Cuba treated her badly because Rita was conspiring against her.

Our compatriots from the Trio Matamoros and Benny Moré's band had to deal with equally dirty tricks. When we asked Negrete about it, he refused to yield and explained that they had entered Mexico without a working visa. 'I'm really very sorry, but it won't be possible to give them permission. I'll do everything in my power, because as an artist I owe Cuba a lot. People have always treated me well there. On the other hand, unfortunately I can't ignore the regulations of my own country!' We realized that we wouldn't be able to soften his steely heart. The incident caused feelings to run high, but ultimately the Trio Matamoros and Benny Moré were allowed to perform. Anyway, this all remained very nerve-racking. Benny Moré, by the way, was so successful in Mexico that he decided to settle down there for good. It's true that Negrete was extremely hard on other Cuban artists. But he never gave us any reason to complain about him. He never put any obstacles in our way.

~ **Anacaona** ~

For the following year we were planning a tour first to the Caribbean island of Curaçao and then to Venezuela. Ada's son, Reinaldo, was four and she thought the time had come for her to rejoin the band. Echarri, of course, was still against it and refused categorically to take care of his son for so much as an hour. But Ada had no desire to miss another tour. She left in secret and took Reinaldo with her.

Millo had already broken up with her boyfriend Oscar, the American, and was suffering greatly. She hoped to be able to shake off her lovesickness. I tried to console her and advised, 'Write him a letter and get it off your chest.' But she remained steadfast.

And perhaps partly to have a companion in suffering she advised me, 'You ought to break it off too. You keep waiting and waiting. . .' Millo actually opened my eyes. What could I expect from Eladio? His mother was joining forces so powerfully with his wife, I could no longer hope he would ever get a divorce. I told myself, 'Fate has decided on another wife for him.' But the decision seemed incredibly difficult for me. I engaged in long conversations with myself, reminding myself that I had been a happy person before Eladio, and that I could be again. I knew lots of people and always had a great time. I slowly managed to emotionally detach myself from him.

Millo helped me a lot. We responded to many things the same way, without ever having to talk about it much. When I bought a beautiful dress and was looking forward to wearing it out on the town for the first time, she said, 'Won't you lend it to me?' I hesitated only briefly. I didn't begrudge her the pleasure of being the first to wear the dress. It was the same way when I was crazy about some piece of jewellery of hers. She simply handed me her sensational topaz earrings and said, 'These are for you. You like them so much, keep them.'

Cucaçao, 1947

By the time we arrived in Curaçao we had left all our troubles behind. Four-year-old Reinaldo was a ray of sunshine. We took turns looking after him. It was fun to teach him the alphabet and how to count. He was so uncomplicated. In the evenings we took him along to the show.

But after a week – we were just setting up for the show at the Lago Heights cabaret – three policemen came looking for us in our dressing room. We knew right away by their expressions that they didn't want an autograph. 'According to this arrest warrant, we have to take you all in,' they explained, and showed

Cuchito the paper. It read: 'THE ORQUESTA ANACAONA HAS KIDNAPPED A WOMAN AND CHILD. THEY ARE HOLDING THEM BOTH AGAINST THEIR WILL.'

'Echarri is behind this, that scoundrel,' Ada blurted out. We figured out that, in his rage, Echarri had gone ahead and lodged a complaint with the police, claiming that we had kidnapped Ada and Reinaldo. He had always been convinced that we – Cuchito first and foremost – incited Ada to rebel against him. According to him, she only clung to her profession as a musician because the band couldn't manage without her.

We explained the situation to the police officers and found out that Echarri had had the arrest warrant issued with the help of his influential politician friends. The Cuban minister of transport had passed the warrant to his colleague in Curaçao and the latter brought in the police. The gentlemen in uniform found it rather strange that a woman and her child would be kidnapped by her sisters. Not to mention that the 'victim' was now vehemently resisting her own 'rescue'. But orders were orders. Ada calmed down and decided that it was better not to pick a fight with the Cuban minister of transport all the way from Curaçao. 'All right, I'll return to Cuba at once. But inform the Señor minister that my husband should be so kind as to send me an aeroplane ticket.'

He did so a few days later, but out of sheer eagerness Echarri booked the earliest flight without noticing that the plane flew, not to Havana, but to Camagüey. He had to drive all the way to the eastern part of Cuba to pick up Ada and Reinaldo. On the drive back to Havana, Echarri raged for hours, giving her quite an earful, complaining that she had no idea of what he had gone through because of her.

At our next stop in Caracas there were more police officers waiting for us at the airport. Apparently Echarri had brought charges against us in Venezuela too, just in case. Cuchito now studied the warrant closely and was utterly furious. Echarri actually claimed that she, Cuchito, had exerted pressure on Ada and forced her to work with the band in a questionable environment. This from Echarri, the man who took every liberty open to him and even bragged about the seedy places he knew about and frequented! That's what Echarri was like; but Ada still stuck by him.

Chapter 10
The Honourable Society

A few days later another telegram set us all abuzz:

'The Casino Nacional will open shortly – Direction of the show given to me – I want the Orchestra Anacaona – Please sign no more contracts – Ernesto Lecuona'

'We're going back to Havana right away. We have to drop everything for this booking. Let's go,' said Cuchito. 'The Casino Nacional is the top venue and, what's more, it's Lecuona who's calling us.' She telegraphed back:

'What an honour – We're coming immediately.'

No sooner had the curtain fallen on our last performance than we packed our bags and flew home.

Ernesto Lecuona had a legendary reputation and was one of the best, if not the very best, of all Cuban composers. And as with all extraordinary artists, there was lively controversy about his music, because Lecuona had no qualms about mixing classical with popular music, as in his songs '*Malagueña*' and '*María la O*'. At the age of almost fifty, he was also reputed to be one of the most virtuoso concert pianists in the world. When he was a child, music critics had prophesied that he would be a second Rachmaninov, but Lecuona had done nothing to nurture his great classical talent. His passion was for popular and dance music. People claimed he was only able to compose while dancing.

In the late 1920s, Lecuona had had a worldwide hit with 'Siboney'. A little later he launched a big band: the Lecuona Cuban Boys. The twenty musicians enjoyed overwhelming international success with their synthesis of Afro-Cuban rhythms and salon music. In the mid-1930s they gave concerts for months on end in Europe, performing in London, Paris, Biarritz and Berlin.

When we arrived in Havana, we saw that we were already included in the billing for the Casino Nacional: 'We are proud to present the *Chinitas* of Anacaona.' They had added us to the programme on Lecuona's word only, before we had even signed a contract. The Casino Nacional was the most modern casino complex in the city – and one of the most elegant in the world. It was only surpassed by the casino of Monte Carlo. Located in the diplomatic district of Marianao, it had been built by an American corporation along with the Hippodrome and the Playa La Concha, a huge amusement park similar to Coney Island in New York. This complex had been leased to the Cuban government for a period of twenty to thirty years. Games of chance were the main concern in the Casino Nacional, and they could afford to pay their artists the highest wages because people with money went there to spend it freely while basking in the luxurious ambience.

We were supposed to work under the direction of Lecuona for two seasons, in each case from October to January. In the winter, Americans came in droves to Havana, many only for a weekend, to play roulette or cards, see the show and drink a Rum Collins. There were thirty flights a day on the Havana–Miami route alone. And in order to prolong the fun, there were even slot machines installed in many aeroplanes. Later the in-flight service was carried to extremes. Passengers didn't even have to miss a show and dance during the half-hour flight. Ana Gloria

In the Bacardí Bar, Havana

and Rolando were among the artists who set the mood with a conga performance on board the plane. They told me that many passengers even danced on their seats with excitement. They were seized by such a fever that if the plane crashed they would all head into the hereafter shaking to the rhythm of the rumba. All courtesy of Pan-American Airways for only twenty-nine dollars!

The Americans went back and forth to Cuba as if it were their home; after all, we live only a stone's throw away from each other. The American lifestyle was, like it or not, a part of Cuba. Everyone could speak a few words of English, at least enough to provide information. Millo and I took English lessons that were arranged by the US embassy and were free of charge. In the department stores such as La Filosofía, there was almost nothing but goods from the States. The newest and most modern things came from there. The taverns and bars, all the hot spots, imitated the style of our northern neighbour, like the Ten Cents, where the meandering bar specialized in milkshakes. Any American businessman who wanted to could open a store in Cuba. And among the businessmen who enjoyed this boundless freedom were those of the 'honourable society' – the Mafia. They were thoroughly at home in the Nacional, Riviera and Capri hotels, and also in the Casino Nacional; in fact the hotels practically belonged to them, so it was inevitable that sooner or later we would encounter them in our dealings.

Millo with Yolanda and her boyfriend

We were still revelling in our excitement at the coming season with Lecuona, and practising daily, when the first hint of trouble arose. All of a sudden the rumour reached us that the other employees of the Casino were against us working there, although nobody could tell us why. The opposition was actually coming from the employees' wives, we were told. Male orchestras were normal, but 'women playing music in the Casino? Good Lord! That can only bring strife and jealousy.' Apparently they were afraid that we would make their men leave them. But Lecuona was not one to give in.

He presented the manager with a blunt choice. 'I'm the artistic director here. If the Orquesta Anacaona isn't allowed to play, I won't work any more and will annul my contract.'

Sadly that didn't solve the problem. One afternoon our doorbell rang. A group of men stood outside, all wearing serious expressions, and behind them stood an equal number of women, with even *more* serious expressions. 'Hello. We are from the Casino Nacional and would like to get to know you.' I realized at once that these were no ordinary employees.

After everyone had taken a seat on the couch or in the rocking chairs in the living room, the guests asked if we would play them a number. This was strange, they could have easily heard us play at any performance. But they insisted on hearing us here and now. 'Why should we be bullied by strangers into playing?' I thought. However, I could sense that the matter was serious and I went to get my saxophone. With the first notes the tense atmosphere promptly relaxed. The men grinned and the women became friendly. Apparently they had believed that we couldn't actually play music, that we were hookers disguised as musicians. Later we found out that the 'inspection commission' had really been made up of gentlemen from the Mafia and their wives. We had to laugh. Apparently even the professional crooks couldn't do whatever they wanted. Their wives had the last word, especially when other women threatened to get in their way.

After we had passed the 'inspection', the rehearsals for the show began. Despite his fame, Lecuona was jovial, uncomplicated and modest. He was an imposing figure, six feet tall and very handsome. His deep black hair was carefully parted and pomade held the elegance of a slight wave in place. He was always coming into our dressing room just to chat, yet he inspired respect in us nevertheless. Everyone called him Maestro. Except for Millo. She was allowed to call him Ernesto because as a child she had always called him by his first name.

With manager and nightclub owner, Havana, 1947

In one of our conversations, Lecuona said that he wanted to play a song with us in the show. I told Cuchito, 'This is embarrassing. Our pianist is no match for the Maestro. I just can't imagine him at the piano next to our pianist. The two don't go together.'

But Lecuona only smiled when he heard that. 'Let's just try it out...'

For our finale we rehearsed a conga. Included in it were the *modelos*, long-legged American revue girls from Miami, beautiful blonde women who provided the visual highlight of the show. Sergio Orta was responsible for the stage sets.

Everyone knew and respected him because he had just done the choreography for Judy Garland in the movie *Ziegfeld Follies*, which was a big box-office hit. Sergio, a heavyweight of a man, was wider than he was tall: five feet tall and weighing 225 pounds. We all stood ready and waited for Sergio's command.

'*Denle con ganas, chicas!*' – 'With feeling, girls!' We strutted down a long staircase together with the *modelos*, who were decked out in net stockings and feather-trimmed bikinis.

'Stop! Stop! Stop! Out!' roared Sergio after a few beats. 'Take her out of there!' Everyone stared. He meant Cuchito. She really couldn't dance. With her awkward movements, and stiff as a walking stick, she stood out from the group of elegant bodies all swaying rhythmically in unison.

His assistant tried to smooth things over. 'Look, Orta, how about we give her the maracas instead of the sax? It might make dancing easier for her.'

'Forget it; just get her out of there.'

Disappointed, Cuchito joined the other musicians, the Hermanos Castro, while we got to dance in the line with the American models.

I was excited by the work at the Casino Nacional. The revolving stage was gigantic. When the heavy red curtain went up, we were on the left-hand side of the room, and as we played 'Siboney', the stage turned slowly until we had reached a spot directly in front of the audience. There was room for at least a thousand people in the audience. Millo then stepped into the middle and played a bongo solo. Above our stage towered a second level and the roof was way up above the third floor. To the right and left of the stage, you could catch a glimpse of row upon row of roulette and card tables. When the show started, the slapping of cards from blackjack and baccarat games and the clicking of the roulette balls instantly stopped. 'We're taking a break for the show!' The gamblers didn't need to fear anyone raking in their winnings during the performance. Anyone who wanted to could join the dancing, and by the end almost everyone was on their feet for the conga. The whole audience snaked its way through the room, kicking their legs and wiggling their hips.

There were also well-known regulars who lent the Casino Nacional its special atmosphere. The boxer Joe Louis could often be seen there as well as Frank Sinatra. Sinatra was already at the pinnacle of his fame and women would practically faint when he stepped up on stage. The eccentric actor George Raft, with his trademark fat cigars, came in and out of the casino. He also happened to be a good friend of the Mafiosi! One time, one of the artists on stage urged him to stand up in the audience so everyone could see him. The crowd went wild. 'Sing! Sing! Sing!' George Raft didn't need any encouraging, and started singing a song. René Urbino, a young pianist from the Julio Gutiérrez Orchestra who accompanied him, later became Yolanda's steady boyfriend.

Naturally there were all kinds of rumours going around about George Raft and Frank Sinatra's connections to the 'honourable society', but we had no idea what took place behind closed doors at the Casino. Only later did we find out that a 'Christmas' party had been held in the Hotel Nacional in Frank Sinatra's honour. The host was Lucky Luciano. The Mafia boss had been released early from Sing-Sing in February 1946, but on condition that he never set foot on US soil again. So he came to Havana, moved into the Hotel Nacional, and began running his businesses in the States out of Cuba. The Christmas party for Frank, as it later turned out, was a Mafia summit meeting at which Lucky Luciano presented his new strategies for prostitution, gambling and the drug trade. The American government got wind of it and demanded that Luciano be deported from Cuba. Our government, which normally rushed to do everything that Washington wanted, took an amazingly long time. Only when the Americans threatened an embargo did President Grau finally give in. He sent Luciano home to Italy. From then on he would have to run his empire from there, which apparently wasn't all that difficult.

From the very outset of our stint at the Casino Nacional, the Mafia den, our friend Lázaro encouraged us to take it all with a pinch of salt. One Sunday, when we were sitting in the dining room, he exclaimed, 'The Mafiosi? *Coño!* I know what I'm talking about. I got to know them in 1933. Our Septeto Nacional was invited to the World's Fair in Chicago. Suddenly, out of the blue, all expenses paid, air fare and hotel impeccably arranged. Terrific! Why should we ask who

Havana's Casino Nacional

financed the whole thing? A professional musician asks no more questions than he has to. When it comes to people with a lot of money, discretion is the First Commandment. We were just happy to be going to Chicago.

'When we boarded the ship with our instruments, we noticed that seven other men with instrument cases had joined us, acting like they were part of the band. Soon one of us discovered that their instruments must have been made of steel, the cases were so heavy. Of course, it turned out there were guns inside. We said to ourselves: if they think they can palm off these cases on us, they've got another thing coming. Then they'll have to prove to the customs officers that they can play those instruments. *Coño*, that would be funny.

'But customs didn't check us and we arrived in Chicago in good shape, with all our luggage. There, our strange "colleagues" vanished as unobtrusively as they had joined us and we were able to concentrate entirely on making music. Then our financiers came to see us, wanting us to play at some private functions in addition to the official programme at the World's Fair. The high point of these parties was the *danza del abanico*, the fan dance. Half a dozen revue girls from Havana stood on stage, armed only with fans. From behind we could see that they were stark naked! But those ladies handled those large fans so quickly and so skilfully that the crucial spots remained hidden from the audience. The "honourable ones" went wild!'

More and more of Lázaro's stories came tumbling out: 'Girls, that's nothing compared to what we experienced at some places in Havana. Do you know what kind of gig we had recently?' He told us what happened to the Septeto Nacional at the anniversary of the electricity company. The musicians were summoned to play in a private club on Calle Lázaro. From the outside it was a completely normal building. No sign, nothing. But Lázaro had barely stepped past security at the door when he found himself in a restaurant with a dance floor and stage.

Before the show started, everyone in the septet had to gather in the kitchen, not to get a hot meal, but to put on a mask. Only then were they allowed to go into the ballroom, where all the guests were wearing masks as well. Lázaro and his colleagues from the septet set the mood with Afro-Cuban rhythms and soon the masks were all that the guests had on. A real orgy was taking place. It was total chaos. The rich and influential celebrated in their closed circles without inhibitions, carrying on with girlfriends and prostitutes, and they hired the best musicians to play for them. Anyone who had money could enjoy a titillating double life.

I knew what Lázaro was talking about, because we all had our hands full fending off the businessmen from the sleazy, lewd side of Havana. The owner of the Shanghai Theatre tried once again to lure us with a high fee. During my childhood they were still staging enchanting Chinese productions there, starring renowned artists from Hong Kong or San Francisco. Since then the Shanghai had turned into a shady nightspot, exclusively for men. Not only would the dancers strip down to skimpy bikinis as thin as dental floss, but the comedians on stage gave performances that were more obscene than the nudity. They made vulgar and suggestive jokes about everything. And the waitresses were the type of women who would do anything for money.

The female musicians who weren't afraid of appearing at the Shanghai were mostly mediocre, but not all of them. A few excellent artists made their reputations there, such as Natalia Herrera, who was initially employed as the vocalist for the house band. She owed her success to being strict about separating her professional, stage life from her private life. In the show she acted lasciviously and drove men crazy. But after the last bar of music had been played, she once more became utterly remote and unapproachable. She curtly refused to tolerate any crude familiarities. Because she was so high class, the manager and patrons had to respect her. Thank God we were spared working our way up at joints like the Shanghai. Luckily, we could afford to decline such offers.

Since my return from Curaçao, Eladio had been pressing me to stay with him. But his views on partnership and marriage were a wake-up call for me. In one of his essays, for which he even won a prize, I could read about it in black and white:

'Men who work at night will never belong to the category "ideal husbands". Journalists and musicians belong to this group. In terms of marriage they are tragic figures. The ideal husband is someone who manages to transfer the order and discipline that he observes at work to his home life... Nevertheless there are men who never marry but are able to transform themselves into ideal husbands. They practise open relationships. If they feel like breaking up, all they have to do is pack whatever they have left in their lover's wardrobe. And this ritual keeps them good humoured and ready for reconciliation. The result is that they never actually break up with the women they could legally leave without scruples.'

'Enough. We can stay friends and still see each other, but not as a couple. I'll see you only if Millo is present too. A steady partnership is out of the question,' I informed Eladio at our next rendezvous, and thus our relationship was dissolved. But although he was seemingly so liberal, he would not let me go so easily. He had a friend of his, the sportswriter Cuco Conde, spy on me. He wanted to know if I had a new lover and whether it was serious. He learned from Cuco that I had no end of admirers. They included a member of parliament, a singer and Guillermo, the congenial jai alai player, who already had three marriages behind him. We enjoyed ourselves at the beach of Guanabo, or I would go out with Millo when she had a date with Cab Calloway. But all at once I noticed that since I'd broken up with Eladio, something inside me had changed: I was no longer in love.

At about that time, during an engagement at the Actualidades cinema behind the Teatro Payret on the *aires libres*, we got to know an ambitious young singer. Her name was Celia Cruz, the artist celebrated today as the 'Queen of Salsa'. She could create quite a sensation with her powerful voice and her repertoire of Afro-Cuban music. I observed how, at our first rehearsal together, the petite and very curvaceous young black woman stepped rather shyly onto the stage. Rodrigo Neyra, alias Rodney – later the great choreographer at the Tropicana club – directed the show. Celia let it rip, launching into the hit '*Mango Mangüé*'.

'Stop. Stop!' Rodney interrupted the song and looked at Celia with the greatest dismay. '*Negra!* Not like that, not like that. You're so thin and you're standing there like a lump of wood in front of the mike. You've got to move. You have to give what you sing more *sandunga*, more spice.'

We had to laugh when he leapt up on stage like a whirlwind to stand next to Celia, swinging his hips and prancing around like a peacock. He put some fire under Celia's behind and taught her how to get people not only to listen to her, but to look at her as well.

We quickly became good friends with Celia, not least because she lived in Lawton and Alfredo León was her boyfriend. We knew him well because he sang in the *son* septet Segundo Nacional, and because his father, Bienvenido, was the vocalist of the Septeto Nacional. Father met Alfredo at the Mercado Único, where he often went after a gig to eat wonton soup. 'Hey, Alfredo, when do you think you and Celia will get married?' Father kept asking him. But like so many men, Alfredo didn't want to tie himself down.

*Anacaona with
Celia Cruz, 1947*

With Celia Cruz

Celia's home was one of those classical-style houses that are built as if for the exclusive purpose of having parties. That's how it seemed to me the first time I walked through the foyer, where she received her guests. Continuing, I entered the large interior courtyard, where musicians were playing and people were dancing. I grabbed a good dance partner, the actor Rosendo Rosell, because, like most of the guests, we wanted to put on a good show on the dance floor.

~ **Anacaona** ~

Surrounded by such an illustrious crowd of famous artists, we were inspired to be innovative as we danced rumba and *son*. Everyone was trying out their own original steps with as much agility as possible, hoping to attract the attention of others with spins and turns, with a shimmy of the shoulders and special flicks of the hand. Ondina danced with *'Bola de Nieve'*, Snowball. Everyone knew the black man with the physique of a boxer as Rita Montaner's piano player, but he was also a great singer in his own right. I liked him best as diseur of the song *'La Vie en Rose'* in which he was unsurpassed.

Now the large black man was wooing skinny Ondina at the edge of the dance floor, sighing, 'This China girl, she has a wasp-like waist and is built as elegantly as a Parisian. I want to marry her. No one else.' Ondina merely gave him a knowing smile and looked pleased, and when she thought no one was watching, she signalled to me. With her upper arms pressed to her side, she raised her hands and fluttered them like a little bird. She wanted to tell me that she didn't take that marriage talk seriously, because Bola had 'feathers'. Everyone knew that he was gay.

During a break I spoke to him: 'Bola, I think your song "*Si Me Pudieras Querer*" is so beautiful.'

'So you like it, Alicia? *Por Dios!* What bad taste you have!' he said, laughing. Years later he confessed to me that in his younger days he had been in love with Rita Montaner. He had dedicated the song *'Si Me Pudieras Querer'* ('If You Could Love Me') to her, the love of his life. I think I was the only person he ever told.

But who was the love of my life? Who was I going to marry? Celia Cruz brought up this topic one day. For fun and out of curiosity, we got the idea of asking the spirits about our future partners. Celia knew how to use ouija board to consult the spirits and took the matter in hand. Late one night she suggested we set out a glass of water to attract the spirits. Millo joined us at the table, on which Celia had placed the lacquered wooden board with the letters of the alphabet painted in an arc. Now Celia set an empty glass upside-down on it and we touched it with our fingers, only very lightly, because you're not allowed to put pressure on the glass to manipulate it. But the glass didn't move. Maybe it's possible, I thought, to influence the glass with your thoughts. I summoned from memory two possible candidates that Millo and I had known in Aruba: Henry and Enrique Trappenberg, two brothers of Dutch descent. Henry worked in customs, which is where we met him. He was serious about Millo and had already introduced her formally to his family. Suddenly the glass moved as if by a ghostly hand from one letter to another. Imagine what the response was to Celia's question: JESUS MENENDEZ. He was a union leader fighting for better working conditions at the sugar mills. Celia got goosebumps. 'Could be that he's in love with me.' Now it was Millo's turn. I was sure that her admirer, Henry Trappenberg, would come up. But it wasn't his name the glass spelled out. Celia said, 'How funny, a K… and I can't make out the rest.' We couldn't decipher it properly, and we didn't know any man with a K in his name.

We obviously weren't going to get married in the near future – I was now twenty-seven – but a child was shortly to come into the world for us to look after: Flora's second son, Willy. González, Flora's husband, was very keen to emigrate to the States. He pictured his sons learning English and studying there. Flora wasn't at all happy about this plan; our neighbourhood meant everything to her. She was constantly going in and out of people's houses and loved to gossip with everybody. She had perfectly mastered the 'gossipography' of the neighbourhood, as Mother put it. As a seamstress she met lots of people and could keep the exchange of information going while she worked. There wasn't any television in those days, so gossip was the main distraction.

Alicia as vocalist, 1947

Time off

González pressured her: 'Let's emigrate. Let's emigrate.'

'You emigrate. I like it here,' Flora would snap back.

But Flora finally gave in and they travelled to New York, where they moved into a small apartment in Manhattan, on 95th Street. The area was later named 'Spanish Harlem' because of all the Latinos there, but at the time almost nobody but white Americans lived there. Willy, who was born in Cuba, soon started running around the apartment. When he got noisy the neighbours grew annoyed and banged on the walls. When Flora and Willy visited us, we discovered we loved taking care of him. 'He'll do much better here,' we told Flora. It made more sense to leave Willy with us in Cuba, and that's what she did. Emma in particular was crazy about him. She could read his every wish. Emma was usually serious, and sometimes grumpy. Maybe that's why she had such a hard time finding a partner for life.

'Everyone asks the same thing on the first date: what's my job and how much money do I make. That's all they want to know. It's obvious that they're only after my money,' she complained. Charming little Willy, though, brought out her soft, more tender side.

Besides working in the band, Millo occasionally played at the Tropicana nightclub. The Mafiosi were putting a lot of money into the former Hacienda Villa Mina, transforming it into a glamorous open-air cabaret and adding on gambling parlours. They decorated the entrance with the statue of a ballerina in full pirouette and a fountain illuminated by multi-coloured spotlights. This showpiece, displaying eight curvaceous nymphs dancing in a circle, had been taken from the Casino Nacional. Outraged, the Jesuits were up in arms against the Tropicana, because this new temple of sin was located close to their seminary, where Fidel

243

Millo, late 1940s

Castro also later studied. Armando Romeu's ensemble became the house band of the Tropicana for over two decades. Armando Romeu was regarded as an outstanding interpreter of jazz and was an expert in musical notation. He could put down on paper even the most complicated music just by listening to it; for this reason we musicians were always after him to provide sheet music for the most current pieces from the States.

One day Armando called us up. He was on the verge of a nervous breakdown. His drummer was an epileptic and had not yet recovered from a seizure. He asked whether Millo could fill in. She agreed. Shortly before the performance Armando gave her the sheet music. He explained nervously to Millo, 'Look at this. There's a break here.'

Millo glanced at it. 'Sure, sure, everything's fine, Armando.' She could memorize pieces like lightning. When she let loose on the drums, Armando could scarcely hide his astonishment. He didn't yet know that Millo's favourite drummer was the same as that of his regular percussionist: the drummer in Benny Goodman's band. Both of them followed his style. After the performance, Armando hugged and kissed Millo out of sheer joy. That's what Yolanda told us later. Pressed into service by Mother, she had to go along as Millo's chaperone.

After this, Armando kept calling. 'Millo, I need you again,' was all he would say. 'You're the only one who can replace my drummer. Say yes or I'll have to call off the show.'

When I met Armando decades later at a cultural event, he recalled, 'Yes, Alicia. Millo was the best there was on the drums. What a woman! When I called her, she could play any piece on the first try, without rehearsing. Nobody else could do that.'

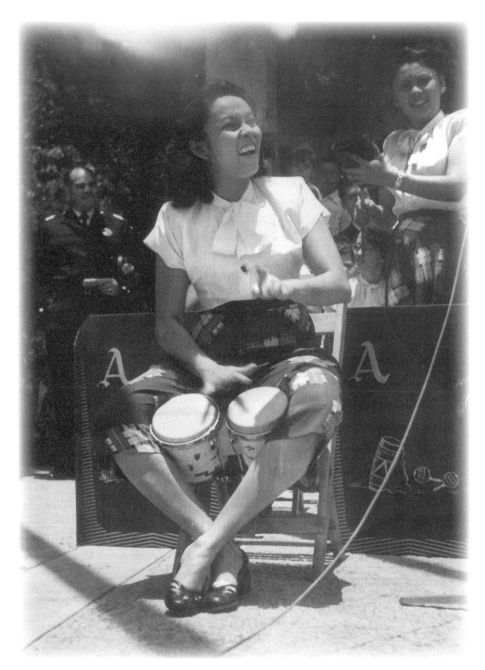

Bongo solo in Medellín, Colombia

Chapter 11

Don't Meddle with the Saints

For all her natural flair and skill, Millo practised every single day and pitted herself against two outstanding percussionists, her teacher Manzano and his nephew Candido Camero. Sometimes one would take the conga drum or play the bongos; then the other would take over and play a solo on the conga. This would go on for hours. I often accompanied them on the claves, just for fun. Lázaro also loved our jam sessions. During one of them he mentioned his idea of arranging an Afro-Cuban piece especially for us to perform on stage, just like the ones they play at the ceremony of *toque del santo*, the 'drumbeat of the saint'. As a *santero*, Lázaro was extremely familiar with this kind of music, played in six-eight time.

His *toque del santo* was to be held on 16 December, the eve of his name day. I was so impatient for the day to arrive! Friends and acquaintances hurried to his narrow terrace house with the tiny rooms in the Barrio Chino. Millo and I grabbed seats near the altar, which was covered with lilac-coloured flowers and decorated with numerous candles. Here we had the best view. In front of the altar the musicians, all men, were busy with the three *batá* drums. These are covered with hide on both sides and it is thought that a magical power resides within them. The drums invoke the saints to come down to earth and to join in the human celebrations. Another musician was shaking the *chekeré*, the bottle gourd, which is covered by a net with seeds sewn onto it. The musical instrument that fascinated me most, however, was the *guataca*. A big, gaunt black man was coaxing fascinating sounds from an iron hoe, like the ones used for field work. Nowadays a cowbell is used instead of a hoe, but those wrought-iron hoes had a brighter, more beautiful sound. After they had finished the greeting ritual in the form of particular drumbeats, the musicians really got going. Captivated, I stood there surrounded by the *batá* drumbeats, the rustling of the *chekeré* and the fine 'tin-tin-tin' of the hoe. Many of the guests were dancing frenetically, while those who, like me, were completely hemmed in, bobbed and swayed amidst the storm of drumbeats. The atmosphere was close and threatening, and amplified the intoxicating rhythms.

Soon the first dancer, a young woman, fell to the floor in a swoon. She was 'receiving her saint' or 'being ridden' as we say. After she had apparently regained control of herself, she danced on, but now quite differently because a saint had entered her body. From her lithe, sensual movements one could tell that it was Ochún, the goddess of love, the ruler of the river. We now squeezed even tighter together to give Ochún room to dance. Then another guest fell to the floor. He was transformed before our eyes into a limping, writhing, cowering cripple – into Babalú Ayé, the leper San Lázaro. As he made his rounds some people moved close to him in order to ask questions about their health. Babalú Ayé spoke to them in Yoruba or Lucumí – in some African language, anyway, that I didn't understand. An initiate translated the messages, and whoever was being addressed often blanched with naked terror. The saint told them things that no one could know: what sins they had committed and what gifts they should offer – flowers, candles, honey, chickens – to put things right. But I wasn't afraid. I didn't have a guilty conscience, and I was happy about the presence of the saints. I could still hear the 'tin-tin-tin' of the *guataca* ringing in my ears days later.

~ **Anacaona** ~

Although religion was a strong anchor in our lives and in our music, we sisters never talked much about religious matters. I discussed such things even less with others. Nevertheless I knew that most people's lives in the neighbourhood were filled with religion. Each had his own discreet way of honouring his saint and securing protection and well-being. You could tell by looking at a person's clothes: the daughters and sons of the love goddess Ochún liked wearing yellow; the offspring of the god of thunder, Changó, dressed in red; while those of the sea goddess Yemayá wore blue. Some people wore the favourite colour of their saints in the form of glass beads, concealing the bracelets or necklaces underneath their shirts.

A person's patron saint also determined their character. A fellow musician I knew, who was always the centre of attention at any gathering with her exuberance and winning smile, was a typical daughter of Ochún. The hot-tempered grocer at the shop on the corner was clearly close to the god of war and thunder, Changó. His domineering wife, who was unforgiving if you occasionally forgot to pay for goods bought on credit, was doubtless a daughter of the sea goddess Yemayá. Harmonious, reticent people who unwaveringly go their own way are children of Obatalá. A song from our repertoire by Ignacio Piñeiro explains how you can tell which saint is closest to whom, even if that person doesn't acknowledge it:

> *Mayeya, don't try and fool me*
> *Mayeya, don't meddle with the saints*
> *Respect the holy necklaces*
> *Mayeya, don't meddle with the saints*
>
> *Don't pretend to fool me with this story*
> *Because we all know each other in little Cuba*

Whoever doesn't dress in yellow puts on blue
Or even shining red or lilac

After his name day, Lázaro talked us into learning his latest composition, 'Ta Macario', which required three *batá* drums. 'That way you can offer your audience something religious too.' Afro-Cuban pieces were currently very fashionable and were part of the repertoire at all the nightclubs in Havana. But for stage shows they had to be altered to keep them from invoking religious power. Lázaro took it upon himself to get the *batá* drums for us. Naturally they couldn't be 'real' ones, which had magical powers and for that reason could never be placed on the floor. But he did make sure that they were blessed by a *babalao*, a priest, and Millo only played rhythms that were similar to those from the *toque del santo*. She didn't dare play the true rhythms. 'Don't meddle with the saints!'

The superb Cuban conga player Chano Pozo should have taken that advice. He had earned a legendary reputation in the States with his drumming, but in 1948 he was shot to death in a bar in Harlem. It was rumoured that this was divine punishment because he had used secret drum rhythms to further his career and played them in public.

Everyday we practised Lázaro's piece 'Ta Macario', until finally it was time for the dress rehearsal. In order to see if it worked, we invited Flora – visiting from New York – and Emma to be the audience in the living room. 'What's this whole superstition thing?' asked Emma, incensed. As a hard-line Catholic, she refused to listen to our performance. She didn't approve of 'superstition', even in a tame stage version.

'If it's all nonsense, then you have nothing to fear. It's just part of our show,' I told her, and she finally gave in.

Ziomara took up her position in front of Emma and Flora and started singing. She had never distinguished herself as a singer before, but this music suited her because her voice is as husky as that of a market vendor. Ziomara bellowed out, 'Ta Macario! He lies in chains. What has happened to him?'

We replied in chorus, 'He's going to make his saint Changó. He's going to make his saint Changó.'

Then Millo started beating the big *batá* drum: *Paaan, panpanpanpanpan. Paaan, panpanpanpanpanpan.*

Abruptly the rhythm changed to *tikitikitikitik* and Ziomara took out seven scarves. The seven colours represented the seven African powers, the most potent saints: Changó, Ochún, Babalú Ayé, Yemayá, Oggún, Elegguá and Orula. Waving the light chiffon scarves, Ziomara began to dance. Rotating her hips wildly, she shook the scarves around in the air as if she wanted to free Emma, who was sitting there as stiff as a board, from an evil spirit. 'Go away! Don't touch me!' Emma shrieked, and jumped up as if she had been stung by a tarantula. She ran off and we laughed so hard that we had to stop playing.

Emma was *calambuca*, even more Catholic than the Pope, and had fulfilled her long-cherished dream of going to Rome to see the Holy Father. She also made sure that all of us observed Friday rituals and ate no meat, even though we didn't pop into church every day like she did. Still, like almost everyone in Cuba, I thought of myself as a Catholic. I first realized that ours was a special type of Catholicism when we were abroad on tour and met Catholics for whom Sunday Mass was a must. I only went to Mass when I had big worries, at those rare moments when I felt a deep need to enter a church.

I mostly honoured the saints and the dead at home, because I'm a spiritualist. I had placed the figures of San Lázaro and the Virgin of Caridad on my dresser and regularly put flowers out for them. But above all I made sure to offer the departed spirits a glass of water set high atop my wardrobe. Spiritualism and

Santería follow somewhat different customs and beliefs, but mostly we call them both simply *la religión*.

Since the breakthrough of the *son*, African culture had become acceptable in the salons and in some parts of Havana society. In the countryside, though, racism still prevailed. When we played at a club in Pinar del Río, the blacks danced on one side and the whites on the other. They were all dancing to the same music, but they had to keep to themselves. And in Santa Clara on Sundays, when everyone was out walking in the plaza, the whites strolled through the middle of the square while the blacks had to keep to the periphery. In the clubs and nightspots of Havana, on the other hand, those who considered themselves white practised more discreet forms of discrimination.

We never had problems like this at performances. We were even invited to play at an important gala at the Teatro Nacional. It was a tribute to the great Mexican comedian Cantinflas and the Cuban singer Miguelito Valdés, who had enjoyed huge success in New York as Mr Babalú Ayé. A few days later our friend Enrique Arceo came to visit from Mexico. One evening he invited Millo, Yolanda and Lenin out. I didn't go. He wanted to experience Havana by night, and on impulse my sisters suggested they go to the Teatro Nacional cabaret. 'You'll love it. Their show is fantastic!'

The doorman at the entrance to the cabaret, in the basement of the Teatro Nacional, stopped the four, stared openly at Yolanda and told Enrique, 'You're not wearing a tie.' Enrique, however, was correctly dressed; he was wearing a *guayabera*, an elegant white pleated shirt. A tie is not worn with this type of shirt. Anyone could get into the most distinguished clubs wearing a *guayabera*, which is a traditional Cuban garment. But the doorman insisted on a tie. The maître d' intervened, offering to lend him one. Although Enrique accepted gratefully, the doorman still refused them entry. Now Yolanda realized what was going on. Our brother Lenin has very light, even milky skin. Enrique Arceo was also quite light, almost tending towards a pinkish hue. Millo's complexion was *café con leche* brown, still light enough. But Yolanda was clearly a shade too dark. The doorman finally said, without beating around the bush, 'No, you see, this is a *club*,' stressing that some people fitted in and some, like Yolanda, very definitely did not.

Millo was seething with rage. 'Do me a favour and call the manager.' When he arrived, Millo struggled to control herself. 'A few days ago we were the Cuban band invited to play here in honour of Miguelito Valdés and Cantinflas. It seems a little disrespectful to now refuse us entry because this is a "club".'

The manager feigned shock. 'Who is claiming such a thing? Please, come in.'

'No, now we're the ones who no longer wish to enter,' Millo shot back, and the four of them went to another cabaret. Not a first-class one, to be sure, but a second-class one, where they weren't quite so particular about the spectrum of skin colour.

Racism didn't even stop for internationally known celebrities. Josephine Baker had been invited to perform at the Theatre América in Havana that same year, and had wanted to stay at the Hotel Nacional. 'All the rooms are occupied,' the head clerk at the front desk told her, without checking for vacancies. He didn't even bother to seem apologetic. That's how high society in Havana was: in the show they praised the diva to the skies, but at the same time they considered themselves too superior to sleep under the same roof.

Millo, 1951

Chapter 12

Irresistible Cuban Women

In the early 1950s, the music known as *el filin*, 'the feeling', was spreading like wildfire. One of the founders of this new musical movement was Ñico Rojas, the son of the architect who had designed our parents' house. Mother had given him his first guitar and Ada had taught him his first song on it. Ñico soon developed into a brilliant guitarist, one of the best in Cuba. The co-founders of *el filin* were the pianist Frank Emilio and César Portillo de la Luz, who were introduced to us by Ñico. Their lyrics and melodies were tender and profound. They took their inspiration from the most varied genres of Cuban and American music. Or more precisely, they didn't give a damn about the artificial categorizing of musical genres according to countries and regions; they were interested in the universal language of emotion.

These musicians were now at the centre of the *rumbantela*, the sweet life, Cuban-style. Ada and Echarri's house, right next door to our parents, became one of the favourite hangouts of these bohemians. They would meet there late at night, eat snacks, sip cocktails, listen to the singing and guitar playing, and dance. By that time most of them would already have played a few sets at the Bodeguita del Medio, one of the most popular haunts of anyone with an appetite for life. Accompanying them would be baseball players, jai alai players, and artists such as Felito Ayón, the son of Félix Ayón, one of Father's old friends. We were amazed when Felito came back from an extended stay in France with long hair. That was considered eccentric, very bohemian and extremely avant-garde. Felito was constantly bringing together the most disparate creative types, either inviting the whole gang to his house in El Cerro or taking them all along to Ada and Echarri's. Among the group would be Carlos Puebla, Felito's printer colleague Plomito and his wife, Dinorah, and 'Las Capelas', the singers Daisy and Marta, who lived only a few blocks from us in Lawton. At Ada's place there was so much happening that one evening we decided to officially christen the house and hang up a sign that said '*El Gato Cojo*', 'The Limping Tomcat'. The sign inspired Felito Ayón when, in 1958, he opened *El Gato Tuerto*, The One-Eyed Tomcat , which soon became the hub of *el filin*.

In the meantime, Mexican movie-goers were worshipping at the feet of female Cuban rumba dancers. These *rumberas* were the protagonists of films such as *La Insaciable (The Insatiable)*, *Noche de Perdición (Night of Perdition)*, *Víctimas del Pecado (Victims of Sin)* and *Piel Canela (Cinnamon Skin)*, in which Cuban women were portrayed as the devil made flesh. A typical plot entailed a *rumbera* beguiling a male protagonist and drawing him into sure but sweet depravity. In the film *Sensualidad (Sensuality)*, for example, Ninón Sevilla plays a prostitute and turns an honest man into an utter *bobo*, drunk and daft with love. All he wants is to be with his lover, and so he ends up both financially and socially ruined. The audience feels only sympathy when the male protagonist sighs at the end, 'Yes, I've lost everything: my honour, my happiness, the respect of my family, but what I've danced no one can take away.' Ninón Sevilla was not only fêted in Mexico, but even became extremely popular in France. They held her in high esteem as an uninhibited woman struggling against outmoded, dusty, bourgeois moral values.

In 1951, at the height of the Golden Age of Mexican cinema, the film production company of the Calderón Brothers from Mexico City contacted us. Ninón Sevilla had pulled strings to make the deal because she very much wanted to work with us. We shared a deep bond, because she was from Havana's Barrio Chino too. Ninón grew up with her grandmother in humble circumstances in our friend Lázaro's neighbourhood. In her youth Ninón was captivated by the rumba, danced the way the local people danced it. You could only experience that in the *solares*, those formerly elegant, now run-down tenements with their big interior courtyards. Poor families lived there in cramped quarters, sharing a bathroom and kitchen. Ninón was enticed into the back courtyards because only the poor understood how to throw spontaneous parties, make music and organize a *real* rumba. One person would take a board, another a frying pan, a third would turn an empty drawer upside-down, and the rhythmic ensemble was ready to play in two-four time. The only real instrument was the conga drum, and whoever was the best percussionist had the privilege of playing it. Then there were the singers. The music was the men's domain, the women's the dancing. With a partner they would start the flirtation game, dancing very slowly at first, then allowing the movements to become more and more intense and direct. The two intoxicated dancers gave cues, firing up the musicians. A singer would improvise the lyrics according to the dance and get everyone going even more. '*Se armó la rumba,*' they would say, 'The rumba has broken loose.'

Ninón first appeared on the stages of Havana together with Horacio as a rumba dance pair – to the horror of her Catholic grandmother. But then she broke up with her partner because he drank too much. She next sought her fortune on her own in Mexico City. As a sensual blonde with a wasp-like waist, long legs and a certain mischievous air, she succeeded in making her breakthrough in the famous Teatro Lírico as a solo dancer and moved to Mexico permanently. Ninón advanced to stardom and from then on had to pay careful attention to

257

House party at Ninón Sevilla's

her reputation. She knew that her fans didn't want to see her associated with love affairs or a marriage, or even a pregnancy. Anyone who wanted to remain successful on stage had to maintain a spotless private life, to seem pure and inaccessible. Ninón took this very much to heart, but also joked that people demanded that she be 'a vegetarian from the waist down'.

We appeared with Ninón in the film *No Niego Mi Pasado* (*I Don't Deny My Past*). In one scene, Ninón dances across a market square wearing a satin bikini and ruffled train, turning men's heads with a jaunty swing of her hip and a shimmy of her shoulders. We supplied appropriately hot rhythms for the scene.

~ **Anacaona** ~

I have to admit, I turned pale with envy when I saw Ninón dance. How I would have liked to be able to dance the real rumba! At parties at Ninón's house I tried my best but could only manage a less sophisticated version. The true rumba dancers have an infinite variety of moves and steps in their repertoire, giving expression to the music with every part of their body – their waist, shoulders and even with their head. I would have most liked to learn the *guaguancó*, for me the most beautiful rumba, with its own unique gestures and a slower pace than the others. But as far as this type of dancing is concerned, I have remained ignorant.

The next movie we did was *Mujeres de Teatro (Women of the Theatre)* at the Churubusco film studio in Mexico City. They had built a nightclub in a studio as big as an aeroplane hangar. This time we played for the Cuban movie

Ninón in a strapless dress

and revue star Rosita Fornés and Emilia Guiú, a Catalan actress. The assistant director explained to us that during our number a man would be shot at and we would have to take cover – that was all. Take one: in the middle of the song the shots rang out. The patrons of the club ran all over the place. Some of us ducked underneath the piano, others spontaneously stormed off the stage. Then I saw Ada trying to escape with her bass, and I couldn't help laughing. 'Cut!' The assistant director was beside himself. 'No laughing!' he yelled at me. 'This is serious. Girls, you have to try to escape the shooting. You're running for your lives, so please leave the instruments where they are. It all has to look real!'

In the third film, *La Noche es Nuestra* (*This Night Belongs To Us*), we were more professional. We were appearing in a theatre, all in long, elegant, light-grey gowns, hemmed with sequins. Each dress was slightly different from the others. One gown was strapless, another had long sleeves, and so on. Flora had designed them and each of us had embroidered our own dress.

While we were busy at the Churubusco studios, Emilio Fernández turned up. El Indio, as he was universally known, just wanted to stop by and see us, he said. Even at the age of forty-seven, he was an imposing figure of a man. He wasn't tall, but he had great charisma, an athletic build and a striking Indian face. He was an actor and director and at the pinnacle of his fame. His films were full of melodrama, all revolving around the theme of love, and from time to time El Indio would play the lead role. He liked to play the part of the man who, with an exalted sense of honour, manages to tame the unbridled sensuality of the woman. In real life, however, it was just the opposite. El Indio repeatedly gave his emotions free rein. When, at the age of nine years old, he discovered his mother with a lover in his parents' bedroom, he had swiftly dispatched the man, a family friend, to the hereafter with a carbine shot. In his younger years he had fought his way up through Hollywood as an extra, dancer and actor, and finally achieved success in the 1940s as a director. His film *María Candelaria* had its premiere at the Cannes film festival.

During the breaks in shooting he would always come over to see us, until finally I noticed that he had his eye on Millo. 'You're telling me El Indio is after me? You're nuts!' Millo didn't want to believe me until her admirer one day behaved quite jealously.

'It will be your downfall if you marry a gringo!' he told her with a menacing smile. It bothered him that many Americans would gaze adoringly at Millo during the concerts and then want to meet her after the show. We eventually found out why he was so interested. He had just separated from his young wife, the actress Columba Domínguez, whom he had discovered and made into the star of several of his films. On screen she personified the prototypical Mexican-Indian woman: proud, resigned to her fate, humble. Her beautiful, perfectly proportioned facial features and her long, blue-black hair predestined her for this type of role. For the first time she had gone to Italy to

El Indio, Emilio Fernández, dedicated a photo to Ziomara

make a movie, without her husband. While there, she had got herself a short, modern hairdo without asking his permission. But El Indio loved the Indian look of his wife above all else and when he saw her with her hair shorn, he had a fit.

'I can't live with a woman who denies her Indian roots as soon as she sets foot in Europe,' he apparently said as he threw her out of the house.

Back in Havana, Xavier Cugat had his agent ask Cuchito whether she could spare Millo for a tour. Cugat was the leader of the best-known Latin American orchestra in the States and he was *the* Latino bandleader in Hollywood movies. He always had an eye-catching singer fronting his band, actually preferring platinum blonde vamps. Although Cuchito felt secretly flattered, she turned down Cugat's offer politely but firmly. From then on she worried constantly about Millo. Musically we were all very professional. Ondina on the trumpet was also a crucial part of our showpiece, but we didn't have to worry about losing her, since her personality was simply much too difficult. But Millo, besides her musical virtuosity, had that certain something. She was a show all by herself. If we lost her, we'd lose our star attraction. That's why whenever she won acclaim, we were happy, but we were also a little afraid that someone would make Millo a fantastic offer that she wouldn't be able to refuse. And that's what happened in the spring of 1951.

Cuchito, Millo and I decided to go to New York just for fun. Millo wanted to buy a new drum kit and look around for new musical arrangements. It was the age of Latin jazz and cubop, and Millo insisted that we should always be able to play the latest hits. The new language of this music appealed to us. Like rumba and *son*, it thrived on the dialogue between the instruments. Added to this was the loose improvisation that is so characteristic of jazz. Dizzy Gillespie, the famous trumpet player, had created this new sound together with Chano Pozo, the Cuban percussionist, who would later feel the wrath of the saints. The new sound united two musical traditions that both had African roots but had blended with different European musical styles in the United States and Cuba, and since then had developed along separate paths. Dizzy Gillespie was perhaps the first

262

American soloist to assimilate our complex rhythms and understand how to communicate them to American musicians.

Chano was a musical genius. His hands glided across a set of conga drums as if over the keys of a piano. Striking the drum with the hand was a new element he had introduced to the world of jazz. Both of them had written famous pieces, such as 'Manteca', 'Tin Tin Deo', and 'Afro-Cuban Suite', and with those tunes they had laid the foundations of Latin jazz on a parallel track with Socarrás, Machito and Mario Bauzá. We were looking forward to seeing Socarrás, Mario and all the others again in New York.

During the day we would brave the crowds in Bloomingdale's on 59th Street – what's the point of working so hard if you can't enjoy spending the money? We then went to Manny's, the famous music store on 42nd Street, whose walls were covered with photos and dedications from famous artists. The owner greeted Millo exuberantly. It was a great feeling to be welcomed so warmly by him. Then we called up Graciela Pérez, our former vocalist, and her brother-in-law Mario Bauzá, who suggested that we all go to Birdland on 52nd Street at the corner of Broadway. "That's the club for jazz musicians,' they said. "They go there after they finish work to have a drink, jam and give free rein to the music in their souls. It's the ideal place to pick up on new trends.'

When we entered Birdland around midnight with Mario and Graciela, a jam session was in full swing. And what a jam it was! The musicians were playing the finest cubop, and even Dizzy Gillespie was there playing the congas. We were escorted to a table where our fellow musicians were sitting: Machito, Gil Fuller, Dizzy's arranger, and Joe Carroll, the bebop singer. Socarrás had recently told us all about these avant-garde musicians who gathered around Dizzy Gillespie. 'They're musicians who take their craft so seriously that they lie around moping all the next day if they hit a false note the night before.'

Millo with Yucatecan musicians in Mérida

Also at the table was Tabaquito, a conga player who accompanied the Cuban rumba dancer María Antonieta Pons in the movies. Tabaquito greeted us heartily, but was surprised: 'Girls, how come you're here? We were sure you were playing in Mexico right now. I read it in the paper.'

'Well, here we are. It's a shame we don't know a thing about this booking, but even better than playing in Mexico is being here and hearing you guys play,' Cuchito replied.

'All right, let's make some music together,' Tabaquito urged us. 'You're

going to join the jam session.' The others at the table got very excited. I was shy about playing with such great musicians. But they insisted.

'No, no, it's out of the question. I'm going to listen first,' I said defensively. 'Why don't you go, Millo? You know the music. Go ahead!' That was my way of persuading her not to take the big stars too seriously, although even musicians observe a hierarchy. In a jam session they will try to make sure that all the players harmonize according to their abilities; not every newcomer is welcomed.

Millo answered, 'Heeeey, why not?' As far as music is concerned, she's not afraid of anything.

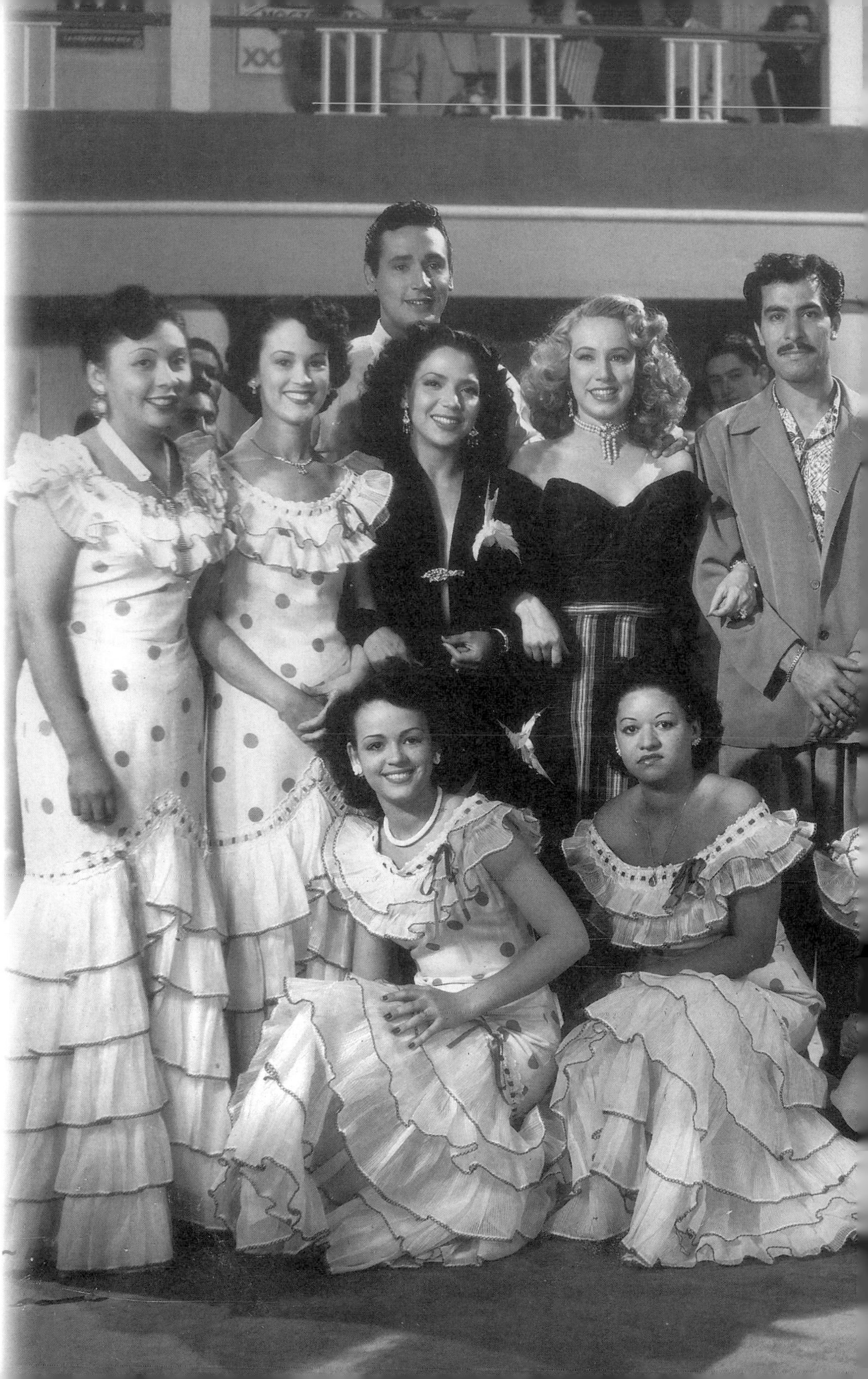

As she walked towards the stage, Mario Bauzá whispered to me, 'Gillespie is playing *"El Automóvil"* right now.'

'No problem,' I retorted. 'Millo knows the tune.'

On stage Millo took up position behind Dizzy and without hesitation began playing the conga. Dizzy turned around at once, as if to say, 'What's going on here? A woman comes up and plays behind me?' The fact that she dared do this was obviously something quite out of the ordinary for him. But he kept playing. Millo followed the tune and beat on the conga with a lot of feeling. She improvised original rhythms and Dizzy reacted to them. When the tune was over there was tremendous applause. Millo was only allowed to leave the stage after playing two more numbers. The others soon came over to our table. Dizzy, with his smattering of Spanish, joked with us and spontaneously gave Millo a nickname: Dreamy Eyes. Everybody was wild about her playing – especially Dizzy. Just before everyone left, Dizzy took Mario Bauzá aside and asked about Millo. He said he was planning a nationwide tour and wanted to take her along.

'Look, you've probably thought hard about this and it all sounds great, but there's not the slightest chance that her sisters will let her go,' Mario explained. He knew us only too well. 'Cuchito wouldn't let Millo go with you for anything in the world. And Millo wouldn't leave her sisters in the lurch either. They're a tightly knit group and nobody can break through.' That's how Mario reported the conversation to us the next day.

So Dizzy Gillespie hired Candido Camero as his conga player, Manzano's nephew and Millo's friend. Mario was right. It was unthinkable that Millo would leave the band for anybody – at least for the time being.

Previous page: On the set of Mujeres de Teatro *in 1951 with (from left) film stars Rosita Fornés, María Victoria and Emilia Guiú and director René Cardona*

After we returned from New York we decided to include a vocal quartet in our programme – that was the latest thing. We made our first appearance featuring the quartet in Medellín, Columbia. For years the head of the local radio station, the Voice of Medellín, had been insisting that we go back. The Colombian listeners were completely crazy about us. Despite the mouth-watering fee, Cuchito had always declined. She was afraid of the risky landing approach, because Medellín was situated in the middle of the Andes, and there had been some terrible crashes there. In 1935, the legendary tango singer Carlos Gardel had lost his life in one of them.

The reception in Medellín was overwhelming, almost scary: hundreds of people lined the road to the radio station, stretching their arms out towards us, trying to touch us. The police had a hard time keeping the crowd under control. In order to ward off the most aggressive fans, Millo even had to wield her drumsticks. When we finally presented our repertoire – romantic numbers like 'Noche Cubana' ('Cuban Night'), 'Quiéreme y Verás' ('Love Me and You Shall See') and blues songs in English such as 'You'll Never Be Free' and 'You're Breaking My Heart' – the audience was enraptured. 'Yo No Sé Porque Te Quiero' ('I Don't Know Why I Love You') became a surprise hit. The manager of the radio station had talked me into singing that bolero.

After a month the engagement came to an end, and our fans were up in arms. In the newspaper *Alerta!* two days after our last concert, an article appeared under the heading 'Exclusive', detailing what had happened that night:

'Anacaona's last performance was overshadowed by dramatic events. Three people were seriously injured, and furniture and large parts of the radio station's technical equipment were smashed up. Angry fans who had been denied entry to the studio because of overcrowding destroyed all the security barriers that stood in their way...'

Our next invitation, from Vale Quintero, the owner of the radio station *Ondas del Lago* (Waves of the Lake) in Maracaibo, Venezuela, triggered a heated discussion among us. He wanted to book us for the Carnival season.

'Me, go to Maracaibo? Never again!' Ondina protested.

'Why on earth not?' I asked dumbfounded.

'Have you forgotten what happens during Carnival in Venezuela? I refuse to play for that uncouth mob again.'

Then I remembered how the Venezuelans indulged in vulgar behaviour during Carnival. Even at a performance at the presidential palace in Caracas, the men had shown no compunction about pouring wine down the fronts of women's dresses. People would also throw eggs and flour at each other. But we knew Vale, the organizer, well, and on stage people had always left us in peace. So we agreed. Two weeks before our departure, Vale called and urgently requested that

Alicia and Millo at the Gran Torta, Bogotá

we bring along two singers. We had one, Haydée Portuondo, Omara's sister. She sang the fast songs, the *guarachas* and the *sones*. We knew Haydée from the days when she was still a chorus girl at the Casino Nacional. She was also an excellent rumba dancer. All we needed was a singer for the romantic boleros. Cuchito asked her friend, the composer César Portillo de la Luz, 'César, do you know a girl who could accompany us? One we'll get along with as well?'

'But of course. Take *La Mora*.' Because of her dark skin she was called the Blackberry. Her real name was Moraima Secada. 'She's the right girl for you. She's an excellent singer and has a warm voice. If you want, I'll bring her over for an audition.' Moraima worked in a laundry, operating the mangle and pressing clothes, and occasionally sang in nightclubs. She was in her element doing the emotional songs of *el filin*. The audition, which was held in our living room, convinced us. The next weekend I drove with Moraima to Emma's beach house

Millo

in Guanabo to rehearse. There I taught her our repertoire. She learned the numbers unusually quickly, and was prepared to try anything, even the difficult songs. Her renditions of the romantic boleros were particularly beautiful. I realized that she was a real gem. Moraima quickly developed her own incomparable style.

Maracaibo had grown into a booming provincial town since the largest oil field in Venezuela had been discovered underneath it, and had a kind of gold-rush atmosphere. Venerable colonial structures stood next to modern high-rise office blocks. In the streets, which were choked with buses, limousines and cross-country vehicles, were Guajiro Indian women with their faces painted red and wearing fancy

Singer Moraima Secada and Millo

tunics. When we learned that they belonged to the Aruak Indians, the same people as the original inhabitants of Cuba and our patroness Anacaona, we decided to find out more about them.

We took a motorboat and travelled along the peninsula to one of their settlements. A few Indian women came to greet us, offering us handicrafts. However, they were instantly so fascinated by Yolanda that they forgot all about their business transactions. They poked her in a friendly manner, pinched her arm and spoke in their language to her. Yolanda could make no sense of it. 'I don't understand what you're saying, I'm from Cuba!' The Guajiro women stared at her unperturbed, touching her unabashedly, as if they were good friends. Then a Venezuelan came up and asked if he could help, because he spoke Guajiro. The man was nice enough to explain to the Guajiros that Yolanda was from Cuba. Incredulous, they looked at her. They were convinced that our sister must be a Guajiro. Maybe they weren't far wrong, we thought later. Our grandfather on our mother's side did come from Venezuela, after all. It was quite possible that he, like many Europeans, had married a native in South America, and so perhaps blood from the Guajiros does flow in the veins of our family.

The next day we were scheduled to do some recording at the radio station. We entered the practically windowless building and walked down the long hallway. Photos of the artists and stars who had performed there hung on the walls. Even we were up there, immortalized. In a small studio we were greeted with hearty applause and shouts. The engineers cut a record of us playing. Behind the big plate-glass window in the control room stood a man, good-looking, of medium height, with dark blond hair. But his expression was serious. Very, very serious. He wasn't going to smile for anything in the world. He just watched. Was something wrong with the music?

At dinner we were introduced to this man, whom everyone at the radio station called 'Carlos, *El Técnico*', and his cheerful friend Egon. 'Your music is wonderful,' Carlos assured us. His real name was Karl, and he began telling us about himself. He had emigrated from Germany in 1950 to fulfil his childhood dream of living in South America. He had quit his job as a sound technician at a movie studio in Munich at the first opportunity, turning his back on

Millo and Nena Neyra in Mexico, early 1950s

depressing post-war Germany. Along with fifty other Germans he boarded a ship in Genoa for Venezuela. Egon, who shared a small apartment with Karl, was from Denmark and liked to tease his German friend about the fact that during the Second World War he had been a pilot with the RAF and had bombed the hell out of the Germans.

For the next few days Karl was always in the control room, monitoring the recording. We soon noticed that his mood had improved visibly. He obviously liked more than just our music. I could feel something in the air. Almost daily we – Millo, Cristina Reyes, who played the second conga drum, and I – would go shopping after work with Karl and Egon. And in the evening they both came to the Club Mara, where we also performed regularly. All at once I realized that during the breaks, or later when we went to a restaurant, Millo always sat next to Karl, and the two of them were getting on splendidly. Then it finally dawned on me.

Even though this wasn't the first time that Millo had fallen in love, Cuchito was feeling uneasy, because at rehearsals and gigs Millo was behaving as if nothing was going on. Since none of us ever went out alone with a man, Cristina and I also had our fun with Millo's new admirer and his friend Egon. Sometimes I would dance a waltz with Karl, and Egon and Cristina were already fixtures on the dance floor. Egon – a big, lanky guy like Karl, but a little older – had his eye on her. But he flirted with me too, the way people in love do when they're in full swing and don't want to reveal who they're really after.

Teatro Cervantes, Mexico

One evening the radio station organized a party for us. We all showed up and had a fantastic time, until suddenly Haydée, our singer, started to do her captivating rumba show in earnest. With undulating hip movements she went straight for Karl, wooing him without any inhibitions and pulling the poor man completely under her spell. When she wasn't actually dancing with him, she kept shouting, 'Charly, Charly...' Was she really serious about Karl? At any rate, Haydée knew how to wrap men around her little finger.

It soon got too much for Millo. 'I'm going back to the hotel,' she whispered to me. The evening was ruined for her. Out of solidarity I went back with her. The next day the episode was over. They made up in next to no time, and Karl only had eyes for her.

Millo revealed the news to me first: 'We're going to get married.'

I was completely stunned. Marry a man she'd only known for three weeks? We were very close, but I wouldn't have thought she'd be capable of something like that. But then I shared her joy and asked, 'When is Karl coming to Cuba?'

'Oh no, we're going to live here in Venezuela.' Millo let me in on her plan. She wanted to stay in Maracaibo and leave the band – only temporarily, as she emphasized. She was so in love that she evidently hadn't given any thought to Cuchito's reaction.

Vale Quintero, the owner of the radio station, was one of the first to hear the news from Karl. He told Millo, 'Listen, I only ask one thing: please don't take Karl away. As far as I'm concerned he can fall in love and even get married, but please don't take him to Cuba.' Vale was afraid of losing his best man.

When Cuchito heard about the wedding plans, she said with a serious expression, 'I won't stand in the way of your wedding, but the point is, we don't know Karl well enough. If he really loves you, then he will come to Cuba and marry you there. It will be all right only when our parents know about your plans

In front of the Club Mara

With Vale Quintero, the owner of the radio station Ondas del Lago

and can give their blessing. Only then will we see if this Karl's intentions are serious.' When Millo wouldn't accept this, Cuchito forbade her categorically from having the wedding in Venezuela. Millo was beside herself. She furiously insinuated that Cuchito only wanted to find an excuse to keep her in the band. The next day she gave in. She could easily have married – she was thirty years old, after all. But she didn't dare. We had been brought up very traditionally. And it was the custom for the bridegroom to ask the parents for the hand of the woman. Even I wouldn't have dreamed of rebelling against Cuchito, who had taken care of us for all those years. And none of us had ever bailed out of a tour and left the band over a man. That would have seemed like a betrayal of the family. So Millo grimly went back with us to Cuba and Karl promised to follow as soon as he could.

In Havana, a period of waiting began for Millo. She realized that she had only known Karl for three weeks, and this worried her. Would he come or wouldn't he? We had endless conversations. I consoled her day after day, night after night, but the more time passed, the greater was Millo's doubt and the more relaxed Cuchito became. She really did always put the band first. After three weeks the postman rang the doorbell early one morning and handed us a telegram: 'Arriving Tuesday at Havana airport. Karl.'

Everyone was ecstatic. We wanted to prepare an overwhelming welcome for Millo's great love. In the dining room we put out hors d'oeuvres and in the kitchen we set out the ingredients for cocktails. We drove to the airport full of anticipation, but there was no solemn-faced German in sight in the arrivals hall. We waited and waited. When the last passenger had come out of customs, we drove back home, feeling dismayed. Karl *had* actually been on the plane; he had just somehow missed us. Disappointed, he had taken a taxi. The driver didn't take him straight to Lawton, but had driven him halfway round Havana, so that

A view of the beach at Guanabo

we were back home before he arrived. We were just starting on the canapés when he rang the doorbell. 'Girls, the *polaco* has arrived!' yelled Father, who was sitting in front of the TV in the living room.

Karl told Millo why he had made her wait so long. Love had put a severe strain on his finances. Every time he had gone out with Millo, he had invited the entire group of sisters along, primarily because of Cuchito's principles. He first had to earn some money for the trip and to pay the wedding expenses, supplementing his own funds by borrowing from friends.

With Karl's arrival, both had come closer to their dream. Yet there were still obstacles to overcome. Father's acid test was a Chinese banquet: a roast duck stuffed with chestnuts and almonds, the skin basted with plenty of soy sauce. Father wasn't satisfied until Karl had cleaned his first plate and polished off a second one. A man who liked his food that much had to be the right one for Millo.

Cuchito was a bigger problem. She was still against the marriage, because she didn't know who could replace Millo. Finally we sisters, along with our brother Lenin, succeeded in convincing her that we had no right to stand in the way of Millo's happiness. Now there was only one more problem: the documents. For the wedding ceremony, the notary needed birth certificates and all sorts of documentation from the authorities. These were generally obtained only after long periods of waiting or in return for bribes. Echarri promised Karl, 'Word of honour. I'll take care of the paperwork.' With his excellent connections he was definitely the right person for this task.

Karl, Millo and I spent a great deal of time with Ada and Echarri, who were always in party mood. The two of them had just moved to Guanabo and were living near Emma's beach house. Ada's son, Reinaldo, was suffering from bronchitis, and the doctor had advised them to move to the peaceful fishing village as soon as possible because of the good sea air. There too, Echarri and Ada continued merrily along in what Mother called the *rumbantela*, and the beach house also became a magnet for musicians, painters and the party set. Naturally, Echarri, the baseball legend with the famous home run, and the even more famous Ernest Hemingway, had met at the local bar. The two had plenty to talk about, drinking cocktails and sharing sports stories. Something was always going on at Echarri's house in Guanabo. Looking out at the sea, Ada and Echarri would sing along with the guitar. They called their duo 'Hacha y Machete', 'The Axe and the Machete'. Regular guests were Fina, a stout blonde bar owner, and the Trio Janitzio. Fina was married to one of them. Millo or Ondina would provide the rhythms on the bongos or conga. I mixed daiquiris from lime juice, sugar, white rum and crushed ice. We didn't necessarily have to go to a cabaret if we

Millo and Karl's wedding at the notary's office, 5 March 1953

felt like dancing and having a good time. Karl was speechless, since we partied for days, moving from one get-together to the next, and from one bar to another. Paying was no problem. Echarri signed for everything. We would end up at the beach house and eat Ada's fried fish cubes. Ada – who couldn't even fry an egg when she got married – knew better than anybody how to make them crispy on the outside and yet juicy inside. Even the fishermen of Guanabo were so taken by her cooking that one morning when we were hung over, they appeared dragging a huge *emperador*, a swordfish, behind them. '*Comadre*, look what we've brought you. Let us know when you're going to cook it. We'll be there!' Swordfish, marinated for a few hours in lime juice and garlic and fried in oil, was Ada's speciality.

Between cocktails and dancing, Echarri made phone calls. He really worked hard at solving the problem. He must have been greatly looking forward to having another man standing by him in this big female-dominated family. By 5 March he had it all worked out: Millo and Karl could get married, and Karl only had to show his passport for identification.

On that day Stalin died. In Cuba, resistance was brewing against Batista, who had come to power again after a coup exactly a year earlier. A few months later, on 26 July 1953, a militant opposition group headed by the lawyer Fidel Castro attracted great attention for the first time. As a prelude to armed resistance they had attacked the Moncada barracks in Santiago de Cuba.

Meanwhile Millo left us – but only temporarily, she promised. She went with Karl to Venezuela, because he had no job prospects here in Cuba. Without connections it was impossible for him to get a good job as a technician in radio or television. In this case, Echarri knew all the wrong people. He was only helpful when it came to finding botellas, 'bottle posts', but Karl wasn't the type for this sort of life, and Echarri had his hands full keeping his own bottles fizzing.

Perhaps Karl didn't try very hard to find a job in Cuba. Even Millo didn't seem too sad about leaving us. All of a sudden it was as though the band and our music were no longer very important to her.

Soon afterwards we were invited by Senator Capestano, an admirer of our band, to his spacious estate near Remedios. We were welcome to bring our friends and relatives along, so ten of us went to stay with him – nine of us sisters and our little brother Lenin. In the basement of the luxurious villa the senator had a bar that was almost as big as the one in the Floridita, Hemingway's favourite restaurant. No wonder that the two Prío Socarrás brothers often went there for a short vacation. We chatted by the swimming pool with other the guests, among them Dolores, Sofía and Lourdes, the daughters of the great composer Alejandro García Caturla. All three of them were studying music. Cuchito hired Sofía as our new drummer that very night, which meant we could accept an unexpected booking in Haiti.

At a party given by Celia Cruz we met Martha Jean Claude, the famous Haitian singer. When she saw us she shouted, 'Mon Dieu, I have some news for you.' She told us that the owner of the Voodoo Club in Port-au-Prince urgently wanted us to play there and had been looking for us. He had asked her to find us. But this had all occurred two years ago. When we asked why she had waited so long to give us the message, she just looked at us with big eyes. Cuchito was quite annoyed, but what could she do? As soon as we got home, Cuchito called up the owner of the nightclub. He was extremely pleased and said that he still wanted us to play there. Along with Moraima Secada, our usual bolero singer, our employer insisted on a second vocalist for the fast *sones* and *guarachas*. The guitarist Ñico Rojas, a childhood friend of ours, suggested asking Omara Portuondo, a slim, lively and talented musician. We talked to her, but she was hesitant because she wanted to specialize exclusively in the music of *el filin* and American songs. I tried to change her mind: 'Why can't *son* and *guaracha* suit you too?' Finally she agreed.

In Haiti, the nightclub owner proved to be very accommodating. 'If you want to go for a walk or to a restaurant, I'll provide an escort for you. Be careful. Don't go out with anyone else. It would be best if you didn't eat or drink at other places. You can get everything your hearts desire right here. Drink as much champagne as you want, it's on the house. I'll pay for everything you want.' We wondered what was behind such generosity, because they actually did fulfil our every wish at his restaurant. Ada guessed that it might have something to do with religion. The voodoo religion is a very strong presence in Haiti. Perhaps the owner was afraid someone would slip something into our food or drink or otherwise cause us harm. Maybe he also wanted to prevent the other nightclubs from luring us away. It was a mystery, but we were drinking champagne for free, at least.

I was the one who had to play trumpet in Haiti, by the way. Ondina had refused to go with us. That's how she was sometimes. She didn't have any particular reason, she just felt like being contrary. 'I'm not playing any more, I'm not playing any more.' She went on like that all day long. Finally I had no choice but to take a crash course in trumpet from Lázaro. And today, whenever the conversation turns to that tour, Ondina asks in all innocence, 'Why wasn't I on that tour?'

'Because you refused to come along!' I'm the only one who can claim to have gone on every trip, without exception.

Back in Havana, Sofía the drummer warned Cuchito, 'Be careful. They want to steal Moraima away from the band.' The news was very distressing. Gradually we learned that Omara was behind it. With Aida Diestro, Elena Burke and her sister Haydée, she wanted to form the Quartet d'Aida but they needed a fourth singer. We also had a vocal quartet in our band, because that was in vogue at the time. Behind our back Omara had made the new group seem tempting to Moraima. Eventually Moraima could no longer resist the offer. She had a daughter to care for and urgently needed steady work. But she was very fair; she asked Cuchito for a meeting before she made her decision and explained the situation to her. With a heavy heart Cuchito had to let her go, because we suspected it would become even harder to get enough bookings in the future. For Moraima the decision was the right one: the Quartet d'Aida soon became successful. The separation hurt us not only because Moraima was a first-class singer, but also because she was a magnificent person. When Moraima later became famous as a soloist, she always made a point of mentioning that she first won acclaim with us. She even said that her time with Anacaona was the happiest of her life. Her life ended tragically. Her husband, whom she loved above all else, was in the Cubana de Aviación aeroplane that fell victim to a bomb in 1976 over Barbados. Moraima started drinking. Despair and alcohol eventually killed her.

The loss of Millo and Moraima was hard. But then the following incident occurred in Havana at the Astral Theater. The manager called us up with the happy news of a long-term engagement. Before the contract was signed, however, Cuchito wanted to talk to Armando Romeu, who had often booked Millo at the Tropicana. His band was still playing at the Astral, and Cuchito wanted to make sure she wasn't taking work away from him. She told the manager, 'I can't

Performance at Radio Haiti with singer Omara Portuondo

accept until I talk with Armando Romeu.' The bandleader happened to live in the building next door and Cuchito went to see him at once.

Armando assured her, 'You can take over the contract. Mine has expired. You have all the freedom in the world.' It was a great weight off Cuchito's mind.

Work was scarce and bands, trios, soloists, artists in every category were increasingly encountering furious competition for gigs. The musicians' union had split up in the wake of the clashes between the Communists and the conservative *Auténticos*. We stayed with the organization which took over Arriete y Bambitelli's union. Cuchito did this out of gratitude for all the things he'd done. The new union was now led by Romero Adams, known as the Tiger. Under him, however, shady wheeling and dealing took place, with large sums of money involved. The musical ensembles staked claims to various parts of town, and you had to pay contributions via the union if you 'invaded' certain venues outside your own territory.

We started our rehearsals at the Astral even though the contract hadn't yet been signed. Suddenly a man from our union showed up, a Señor Amargoso He played the conga and was a brother of Romero Adams. Without beating around the bush he informed us that he had decided that a Spanish group, Los Chavales de España, was going to get our booking. We didn't take his meddling very seriously. Amargoso treated us as if we were nothing, so we behaved in the same way.

The next day a trio that was supposed to appear with us didn't show up for rehearsal. Neither did the master of ceremonies, a vocalist, a magician and all the lighting technicians and stage hands. It was plain to see that Amargoso had called a strike against us. Although we were on good terms with these colleagues, they now refused to work with us. Presumably Amargoso, who could exert great influence with the help of his brother, had threatened them with unemployment if they didn't cooperate. Even so, we decided not to give in, and we continued our rehearsals in spite of the strike. When Amargoso came to the theatre and saw us playing, he stormed up on stage and yelled as if he had lost his mind, 'Get out of here! You have no business being on this stage!'

I was speechless. Ondina and Yolanda, however, didn't mince their words. 'You don't seem to care a damn about music, for you it's all about money. You prefer artists who can be useful to you – the kind that slip you some money.'

Amargoso then flew into such a rage that he took the conga drum and ran towards Yolanda, threatening to smash it on her head. Yolanda stared him straight in the eye and said calmly, 'Go ahead, hit me. Let's see if you're really as tough as you think you are.' We only just managed to prevent a fight and get all the instruments back home in one piece. But the next day we found out the price we had to pay: Ondina and Yolanda were barred from the union. The news was posted on the bulletin board at the union hall. We were seething. We had always paid our due, and we were only suspended because we had dared to speak the truth. Another contributing factor may have been that we were less pliable than others and never succumbed to the demands or flattery of influential union men. But that wasn't all. Letters with offers from abroad that were normally sent care of the union mysteriously disappeared. Only later did we learn, from friends in Venezuela and elsewhere, about the bookings we lost out on. When José María Arriete y Bambitelli had led the trade organization, there had never been any problems like this. His successor now left us out in the rain. Our union had gone to hell.

~ **Anacaona** ~

Chapter 13
With a Needle and Thread on Wall Street

After the problems we'd faced in the Astral Theatre, Cuchito couldn't find work for us anywhere, despite all of her good business contacts. The union bosses had pulled the rug out from under our feet. Male bands on their way up such as Arcaño y Sus Maravillas, Aragón, América and Riverside, all good show bands, ruled the scene. Even though Cuba's sugar was selling well and the economy was picking up, most people still weren't in the mood to party. Many people were suffering from unemployment and bitter poverty. Sometimes when we were returning from a gig in the early morning, we would see neighbours shoving a cart on the street. Father told us that in the Mercado Único people were gathering up bananas that fell off the trucks during unloading. Then they would go out onto the streets and sell the fruit for a couple of centavos to people who had also been forced to tighten their belts.

One day, after rehearsing in the living room, Ondina said, 'We have Flora in New York. What if we tried going to New York, one at a time, and try to establish our band in the States?' As Flora's relatives, we were entitled to residence visas. Maybe our colleagues and friends there would help us, and maybe the musicians' union wouldn't make too much of a fuss.

I had my doubts as to whether the plan could work and whether I really wanted to live in the United States long-term. But on the spur of the moment

Ondina decided to make the trip. Cuchito, Ada, Bola, Ziomara and I followed. Four weeks later we were all reunited at Flora's modest three-room apartment. The front door opened directly onto a big eat-in kitchen. It also doubled as a bathroom; the bathtub was to be found hidden away underneath the long kitchen counter. If one of us wanted to use it, she would lift up the counter, run the water and bathe right there in the kitchen. If a neighbour rang the doorbell, you just had to yell loudly, 'Not now! I'm in the tub. Please come back later.' Next to the kitchen was a small living room where, as guests, we slept. And the tiny third room was more like a broom closet. Flora and González had temporarily set up camp in the long, narrow passageway.

All eight of us lived in this sixty square metres of space; Flora's eldest son, Albertico, now in his mid-twenties, often came to visit. He made himself useful, guiding Ondina and me around in Spanish Harlem and showing us the Puerto Rican grocery stores. I also felt right at home because everyone in the stores spoke Spanish. All the foods we loved were there: avocados, limes, bitter oranges, sweet potatoes, malanga and plantains. We could easily find fresh, ripe fruit and the best cuts of meat. Albertico was a passionate cook: pork ribs were his speciality. The only thing he couldn't do was bake, and so he heaped flattery on Ondina. 'You know how to make *masa real* [royal dough] – and I'm really craving a dessert from home.' This cake, made of buttery dough heavily spiced with nutmeg and finished with a layer of guava, was Ondina's forte. Her *tocino del cielo*, a kind of flan, or pudding, with a caramel glaze, made from an amazing twenty-four egg yolks, also became legendary among our circle of sweet-toothed New York friends.

Music colleagues and friends doggedly tried to find work for us, but with-

Previous page: Dinner in Flora's apartment in Spanish Harlem

~ **Anacaona** ~

out success. The American unions were very strict and consistently prevented Cuban musicians from getting a break. When our money threatened to run out, Ziomara and I looked for work through an agency that specialized in finding jobs for Latin Americans. They sent me to Long Island, to the Bestform brassiere factory. I had to get up very early to catch the subway to the factory. Ziomara had better luck. She got a job in a Quick Lunch self-service diner in Manhattan. There it was, just like Eladio had once described in his column:

'At the sight of brightly illuminated dishes displayed in glass cases, we Cubans think, "Oh, how lovely!" rather than "Oh, how delicious!" Gazing in at plates decorated with red beets, pale smears of mayonnaise and vibrant yellow-green lettuce leaves, we behave as if we're in a gallery, and always look first and foremost for the signature of the artist. But when we open one of those glass cases, we get the funny feeling that we've been taken for fools – as if some joker has shoved a plate of fried eggs through our mailbox and shouted "post's here!".'

Flora found a much nicer alternative. She worked at Nanty's, an exclusive dressmaker's workshop on Wall Street. The studio took up almost the entire floor of a very elegant skyscraper and belonged to a Frenchman – an eccentric, conceited man, although he did pay good wages. He sewed the wardrobes of Hollywood stars such as Elizabeth Taylor, Mitzi Gaynor and Doris Day. The actresses would look for *haute couture* fashions in France, buy the patterns and bring them to Nanty's to be made up. Even this was quite expensive, because the couturiers demanded a high price for exclusivity. Nevertheless it was more economical to have the clothes sewn in New York than to buy them finished at the boutique in Paris. A total of forty employees worked meticulously from the patterns to produce the most extravagant creations from satin, lace, chiffon and tulle. Flora was one of six especially skilled seamstresses in the workshop, along with another

Cuban woman, two from Spain and two Italians. The assistants, who merely cut the fabric, ironed, or sewed hems, were almost all Latinas.

I knew nothing about sewing. But when the work at the brassiere factory began to bore me, I asked Flora whether I might give sewing a try. She arranged to have me hired as her assistant. My first assignment was in the cutting room, ironing the pieces, piling them up and finally sewing certain parts together in Flora's department. Then I was moved to be with Aida, the other Cuban head seamstress. It was her ambition to train me to be a skilled worker. She took me under her wing and revealed all the tricks of the trade. With her help, after a few months, I dared to sew a simple pattern. When I tried on the dress, the French owner of the business came to examine my work in person. He walked around me, evaluating my layman's effort. 'How clever! Very smart!' he exclaimed. 'Your sister has tailored the pattern well, she has style,' he told Flora. And I was allowed to sew more dresses, which was an amazing feeling. I had started as an apprentice and, all modesty aside, had practically become an expert overnight. His compliment was all the more flattering because he was a meticulous boss. There was a high turnover among the unskilled employees; people were thrown out for the slightest mistake, like incorrectly cutting expensive fabric. And if monsieur took a dislike to an employee, he would fire her at once, no matter how talented she was or how hard she worked.

From the very beginning Ondina worked in the 'finishing' section, where the last touches were put on the elegant ball gowns by hand. She worked on the gowns from the inside, attaching the bodice with invisible stitches. Zippers were also her domain. And her real speciality was the hems. The trick was to sew everything so that not a stitch could be seen inside or out.

For weeks there was intense activity in our dressmaking studio. We were under a deadline to finish some movie costumes for Mitzi Gaynor, the high-spirited dancer and star of the film *There's No Business Like Show Business*. Each head seamstress was in charge of one dress. The one assigned to Flora consisted of black lace and lots of frills. We lined the lace with satin patterned with bright red roses. A magnificent combination. Finally the big day arrived. Mitzi Gaynor floated into our workshop and, in a good mood, she undressed for the fitting. She had a first-class figure, thin with a tiny waist. When the moment came for her to try Flora's dress, we all held our breath. It fitted like a glove. Not a single stitch had to be altered. Mitzi Gaynor was enchanted. This slender beauty went over to Flora – I was standing beside her – grabbed her by the waist and lifted her right off the ground with joy! That was quite some feat, because curvaceous Flora wasn't exactly as light as a feather. Then Miss Gaynor spun a pirouette like in her movies – she was dancing for joy. All the seamstresses came running into Flora's workroom. There was no stopping the Hollywood diva. She gave Flora a kiss and a warm hug. Ondina was practically bursting with pride, because she had helped by sewing the bodice on this dress.

Flora even got Ada a place at the dressmaker's workshop, for a trial period at first. The fact that she ever passed this test was more due to good luck than her sewing skills. Julia Fletcher, the workshop supervisor, had been feeling poorly for a few days and needed an injection, but she didn't have time to go to a doctor. 'That's no problem, Ada knows how to give injections,' Flora informed her; and so Julia called for Ada. Julia had the syringe and needle, but no alcohol.

Ada had a bright idea. 'Have you got something to drink in your cupboard, maybe whiskey? That's good for cleaning the skin.'

'Yes, I have a bottle, an especially good one. We can use that.' Ada rubbed Julia's skin with a few drops of the fine liquor and carefully stuck in the needle. Relieved, Julia immediately poured two glasses of whiskey, and that was the start of their friendship. So, Ada was allowed to keep her job, although she wasn't always a reliable employee. As one of her tasks was to carry the takings to the bank, Ada would walk down Wall Street every day carrying a lot of money. One day on the way, she made a detour into a department store to look for a present for Echarri. Characteristically, she soon forgot about the time. Suddenly she heard her name being called out, and whipped around to see Julia standing right behind her. 'I'm not so sure this is the bank, Ada! What are you doing here with all that money?'

'I'm looking at the merchandise on display,' was all Ada could think to say. Julia would have fired any other employee, but in this instance she let it pass.

The loveliest thing about being in New York was that we were always together, just like on our tour, both at work and during the evening. So we never felt as if we were in a foreign country. We didn't even have to speak English: at work we heard more Spanish and Italian than English. Even Flora, after all her years in New York, barely knew a word of English. She never really learned it properly because she never really needed to – well, that's not *entirely* true. At work one day, Julia told us that when Flora needed to ask the boss for a raise she would suddenly become fluent!

Although things weren't going too badly for us, since we lived with Flora and worked at the workshop, in the long run it was a soulless existence. We missed the music. We had to abandon, temporarily at least, our plan to establish ourselves in New York as a band, because the immigration authorities and the union had set up insurmountable hurdles. So Cuchito resorted once again to contacting promoters in Cuba and South America. In 1955 we finally got an attractive offer from Peru to play for three months during the Carnival season. We didn't hesitate for long. We left for Havana, where Millo and Karl also happened to be. They were planning to settle in California and were waiting for the correct documents, which could take months. Millo was excited about the idea of performing again and she persuaded Karl to come with us. Yolanda also brought her boyfriend on the trip, the pianist René Urbino. Cuchito planned to work him into the show. He loved to play piano with all sorts of acrobatic tricks, such as standing on a chair and bending over, or turning his back to the piano and stretching his hands behind him to the keyboard. When people from the press heard about the tour, they wrote it up as big news.

As soon as we set foot on Peruvian soil at the harbour of Callao, we felt like were stars once again. A reporter interviewed Cuchito and the next day we read the article in the hotel: 'With 250 of the most luxurious gowns, thirty-eight pieces of luggage full of musical instruments, and thousands of smiles, the lovely members of the Orquesta Anacaona disembarked from the steamship *Queen of the Pacific*.'

And because the reporter must have been particularly intrigued by the fact that almost all of us were unmarried, he put the following words in Cuchito's mouth: 'Musicians who are accepted into our band have to sign an agreement stating that they will remain single. Anyone who gets married is automatically dismissed from the band. Since I'm aware that the men of Lima are persistent suitors, I'm worried that my sisters will be struck by Cupid's arrow and decide they want to stay here.'

Even Ziomara was quoted: 'I heard so much about Peru in Cuba. I like the Peruvian men. They are daring and brave – just my type!'

Soon afterwards other newspapers also heralded us as 'the orchestra of single women'. This aroused so much curiosity that all the shows sold out in an instant. After our performances we would be invited to nightclubs, radio stations and once even to the presidential palace.

Millo confessed to me during that tour that even though she was happy in her marriage, she also yearned for life in the spotlight. Five weeks after our

Anacaona in Santo Domingo, 1953.

arrival, Emma called from Havana to say that Karl's work permit for the United States had arrived. His friends in Los Angeles had pulled some strings. Millo and Karl immediately left Lima, earlier than planned, to emigrate to Los Angeles via Havana, and we continued with the tour, heading for Ecuador. I had doubts as to whether it was right for Millo to choose a bourgeois married life over music. It later turned out that Millo had received fantastic offers of work from the USA. First, Nilo Menéndez, bandleader and composer of the standard 'Green Eyes', wanted her for a tour. Then Candido Camero, Manzano's nephew, with whom Millo had always practised, urged her to go on stage. In the meantime he had been extremely successful in the States, playing with Dizzy Gillespie, Stan Kenton and Machito. Millo introduced her husband to Candido, an unusual musician and unusual person, who drank no alcohol, didn't smoke and never argued. If you offered him a cocktail he would decline in a gentle voice, 'No, thank you, please bring me a glass of milk instead.' Yes, Millo had some really great opportunities to work, but her husband didn't want her to. Such is *machismo*.

Two years later Millo visited us again in Havana. She brought her young daughter Ingrid with her for the first time. She told us that the little girl had not yet been christened, because as an atheist Karl believed that his daughter should decide her religion for herself later in life. A child without a christening? We couldn't imagine it, especially not for our first niece. It was clear that we would have to trick the atheist. Without discussing it with Millo, we invited her to visit the church and to bring Ingrid along as well. When they got there the priest was waiting to greet them, ready to perform a baptism. Our youngest siblings, Yolanda and Lenin, were the godparents. Millo couldn't and wouldn't object. 'By the time Karl finds out, it will be to, late for him to get worked up,' I reassured her. 'After all, he's an atheist and doesn't believe in all this humbug, so what does it matter to him?' We threw a big party and Millo had a photograph taken of her with Ingrid. For the photo Millo put on a dream of a dress made of red chiffon, a creation from the studio on Wall Street. Unable to resist the temptation, knowing how well it would suit Millo, Flora had secretly made an exact copy of an design created exclusively for Elizabeth Taylor.

Millo and I were still very close and went out together a lot. One evening we went to the opera to see *The Medium* by Gian Carlo Menotti. It was the hottest ticket in Havana at the time. Rita Montaner, the revered singer of 'The Peanut Vendor', who had honoured us at our debut and later often performed with us, was now singing arias. Everyone was in

Christening of Ingrid: Millo in a dress designed like Elizabeth Taylor's

an uproar because they had forgotten that Montaner, who had won fame and fortune with her gravelly voice and Afro-Cuban songs, had previously been an excellent opera singer. Now, in her fifties, Rita had returned to this genre. I saw her standing on the stage, unmistakable with her expressive eyes, her winning smile, the large beauty spot on her forehead, but now with grey strands in her hair betraying her age. Rita was playing the role of Madame Flora, who pretends to be a medium and tricks people out of their money. Then at one of her seances a spirit actually appears and takes possession of her. Rita played Madame Flora so convincingly that I was sure she was indeed possessed by a spirit. A chill ran down my spine; a deathly silence gripped the audience. Everyone felt paralysed. Only Rita's crystal-clear voice could be heard as she sang the 'Aria of the Dead'.

That evening instantly came to mind when, less than a year later, the newspapers announced Rita's death. Eventually we learned the circumstances. Apparently, she had been experiencing increasingly serious health problems during rehearsals for *The Medium* and had learned that cancer had begun to attack her oesophagus. Many years earlier she had been told by an oracle that she should 'make her saint'. She was supposed to dress in white, from head to toe, for a whole year. She would then become a daughter of her saint. She would also have to host a big celebration every year on her saint's day, and slaughter animals as a ritual offering. She had consulted the *babalao* because she had been feeling ill, but she hadn't taken the advice seriously. It was only when she began to notice the illness more and more that she decided to implement these measures in earnest, by which time it was too late. The saint had rejected her. In despair she had undertaken a kind of emergency ceremony, making offerings to Obatalá, *la Virgen de las Mercedes*, the Virgin of Mercies. But death could no longer be held at bay. Her last wish was to be laid to rest perfectly made-up and dressed in her best clothes, with the scent of her favourite perfume, 'Femme'. This took place on 18 April 1958.

When I visited Flora and her family again in New York, our conversation turned to the subject of death. I commented, 'Isn't it funny? Whenever you're feeling completely content, suddenly you think about death.' Flora's husband, González, insisted that when his time came, we should throw a big party and invite all his friends.

A short while later, when I was back in Cuba, the following happened.

Flora was already at work and González and Albertico wanted to have breakfast, but they had run out of coffee. Albertico went to borrow some from a neighbour, and when he got back he found his father lying motionless on the bed.

At first, Albertico thought he was play-acting – González often played practical jokes. He chided him, 'Father! I'm too old for this kind of nonsense.' But he just lay there. Then Albertico noticed that he wasn't breathing. González had suffered a massive heart attack.

That same evening, while Flora and Albertico were busy making arrangements to have his body transported back to Cuba, the doorbell rang. A group of their friends had come over, all dressed up and ready for a surprise party – apparently González had invited them the day before. Flora and Albertico immediately realized why the refrigerator was so stuffed full of food. González must have been on a big shopping trip the day before, to stock up for the party. It was almost like his final practical joke… Everyone was astounded and horrified. But there was nothing for it: Flora, Albertico and the guests set about preparing the food in accordance with González's last wish. They grated malanga, fried plantains, put the marinated steaks in the pan, and all took part in a memorable banquet that – may González forgive them – was not quite as cheerful as he had wanted.

Poster advertising the South American tour, 1958

Chapter 14
Rebellion and Mambo

*L*os *barbudos*, the bearded ones, were the talk of Havana after they stormed the Moncada barracks. When they came to trial Fidel Castro, who was an attorney by profession, used the situation for his own political agenda. During his self-defence he gave long, fiery speeches in which he demanded democracy and social justice for all Cubans. He also ridiculed Batista's corrupt regime. However, in late 1954 Batista once again succeeded in winning the presidential election – through manipulation. After that he felt strong enough to grant an amnesty to the political prisoners and release them from prison. Fidel, like many opponents of the government, sought safety in Mexico. In late November 1956 he returned. With Che Guevara and others he set out on the yacht *Granma* on a secret mission to Cuba to instigate a war of liberation. At first no one believed that they had even the slightest chance, because no sooner had the revolutionaries come ashore than Batista's troops tracked them down in the mangrove swamps. Out of over eighty men, only about a dozen escaped with their lives. They fought their way through the wild mountains of the Sierra Maestra, suffering great privations, but gradually they gaining new comrades-in-arms. An American journalist had visited them in their hideout and published photos of these good-looking, deadly earnest young men in the *New York Times*. Now the *barbudos* were also the hot topic of conversation in the USA.

So as not to lose our residency visas and green cards in the United States, we spent a couple of months of each year in New York and worked, as before, at our dressmaking studio. Cuchito also cultivated many promising contacts, still hoping to establish the band there. When Ondina went to take the plane to New York via Miami in early 1957, she was confronted at the border with a new kind of difficulty. The official carefully studied her passport.

'Your name is Ondina Castro?'

'Yes, of course.'

'So you're related to Fidel?'

Ondina was baffled. 'My name *is* Castro, but I'm no relative of Fidel's. I'm Ondina Castro Zaldarriaga and not a Castro Ruz!'

The official wasn't convinced. He made Ondina wait while he dealt with her friend. Her name was Lola Guevara.

'And you are obviously related to Che Guevara. You are also denied entry.'

'I'm not related to Che either by family or by marriage. I don't even know him. It's just like here in the States,' Lola defended herself, pointing to Ondina. 'Look, you can see that she's of Chinese descent. How could she be related to Fidel?'

'So you're Chinese, eh? There's a general entry prohibition for Chinese!' The official became obstinate and sent Ondina to a special hotel where they housed people entering the United States who need further investigation.

It was common knowledge that such procedures could take several days or sometimes weeks. Flora, who had come down from New York to pick up

Previous page: Anacaona, 1958, with (from left): Olga Duchesne, Alicia, Ziomara, vocalist Berta Rodríguez, Liliana, Nena Neyra, Delia Valdés, Yolanda, Sonia Duchesne, Cuchito, Ondina and Olga Valdés

Ondina, also stayed in the hotel but, unlike Ondina, she had to pay for her room. Together they waited until the misunderstandings were cleared up. Fortunately Flora knew an American with money and influence who was able to secure Ondina's entry. I no longer remember his name, but I recall that he had once been in love with Millo. I had no problem entering the States, but a surprise did await me in New York. The day after I arrived, I happened to glimpse the front page of the *Hispano* in a Puerto Rican grocery store – 'FINALLY IN NEW YORK: THE ANACAONAS!' Our friends and acquaintances had informed the press about our arrival. Our fans wanted to put pressure on the union officials, but certain obstacles were impossible to remove. After a few days it was clear that, once again, we would have to make our money at the dressmaker's workshop.

In 1958 the band's fortunes were on the rise once again. Cuchito negotiated contracts with several impresarios, resulting in a year-long tour of South America – Brazil, Argentina and Uruguay. We had innumerable bookings to appear in big theatres, as well as on radio and television. Cuchito then hired Berta Rodríguez, a vocalist with an enchantingly husky voice whom Lázaro had discovered. When it was finally time to leave and I was saying goodbye, I had a bad feeling about it. With Fidel Castro, the rebels had managed to hold their ground in the Sierra Maestra and expand their radius of action in the eastern part of Cuba, despite vigorous pursuit by the government. Everyone was in turmoil. Did the *barbudos* really have a chance of coming to power? What did they want? Like Father, I was sometimes seized by a feeling of enthusiasm and hope that the revolutionaries might be able to implement a more just society: work for all, equal wages and so forth. Sometimes I was overcome by scepticism. Politicians had made these kinds of promises so many times and never kept them. Father still admired the philosophies of Marx and Engels, but he didn't trust all their Cuban representatives. No one could predict what the future had in store for us.

Celia Cruz with friends, Millo and Karl on the right.

It was the age of mambo and cha-cha-chá. '*Mambo en España*' ('Mambo in Spain'), '*Los Salvajes Bailan Mambo*' ('The Wild Ones Dance Mambo') and '*Mambo Mamb'í* – those were the tunes at the top of our repertoire. Jazzed-up tunes like '*Güempa*' were very popular. The special thing about the mambo is its so-called climax, during which every instrument is played as wildly and unmelodically as possible to create absolute musical chaos. 'When the Cuban composer Pérez Prado discovered he could thread every urbane noise through the needle-eye of a saxophone, he instigated a coup d'état against the sovereignty of all existing rhythms,' gushed the Colombian writer Gabriel García Márquez about the creator of 'Mambo No. 5'. Pérez Prado himself gave us many of his own arrangements when we appeared at a party in our honour in Mexico, in

1951. He had always admired us, and particularly loved the way we played and danced to his song 'Qué Rico el Mambo', 'What a Delicious Mambo'. The anarchy spread to the dance floor. Arts columnists celebrated the mambo as a union of the sensual rumba and the jerky jitterbug. In my opinion, mambo is quite similar to rumba, but while in the rumba the man and woman incessantly court each other with circling movements, in the mambo it's as if the display of courtship has gone a little out of control with leaps, turns, bends and a kind of trembling of the upper body. This music utterly transformed a person. It really was just as the title of the song promised: 'The Wild Ones Dance Mambo'. The most reserved people suddenly went crazy on the dance floor – they were on a mambo high.

I took a rather sober view of the year-long concert tour. Of course I was happy to be on stage again with my sisters, and to still be in demand over twenty years after our debut, which was a novelty in Cuba. But to do several shows a day – to spice up the mood and radiate good humour. . . we certainly had an exhausting routine ahead of us. Nevertheless, I had never been to Brazil and at our first stop, the city of Salvador da Bahia, I got the feeling that I would like the country a great deal – it seemed so familiar although everything was quite different from Cuba. In the old town I saw how here too the people celebrated their religious festivals with lots of music and dance. But the Brazilians danced in their own style, with lots of small, shuffling steps – their feet seemed to stick to the floor – and they also moved their hips more quickly and with fewer sweeping gyrations. That was their samba.

At our first performance the Brazilians watched our mambo with excitement. Apart from music, the new show also included a lot of dancing. We wore high-heeled shoes, plastic slip-on pumps with shiny metal buckles in front. These were very fashionable at the time. For 'Mambo Habanero' we stood in a line,

On our way to Brazil

took a step forwards with the rhythm, paused, took a step back, froze, then took a big step forward. Precisely at this moment, the climax of our show, Ziomara's shoe came loose and flew in a high arc into the midst of the audience. Everyone saw the shoe hit a guest on the head. 'So that's how Cuban women dance,' the promoter teased us after the show, as he treated us to one of those strong little Brazilian coffees.

The next stop was Rio de Janeiro. First we went into the studio for a week to record a long-playing record. A television show followed. Then we began our engagement at 'Fred's' – an open-air cabaret on the Copacabana. From the stage I could see the fine white sand – not quite as beautiful as the sand at Varadero, of course, but almost. The extraordinary thing about this world-famous bay is that

312

the hotels, with their bars, cafés and nightclubs, are located right on the beach. So I constantly had the azure sea in view, even during rehearsals, and could think only of going for a swim. The famous Mexican trio Los Panchos were appearing with us, and before long one of them noticed how intently we were gazing out at the Atlantic.

'Girls, have you been in the water yet?'

'No, sadly not.'

'Want to bet that you can't stay in the water for more than ten minutes?' one of them dared us. 'Whoever can't, has to buy a round!'

Ondina and I took the bet. It was August and therefore winter, but the sun was shining and it felt like summer. How difficult could it be?

'Have fun,' they shouted after us as we stormed towards the water during a break. Ave María! I had counted on the water being cold, like it sometimes is even in Cuba, but this was like pure ice water. After one minute we were back out. Ten minutes? We were already frozen stiff! On the beach the trio continued to play, but they were cracking up with laughter.

From Rio de Janeiro we took the bus south, making stops in São Paulo and Santos, until finally reaching Curitiba. I couldn't believe that I was in Brazil. The majority of the inhabitants were descendants of Polish, German, Italian, Slavonic

At Copacabana Beach

and Japanese immigrants. In the Ile-de-France, Bavaria, Matterhorn and Silver Dragon restaurants you could try specialities from every corner of Europe and Asia.

We were contracted for several weeks at one cabaret. On one of our days off we were supposed to play at an important soirée – the governor of Paraná and other prominent people of the region were expected to be there. Shortly before the performance I noticed that my saxophone wasn't working. I was flung into despair, as I didn't have a spare. A musician from the male band on the programme with us said, 'Wait until Charlie gets here, he knows how to fix things like that.' Finally, after what seemed like an age, this 'Charlie' showed up and walked right over to me. Before I knew what was happening, he took my saxophone and blew into it. I was struck dumb in horror. Never before had anyone dared to use my mouthpiece! But what could I do? He had it in his mouth already and was trying to play. Charlie looked baffled because I was staring so hard at him – he was only trying to make it work.

Finally he managed it and said with a disarming smile, 'Try it now. Go on, try it.' I had no choice but to put the same mouthpiece to my mouth. I felt quite queasy about the whole thing – but I must admit it played like a dream.

The other band played first. After that they heard us play for the first time. When we were sitting around after the show, they were full of praise. We felt flattered, returned the compliment and, inevitably, some flirting ensued. The next day several of us were standing on a balcony on the top floor of the hotel, gazing out over the city, when Berta, our vocalist, shouted happily, 'Look who's standing down there. The young man who fixed Alicia's saxophone!' It was Charlie, looking up at us without moving. Then I realized that all of us up there on the balcony were interested in this good-looking guy. 'Which one of us has he come for?' I asked myself as I peered over the ledge at him. He stayed there for a long time and finally walked on with a friendly wave. Presumably he didn't dare come into the hotel because so many women had their eye on him.

Over the next few days he came to every one of our shows at the nightclub, but just sat and listened to our music. I noticed that he often looked at me with a dreamy gaze. After the show he would go out with us to have a bite to eat. We talked and had a lot of fun, but nothing more – he was so shy.

On the third night I took the initiative and suggested that we go for a walk together on our day off. He took me to an impressive Art Deco building, the former seat of the regional government. We strolled past the imposing cathedral, which was modelled on La Seu in Barcelona. Then Charlie told me about the beautiful St Oxum, who is identical to the Virgin Mary. She was one of the three wives of Changó, the Lord of Lightning.

'In Cuba we call her Mary, Caridad, Virgin of Mercy or Ochún,' I said. We kept finding more parallels between the saints in Cuba and Brazil. In a lively shopping street, Charlie pointed out the beggars on the sidewalk who were missing an arm or a leg. Almost everyone who walked past tossed them a coin, so they accumulated quite substantial heaps of money in front of them. We strolled through that wonderful colonial city with no particular destination in mind and lost all track of time. We were in love.

The following Sunday, Charlie introduced me to his parents. They were both French and had emigrated to Brazil when Charlie was a few months old. That day he said, 'Alicia, I want to marry you and I want us to live here.' I thought about it very seriously. It was the first time for many, many years that I had fallen head over heels in love like this. But I didn't want to leave Cuchito in the lurch. I couldn't. We still had bookings in Uruguay, Chile and Argentina to fulfil. How could Cuchito go on without me? It wouldn't work. I couldn't simply surrender to my feelings, as Millo had done, and turn my life upside-down.

My heart may have desired it, but my head wouldn't allow it. Charlie understood my feelings and offered to accompany me on the rest of the tour. But I didn't want to give him any false hope. It wasn't easy when we said goodbye at the bus station. We stayed in touch; every two or three days Charlie would write me a long letter.

The newspapers were full of news about Cuba. The rebels were giving the dictator Batista and his military a hard time. Since June 1958, the unimaginable had started to happen: Fidel and Raúl Castro, Camilo Cienfuegos and Che Guevara, each with a handful of comrades-in-arms, were gradually gathering support from the people, and were threatening to overturn Batista's regime. They were advancing on Havana from the east, the west, from all sides. At every stop on our tour, people talked to us about these events. What could I tell them? I was so far away from my homeland; everything I knew came from the newspaper or the radio. The situation was baffling, because so much of what we read in the press was rubbish. They were making mountains out of molehills. One day the headlines would be: 'They have eliminated Fidel', 'They have killed Fidel.' The next day it would be: 'Fidel is alive!' In one article we read that dead bodies were lying in the streets all over Cuba. It was agonizing for us, because we hadn't received any letters from home in a long time; the postal connections were no longer functioning. I thought a lot about Father, Mother and the rest of the family. At the beginning of January we reached Porto Alegre, the modern metropolis in the south of Brazil. Suddenly it was reported on the radio that, right in the middle of the New Year's celebrations in the military city of Columbia, Batista had conceded defeat and announced his resignation. The very next morning he fled urgently – with relatives, friends and suitcases stuffed full of money – to the Dominican Republic. It was unbelievable. The revolution was won.

Then, of course, we had to run the gauntlet.

'Are you from Fidel Castro's family?' 'Is Fidel Castro a relative of yours?'

People everywhere asked the same thing.

'No, we have never met him. It's just a coincidence that our name is also Castro,' I replied day in, day out. 'No, Fidel did not send his sisters on tour!'

From Brazil we travelled on to the Uruguayan capital, Montevideo. Now that Batista had fled, the newspapers were falling over themselves to print ever more outlandish reports – stories of atrocities, articles about power struggles, the settling of old accounts, and counter-revolutionary attacks. And all that in the middle of Carnival. Despite this, the most disparate groups were organizing rallies in solidarity with Cuba. There was even a demonstration in the big park at the Plaza Independencia immediately before our performance. As we stood ready with our instruments on stage, the speaker said, 'Our brothers are being killed simply because they want to return the riches to their rightful owners, because they are fighting for economic independence and social justice. Our brothers are dying in Cuba. No one knows the number of victims...' We all had tears in our eyes.

Suddenly the master of ceremonies stepped forward: 'And now, ladies and gentlemen, here are Anacaona, the Cuban ambassadors of effervescent joy and pulsating rhythms.' I wiped the tears from my eyes and let it rip.

We were all sitting in the foyer of the Hotel del Prado when Ziomara opened the newspaper and read the news out loud:

'Today, Wednesday, the first delegation of the new revolutionary government of Cuba sets foot on the soil of Uruguay!'

Far away from our home, we suddenly saw our chance to communicate with the *barbudos*. According to the paper, the Cuban delegation would first be visiting Montevideo and then continue on through several Latin American countries. Violeta Casals, an actress and well-known moderator, was a member of the group, as was Jorge Enrique Mendoza, the editor of the newspaper *Granma*.

At the Saeta television station in Montevideo, Uruguay

Both of them had served in the revolutionary army – she as a lieutenant, he as a captain. Father Guillermo Sardiñas was also with them. The priest had joined the revolutionaries in the Sierra Maestra and had been asked to serve in Fidel's government.

'How about welcoming the delegation with the Cuban national anthem?' Ondina suggested. We all thought it was a great idea. We took a taxi to the airport at once and arrived in time to present our request to the security officials. They were friendly enough, but declined permission. 'According to protocol, during a state visit you have to play the anthem of the host country first and then that of the visitor. So you would first have to play the Uruguayan national anthem.' The national anthem of Uruguay? We didn't even know the tune. The aeroplane had landed and time was short. To hell with protocol. We set up right by the exit from the terminal, and when the delegation arrived we simply launched straight into 'La Bayamesa'. The revolutionaries were delighted. Father Sardiñas came over and gave us an extensive account of the situation in our homeland. It wasn't half as bad as we had thought. A great weight fell from our shoulders, since we could be almost certain that Father, Mother and the others were safe.

We crossed the Río de la Plata to Argentina, and in Buenos Aires we performed in the city's premier theatre, the Colón. Many famous musicians came to

At the border of Brazil and Uruguay

hear us. One evening Pelé and the entire Brazilian national soccer team showed up, and we immediately played a medley of dances from different regions of Brazil, with plenty of samba. Some fellow musicians in Bahia had given us the arrangement. As soon as we played the first notes of the song 'Brazil', the soccer players all stood up and started dancing, even on the tables. For half the evening we played nothing but samba, just for them.

Here in Argentina too the revolutionaries followed hot on our heels. The delegation we had met in Uruguay arrived in mid-March 1959. And this time Fidel himself came along. We were playing in the El Cabildo café when some Cuban reporters tracked us down. 'Fidel sent us. He wants to ask if you'd like to have dinner with the delegation.' Fidel Castro! That evening, full of excitement, we entered the room in which the government delegation was eating at a long table. There we sat side by side with the young revolutionaries in their olive-green uniforms, all of them in their mid-twenties to mid-thirties, including Captain Jorge Enrique Mendoza with his wispy beard and long, dark hair plastered down with pomade. Fidel didn't come to the dinner because he wasn't feeling well, but sent his regrets. We chatted with the guests, among them numerous journalists, the sportswriter Eddie Martin and Father Sardiñas. He told us about the days in the Sierra Maestra with the rebel farmers, whose children he had baptized.

We were flooded with offers of work and could have continued touring for months, but even in Uruguay we'd had some problems with our finances. First the promoter, Diego Ortiz, had withheld three and a half months' wages. Then Cuchito negotiated a contract with the Argentine José Barrios, who took advantage of the fact that we weren't familiar with the exchange rates of the different currencies. He also failed to mention that it was terribly cold in Chile.

It was already freezing we boarded the Transandino train from Buenos Aires

Ziomara, David and Alicia in Chile

to Santiago. We couldn't begin to imagine how cold it would be by the time we arrived! At one station before the Chilean border, our vocalist Berta was able to touch snow for the first time in her life. Even in the capital, Santiago de Chile, it was bitterly cold. At first we appeared in well-heated rooms at the Goyescas café and in the Viña del Mar casino. But then they sent us to simple dance halls in the countryside. Even the numerous barrels filled with glowing charcoal that they used as radiators were not sufficient to stave off the chill. We were miserable. Ondina and I had problems with chapped lips. Then Berta, Ziomara and Yolanda all fell ill. After a few days it all became too much for Cuchito and she called the police, because the contract had provided for quite different working conditions. Even the press reported on our predicament. The newspaper *Vistazo* said:

'*A deception in defiance of all the rules of art, perpetrated against the Cuban all-female Orquesta Anacaona, has forced the foreign ministry and Interpol to get to grips with the cha-cha-chá. In this case it's the promoters who are the villains.*'

With no solution forthcoming, we cancelled our appearances for the promoter Barrios. We briefly discussed an offer to tour Peru. Should we continue or go home? By chance Comrade Inchaustegui, the new ambassador to Chile, burst into our conversation at the Hotel Claridge and made us an offer: 'Would you like me to arrange an aeroplane for you tomorrow, and get you back to Cuba right away? I'll talk to Fidel tomorrow and ask him to send you a plane.' A reporter who went by the *nom de plume* Zurita overheard the conversation. Although he lived in Chile, he worked for the Cuban newspaper *Show*. Their front-page headline the following day read, 'FIDEL CASTRO SENDS AEROPLANE TO BRING BACK HIS DAUGHTERS'. Well, that would have been nice, but we were realistic enough and sent Emma a telegram asking her to send us money for the trip home. Then we took the steamship *Reina del Mar* back to Cuba, after almost a year away.

After a show in the Gran Torta of Bogotá, Colombia

Chapter 15
Music and Love in Times of Change

Enrique, Ziomara's boyfriend, picked us up at the harbour in Havana. While our cab driver tried to get through the crowds of porters carrying the luggage, trunks and sacks off the ship, Enrique told us about the turmoil. Before Fidel and his comrades-in-arms made their entrance into Havana, they had made a broadcast on the radio calling a general strike. 'It was terrible! People jumped into taxis and ripped out the meters and cash boxes,' he told us; the cab driver nodded. 'The mob stormed the casinos and went down the rows of slot machines, the "traganickels", breaking them open to get at the coins.' It had been just like during the coup in the thirties. Batista's police were scared to show their faces, new law enforcement officers had not yet been mobilized and criminals were quick to seize the opportunity. Looters helped themselves to whatever they could lay their hands on in clubs, offices, department stores and private villas, and no one came after them. Enrique had witnessed a lot of it because he worked as a graphic artist in the *Bohemia* newspaper building, and people in the media were exempt from the general strike. All around his workplace in the Old City everything had collapsed into chaos.

By the time we arrived these attacks were already history and Cuba was experiencing a fresh political start. In the Declaration of Havana, the revolutionaries had vowed to make fundamental changes for the poor and the farm workers, and they had actually already begun to make good on their promises. They founded cooperatives in the countryside and erected proper stone houses for the workers who lived around the factories in wooden shacks. They built schools everywhere and abolished tuition fees. Even transportation to school and university was free. Everyone who had good enough grades could go to university and study to become a doctor or an engineer. I saw Father's dreams, and those of many Cubans, finally being realized.

I was also impressed, but I found it hard to understand the change in my sister's views. Emma, the hard-line Catholic who had travelled to Rome just to see the Pope, abandoned her faith suddenly and without any warning. One Sunday morning she started removing all the countless pictures of saints, the holy figurines, rosaries, prayer books and candles from her room – including the shrine of the saints – and set about packing them up in boxes. Ada shrieked when she saw this, and we all rushed upstairs. Instead of the framed painting of Jesus and the Virgen de la Caridad, Emma had put up posters of Fidel Castro, Camilo Cienfuegos and Che Guevara. From now on her fervour was reserved for the handsome *barbudos*. She spread out the 'junk', as she now called it, on the dining-room table and gave it away piece by piece. I had my eye on a missal, bound in leather and stamped with gold. 'Emma, if you don't want this any more, I'll take it. I never go to Mass, but I'd like to have this book anyway. It's such a lovely object. When I'm sad, maybe I'll find some consolation in reading it.' I said this just so she would give it to me, but to be honest, I had never really found enough hours in the day to be sad.

For days we speculated about what could have caused Emma's radical change of heart. Gradually I learned that it all stemmed from her job at the department store. Many of Emma's colleagues there were revolutionaries from the outset. At first Emma hadn't noticed a thing, because she had never been interested in politics. But she got along well with her colleagues such as Hilda Mataloa, because they were conscientious. Hilda's fiancé belonged to the rebels. Batista had put a price on his head and hung 'wanted' posters everywhere, so Hilda had offered him and other revolutionaries shelter under her roof, even though she also had to take care of her blind mother.

Back then, Hilda wanted to talk to Emma about armed revolt, but Emma had refused to listen: 'Stop talking about such things, or they'll come and arrest you!' But after the victory of the revolution, Hilda revealed all that she had been through, and Emma began to admire her. Hilda's devotion to the revolution impressed her so much that she became convinced that the *barbudos* might actually be serious and might build a better society for Cuba.

Emma's conversion was total. Not only did she give away all her figurines of saints, but when a musician whom she suspected of sympathizing with the revolution came to visit, she would get very nervous. 'Get rid of the saints, the water glass and the flowers on the dresser!' she would order.

Even the statue of St Martín de Porras, which Celia Cruz had brought home from Peru for Mother, suddenly bothered her. This large and very delicately made figure was the centrepiece of the living room. 'For goodness' sake, why?' I asked. 'What does this statue have to do with Communism? If a person believes in a saint, it's not hurting the revolution or anyone else.'

'All this stuff in the living room makes a bad impression,' she said, clearing the dresser. She could be downright fanatical.

From then on Father would tease her about it: 'Where's our little skirt-wearing Fidel?'

One day Emma suddenly decided to donate a pearl necklace and an eighteen-carat gold Mexican bracelet decorated with a replica of the Aztec calendar stone to the revolution. She presented these valuables to the revolutionaries in full view of the entire neighbourhood as they came marching down the street with the Cuban flag, exhorting the people to donate to the new state. '*Hay que sacudir la mata*' – 'You have to shake the tree' – was their slogan. Emma wasn't the only one. The enthusiasm was contagious. Many people in our district were so taken with it all that they spontaneously stripped off their wristwatches or went to get their jewellery boxes in order to aid the revolution.

Fidel Castro was present at a soirée where Celia Cruz and her band Sonora Matancera were playing and after greeting her he asked, 'Wouldn't you like to help out with a donation?' Celia loved jewellery more than anything and she was wearing several valuable pieces at the time. Without a moment's hesitation she stripped off all her gold and handed it to Fidel. At least that's how the story was told to me.

Soon afterwards the radio reported that the revolutionary government had run out of dollars for international trade, because Batista's henchmen had emptied the treasury before the takeover and fled to Miami. The *barbudos* asked the people to turn in their dollars for pesos. Cuchito didn't have to think about it for very long. She took ten thousand dollars to the National Bank – the money we had earned on the tour in South America. It was her decision, no one pressured her to do it, and none of us tried to stop her. Like many people, Cuchito wanted the revolutionaries to continue. Che Guevara, the head of the National Bank, thanked her personally for it. They gave her a certificate of acknowledgement with his signature.

Meanwhile the nightlife of Havana was undergoing a radical shake-up. One by one, the brothels of the Old City and the harbour district closed down: no easy feat, because not all revolutionaries were angels. Enrique confided to us that the very capitanes who had been in charge of shutting them down often secretly kept some business going, and pocketed the prostitutes' earnings. They were nothing but glorified pimps. Eventually, Fidel's brother, Raúl Castro, got wind of it. He went to the police station in person and challenged the capitán, who was running around with a gun. 'Put your gun down. You're under arrest.' When the capitán showed no sign of complying, Raúl took another tack: 'If you're a man, then draw your pistol so I can have the pleasure of killing you.' That's how the story was told to Enrique anyway. Raúl Castro swept the city clean with an iron broom and closed down all the brothels. That kept him busy for a whole two months.

The cabarets were another thorn in the revolutionaries' side. They were regarded as decadent. The Sans Souci, which stood outside the city, was closed down immediately, and the military converted it into a warehouse. The Montmartre cabaret became the Moscú restaurant. The Zombie Club cabaret, in the basement to one side of the Hotel Inglaterra, was pulled down. Across the street by the fire station there were countless cabarets and they, too, were all shut down. At the Marianao beach they shut down the Havana Yacht Club, the Country Club and El Naútico. Even the Casino Nacional's time had come. When people got wind of this, all the ornaments inside suddenly disappeared. The managers in particular walked off with what they could: chandeliers, silverware, carpets, crystal glasses, oil paintings and antique furniture. The Country Club was turned into a cattle ranch and the dog track was turned into a public bicycle track. The new slogan was: 'The beaches are there for the people!' For this reason they were getting rid of the elegant clubs.

Even the *aires libres* became more accessible. The airy awnings were replaced with practical ones of sheet steel, but over the years the cafés fell into disrepair, as did parts of the Old City. The great musician Odilio Urfé became musical director of the National Culture Council after the revolution and was very committed indeed. He had ambitious plans to restore the elegant Hotel Pasaje, where our career had started all those years ago, to its former splendour and flair. But his idea found little favour among the bureaucrats. There was always something more important to attend to than the preservation of architectural jewels. And one day the Hotel Pasaje simply fell down.

Thus the revolutionaries cleaned up the swamp of sinful Havana; and thus, as a result, many popular artists and club owners turned their backs on Cuba. A few of them had certainly been supporters of Batista, but most of them just left because there were hardly any opportunities to make money. The city's nightlife collapsed. The American record companies closed down their branches in Cuba. And for the many journalists, gossip columnists and sportswriters, times became hard. My great love, Eladio Secades, was among those who left. Before emigrating to Mexico he inscribed a copy of his last book, written in 1958, to me. I never saw him again. Eventually I heard that he had died there.

Carlos Puebla was one of Ada and Echarri's close musician friends. The former mechanic regularly sang and played guitar in places like the Bodeguita del Medio, a popular club in the Old City. The walls of the narrow tavern, full of nooks and crannies, were covered with the signatures of celebrities. Carlos had often been there in the days when the crowd of bohemians went from one party to the next and finally ended up at Ada and Echarri's house, playing music into the small hours. A true *bon viveur*. At least that's how we had come to know him. Now he sang, 'Se acabó la diversion! Llegó del Comandante y mandó a parar' – 'The party is over! El Comandante has arrived and ordered the end of all that.' His change in attitude occurred as suddenly as Emma's, and we couldn't get over it. He wrote one song after another celebrating the agrarian reform, the militia and the committees defending the revolution and became immensely popular.

Ada, Echarri and Carlos Puebla, around 1960

In February of 1960 we went on tour again, this time to Colombia. We were performing in a town on the border with Venezuela when a serious crisis between Cuba and the United States shook the world. The French ship *La Coubre* had been blown up in Havana harbour. On board the ship were munitions that the Cuban government had purchased in Belgium. Fidel suspected an act of sabotage by the Americans. '*Patria o muerte*', 'Fatherland or death', was the motto with which he now denounced the USA and turned to the Soviet Union. Wild

Barranquilla, Colombia, 1960

~ **Anacaona** ~

rumours were circulating once more. In Colombia we were told that Fidel had planted the entire island with dynamite and threatened to blow it sky-high if the United States attacked.

An offer of a tour in Spain was waiting for us on our return to Havana. We were ecstatic at the prospect of being able to play in Europe again after such a long time. There was just one problem. For some reason the Spanish promoters were unable to pay for the trip in advance. Iberia Airlines insisted that we buy the tickets in Havana – and pay in dollars – but Cuchito had exchanged all our dollars at the National Bank. We were at our wits' end. Since our long-desired tour of Spain was about to slip through our fingers, I suggested to Cuchito, 'Talk to Che. Take his letter and go to the National Bank. I'm sure he will allow you to change some of your pesos back into dollars.' But Cuchito wouldn't do it; she was afraid. There was a general mood of suspicion because many musicians had defected abroad. Celia Cruz and her band Sonora Matancera, for example, went on tour to Mexico for several months and simply never came back, travelling on through to the States. Artists were interrogated extensively before leaving on foreign tours. But Cuchito was offended by the thought that anyone could suspect her of wanting to defect to another country.

'Everything is different now. It's no longer possible to simply leave the country,' our little skirt-wearing Fidel explained.

So our trip to Spain fell through. Similar things were happening to other artists. Prospects in Cuba were not so rosy, and state authorities were in charge of the few appearances available. Famous bands such as that of Enrique Jorrín, the inventor of the cha-cha-chá, and that of Antonio Arcaño, whom people called El Monarca, the monarch, had to break up – for the time being at least. Many musicians were forced to take other jobs – and so, too, were we.

Ondina set all scruples aside and returned to New York. Again she stayed with Flora and went back to sewing hems, zippers and bodices for the gowns of movie stars. Cuchito began teaching at the Fernando Carnicer music school. Ziomara found a job through Emma, working as a switchboard operator at La Filosofía department store, where Bola was already employed as a cashier. Ziomara liked the work because of the pleasant atmosphere there. Even after hours, the employees spent a lot of time together. Ziomara offered to give her colleagues conga lessons after work, at no charge, of course.

Among her colleagues were female militia members who took care of security in the department store and carefully inspected the merchandise on display, because the opponents of the revolution were setting off bombs to destabilize Havana. These young women always wore a uniform consisting of a blue blouse and olive-green trousers, and showed a lot of courage doing so, because several militia members had already been shot from passing cars. One day the El Encanto department store on Calle San Rafael suffered a bomb attack and burned to the ground. One of the saleswomen, a good friend of Emma's, died in the flames.

My brother Lenin, the baby of the family, had finished his studies to become a hydraulic engineer years before, and had searched in vain for work under Batista. Now he found a managerial position in the Ministry of Construction – it probably helped that his name, Lenin Castro, suddenly had a certain cachet. He helped build the modern housing developments in Alamar, on the east side of Havana.

Lenin often picked up Emma at work. One day she introduced him to Nancy, a militia member, beautiful, tall, blonde and athletic, who worked as a model at fashion shows in the department store. Otherwise she was a saleswoman in the menswear department and extremely popular with customers. (Men were *always* coming in to be measured by Nancy, ostensibly to find out what size they were…) Lenin immediately became besotted. Overnight he became a volleyball fan, because La Filosofía's team, led by Nancy, played several times a week. And while chatting after the match they discovered that they shared two big things in common: their passion for the revolution and their passion for target shooting. A romance blossomed! Soon they went to the altar – not in church, of course, but at one of the magnificent salons that the revolutionaries had set up for wedding ceremonies. They signed their names, exchanged rings and then Lenin surprised his wife with a wedding present: a pistol. Soon after that, private ownership of weapons, even by their supporters, was forbidden by the new government. They were only allowed to carry weapons when doing sentry duty as members of their local militias.

Emma soon moved from the department store to the Ministry for Interior Trade. Her greatest wish was to meet Fidel Castro in person. In order to pull this off, she thought up a special gift for him… Che Guevara bred German shepherds on his estate near Havana. Emma also had two German shepherds, Reina and Golfo, pedigree dogs that had been given to her in Yucatán by our friend the bandleader Arturito Núñez. Emma had the idea of mating Reina with one of Che Guevara's German shepherds – and Reina actually did become pregnant by Che's dog! Sadly all eight puppies in the first breed were stillborn, but after a second try she finally had a pair of puppies that she could present to Fidel. She would have liked to give Fidel her present in person, but obviously he had more important things to do – he was busy with the agrarian reform, the expropriation of American companies and the invasion in the Bay of Pigs for a start. Emma settled for delivering the pair of puppies to his office. Eventually she received a thank-you note; Fidel had received the gift.

That same year on 26 July the new national holiday commemorating the storming of the Moncada barracks was celebrated in grand style in eastern Cuba.

Emma travelled to Santiago to attend Fidel's speech accompanied by her friend Mercedita, who had fought with Fidel in the Sierra Maestra, and a Japanese woman, an enthusiastic supporter of the revolution, whom Mercedita had met in Moscow. Just before the holiday, a tour through the train station was organized for the visitors. Surprisingly, Fidel showed up to greet the crowd and, as fate would have it, remained standing next to Emma for a while. She asked him at once, 'Fidel, the puppies that I gave you, do you like them? How are they doing?'

'Ah, you're the one with the dogs? What's your name?'

'Emma Castro.'

'That's my sister's name too, Emma Castro.'

So Emma got talking with Fidel. Meanwhile Mercedita and their new acquaintance were standing some distance away. When Fidel noticed the lovely Japanese woman, he forgot his conversation with Emma, whistled through his teeth, and sighed dreamily, 'Uuuy! I think I'm going to have to learn Japanese.'

And what was our playboy Echarri doing during this period of violent change? His prospects could have been quite bleak. Most of his influential pals had fled to the United States or emigrated elsewhere, and in the meantime he was almost sixty and of course he hadn't saved one centavo. If he wanted to draw a pension, he desperately needed a steady job. No matter whether it was capitalism or socialism, Echarri was like a cat; he always landed on his feet. And, as so often before, a good friend helped him out, installing him at the Ministry of Construction in an office responsible for especially urgent street repairs. These were done at night so they wouldn't disrupt traffic as much.

Echarri became a sort of inspector in this department, and was responsible for processing paperwork and the inspection of construction sites. But did Echarri actually work? Not on your life! Why break the habit of a lifetime? Even in this position he didn't actually do a thing. Once in a while he would show up at a site, but that was it. And even then he always had a friend drive him.

In the end, Echarri never did learn the meaning of work. But he did bring our youngest sister 'Yolanda' together with her future husband. One day the staff of his office threw a party in the province, near Santiago de la Vega. Echarri, lazy as he was, was looking for a car and driver and talked Yolanda and her friend Dagoberto, who had a car, into coming with him. When they arrived, the party was in full swing and there was a lot of drinking going on. Panchón, Echarri's colleague and good friend, quite brazenly went right up to the new arrivals and asked Echarri about Yolanda: 'How on earth is it possible that such a beauty shows up here? Who is she? I have to meet her.'

From the first minute he laid eyes on her he was interested in Yolanda and wooed her persistently the entire evening. He was even so bold as to tell Dagoberto, 'You ought to dance with her one more time, because I'm going to drive her home!' Gradually Yolanda began to take an interest in Panchón. She actually got along well with Dagoberto, who was very striking and had a good job as an engineer in Matanzas, working directly with Che. But Dagoberto was moody. Yolanda preferred Panchón's temperament and felt more comfortable with him, even though he wasn't as well off. Better to be poor but happy, she thought. They were married in 1962. Because of the difficult work situation Yolanda then applied for a job with a big band, the newly formed Banda Provincial de Marianao.

Ziomara and Enrique were the last of the wedding boom. Enrique, who was considerably younger than Ziomara, had grown up in our neighbourhood and his parents were Galicians. He was one of the youths who used to gather in front of our house to watch us rehearse in the living room. Some time later he started courting her. He asked whether she could teach him to play percussion, but after two days Ziomara broke off the music lessons, saying Enrique had no talent at all. After that he allegedly wanted to learn to play the flute, again with Ziomara. And again she could only stand it for two days. But from then on they started going steady. Until one day Ziomara issued an ultimatum: 'Listen, either we get married or it's over.'

Why was she so resolute? Enrique was doing his military service at the time. After the Bay of Pigs invasion and the missile crisis that almost plunged the world into nuclear war, the government announced in 1962 that they were sending Cuban soldiers to train in the Soviet Union. However, married men were allowed to stay in Cuba. On the very same day, at nine in the evening, they went to the notary and sealed their bond for life. They were able to work things out so quickly because Ziomara had secretly prepared everything in advance. The next day, a Sunday, she signed her name in the guest book of the former Hilton Hotel, renamed by the revolutionaries Hotel Habana Libre: 'Free Havana'. Now that everyone had access to this luxury hotel, not just the privileged few, the newly-weds could honeymoon there at a special rate.

That evening Lenin invited them to the show at the Tropicana. But the next day at three in the afternoon they were unceremoniously put out onto the street by the hotel management – a group of important foreign visitors had arrived unexpectedly and their room was needed. So much for 'Habana Libre'. All Ziomara and Enrique could do was to shrug their shoulders, stroll through New Havana and visit the Rampa, the post-revolutionary amusement district on Calle 23. In the evening they went to a newly opened movie theatre and then ate at Monseigneur. Finally they returned home in an overcrowded bus.

Throughout these new and changeable times, music remained my life, my passion. If I needed a second profession to fall back on, it had to be in music; that was my idea. I was seized once again by my old ambition to learn the classical double bass. Even before the revolution, Roberto Sánchez, the conductor of the symphony orchestra, had put this idea in my head: 'We definitely need a woman in our orchestra. Alicia, you're ideal for it.' I wasn't afraid of playing classical music professionally. There were so many role models: Alberto Socarrás, Ernesto Lecuona and many others who devoted themselves to classical as well as popular music and mastered both genres. On several occasions I had started courses, but was always forced to break off because of tours with the band.

Before long Orestes Urfé, the great double bass player, offered his services as a teacher. He was very eager for me to join the house orchestra of the Teatro Nacional, of which he was a member. 'This is an orchestra of international stature,' Urfé assured me, and he knew what he was talking about. A renowned classical musician, Urfé had been a member of the Boston Symphony Orchestra in the early fifties.

There, he told me, the conductor kept asking him, 'Urfé, what do you think of the quality of our Boston orchestra?' That was his way of fishing for compliments.

Urfé always answered obediently, 'It is excellent, Maestro, quite excellent.' But one day he finally admitted, 'In my view the strings in Cuba play a tiny bit better.'

The conductor probably thought to himself: what a show-off. If I ever go there I'll check up on this myself. One day the Maestro was indeed invited to visit and conduct in Cuba. He instructed the orchestra to play a certain passage, then asked the musicians to stop. 'We'll take a short break. Five minutes.' He took Urfé into the dressing room with him.

'Well, Maestro?' Urfé asked expectantly.

'You're absolutely right,' he replied. 'The strings here truly are better than the ones in Boston.'

The course for studying the classical double bass at the conservatory actually lasted seven years, but Urfé compressed it into two years for me, because I had already mastered the instrument. I had gained a lot of experience of playing the double bass with a bow in the orquesta típica. When I had completed my studies, I sat the entrance examination for the Orchestra for Opera and Ballet.

Together with Urfé, I went to the Teatro Nacional, a building that stands a class of its own, hopelessly overloaded as it is with endless balustrades, ledges and windows flanked by ornate shutters. Inside the conductor, Félix Guerrero, was waiting for us, along with the best musicians in Cuba; they would be judging my performance. Before the examination, I had to play with the entire orchestra. It was the first time I had ever auditioned on my own, let alone played with a full orchestra – *let alone* one composed of musicians I'd never set eyes on before. Suddenly I did get nervous... I took a deep breath, closed my eyes and began to play.

Afterwards, the conductor announced his decision: 'Alicia, starting today, you are a member of the orchestra.' Turning to Urfé, he explained, 'The fact that you brought her here means you are absolutely sure of her abilities.' I was thrilled... It felt fantastic to have a steady job and to be able to go freely in and out of that magnificent building. Later on, I even played as a soloist of classical music on the double bass and the clarinet.

340
≈

Father, now seventy-nine years-old, was suffering from a deteriorating heart condition, so he was forced to turn over his market stall to Otto. That proved to be a risky move because Felicia, Otto's wife, began meddling in the business. She had the splendid idea that Otto should sell the shop, take the money and emigrate to the States with her. So what did our dear brother do? Without telling Father a thing, he sold the beloved shop to the first buyer. How could he do that? We were stunned and angry at Otto and determined to hold him to account. However, three days later, the government nationalized all businesses – the upshot being that, by complete fluke, our brother had pulled off an incredible deal. Father's shop, unlike so many others, had at least made a little profit when it was sold.

The doctor confirmed that Father had worked too hard all his life and was exhausted, his heart terribly strained. His health was declining to such an extent that we had to notify our sisters abroad. Millo was with Karl and their little daughter in Brazil, where Karl was working as a cameraman. He was constantly travelling because he worked for the South American production department of a German television company. Flora was still living in New York, and Ondina had been with her there for two years, she liked it so much. When she heard about Father's illness, though, she packed her bags at once.

Here in Cuba, in the meantime, the embargo imposed by the USA in 1960 was having a noticeable effect. American goods were gone, and we had a hard time getting used to the products from the Soviet Union. The Cubans in New York knew about this situation. When friends heard that Ondina was planning to go back to Cuba, they showered her with gifts to take along. One woman who worked in a ballpoint pen factory forced a thousand pens on her, to pass out to the people here. Another provided a hundred packets of razor blades. And Aida, my supervisor at the dressmaking studio on Wall Street, bought a whole Galician ham on the bone and insisted that Ondina take it with her. It was pointless to protest. Skinny Ondina set off with a huge suitcase in her right hand and the gigantic ham in her left. She took the ham onto the plane as carry-on luggage, and was pestered relentlessly by her fellow passengers, who all wanted to get their hands on the meat. 'Won't you sell me that ham?' Even in the arrivals hall at Havana airport people were shouting, 'Hello, please sell me that ham!'

'I'm not selling anything!' Ondina shot back, clutching the ham as if it were made of pure gold. It was like running the gauntlet. 'I don't care how much duty there is on it, I'll pay it. I need this ham for my family!' Ondina instantly went on the offensive with the intimidating customs officers.

One of them took a closer look at her baggage and discovered the huge number of ballpoint pens and razor blades. 'You're a smuggler!'

Ondina just looked at him, her eyes wide. The sheer quantity did make it look like a wholesale operation, but somehow she wriggled out of the jam, even though she had to pay a stiff duty on all that merchandise. Echarri, Lenin and Panchón, who picked her up at the airport, were extremely impressed when they saw her coming out of customs with the meat, and found that she also had enough razor blades and ballpoint pens for the whole of Lawton.

By the end of September 1963, after weeks of persistent negotiations with the Cuban embassy in Rio, Millo and her daughter, Ingrid, were also allowed to come to Cuba. Re-entry for Cubans living abroad had been severely restricted. The government wanted to make it impossible for those who had left the country for political reasons to visit their homeland, but this measure also affected people like Millo, who had quite different motives for leaving, and had done so long before the revolution.

Millo had almost given up hope of ever seeing Father again when, at last, the visa was issued. By the time she finally arrived at our front door, Father was already confined to his bed. She was just in time to say goodbye. One after the other we went into his bedroom. Then he lost consciousness. We took him to the hospital. 'On the day I die, I don't want you to wear black,' Father had told us. 'Think of me as if I were still alive. Make music, dance...' But when he died, we couldn't fulfil this wish. We just weren't in the mood to play music. For the first time ever, no instrument would be heard in the house for days.

Millo and Ingrid, who was now seven years old, stayed for two months. We enjoyed our time together despite the sadness. We taught Millo's daughter to read and write, as we had done before with Ada's son. Since she had grown up in the States and in Brazil, she knew only English and Portuguese, but had never had any lessons in Spanish. We wanted her to master her mother tongue properly. The child complained that every day at our house we had only rice and beans to eat. I thought to myself: she has Cuban blood, so she has to like it. We laughed a lot at her contrariness. She also complained that the water in the glasses on the dressers was stale. Whenever she was thirsty she would take a glass from the dresser. 'Dios mío, child, those are for the spirits!' Children are so direct and uncomplicated, they can really make you laugh. Maybe we were especially happy because somehow we knew that Millo and her daughter might not be able to come back for a while due to the political tensions and the complicated entry formalities; we wanted to enjoy every minute with them.

In the first years after the revolution great strides forward were made in the social sphere. As far as music was concerned, however, they were uncertain times. Son, rumba, mambo – everything seemed passé. It was the dawning of an age in which many people believed they had to use their art solely in the service of the revolution. The melodies of the new songs were Cuban, *son montuno*, *guaracha* and *guajira*, but the lyrics sounded about as exciting as a party newspaper. Songs honoured the martyrs and heroes of the revolution, the merits of the literacy campaign and our new sense of national identity. Boring they may have been, but they did have their uses: in a situation in which Cuba's David was confronting America's Goliath, they kept spirits high. After the United States severed all relations with Cuba in early January 1961, this song by Carlos Puebla could be heard on the radio:

The goddamned rats have long deliberated
And after much thinking, they broke off relations

[Chorus]
The milk that the cow gives is meant for the calf to drink. . .

And breaking off relations doesn't scare us
Because we have cannons and we have even more
And imperialism must know if it picks a fight with us
That those famous rockets aren't merely symbolic
We want to live in peace in our beloved land
But if it comes to war, nobody will stay behind

[Chorus]
The milk that the cow gives is meant for the calf to drink. . .

The new social ideals may have had their merits, but I missed the songs that were a treat for the soul, songs that dealt with love, disappointment and the hope for new joy in life. With Ada, I recalled the romantic tunes we had always heard as children and how Mother had sung them with Aunt Pepa. In terms of the public stage, they had been abandoned, but in the dining room of our house they remained as popular as ever. When Cuchito came home from her teaching at Fernando Carnicer and Ziomara dropped in after work at La Filosofiá department store, we would often sit together. Ada would pick up the guitar and sing 'Vivir Sin tus Caricias' ('Living Without Your Caresses'), 'Como Arrullo de Palmas' ('Like the Rustling of the Palms'), 'Para Adorarte' ('To Adore You'). Mother, with her grey hair held in place by combs and her body bent over with age, was transported by the songs to a different world. Ada knew a tremendous number of the old songs. 'The best present Roberto del Cueto ever gave you wasn't the diamond ring, but the guitar!' I teased Ada, about her former fiancé. We decided to try singing the way Mother and Pepa had used to do, with me taking the lead, she the harmony, and both of us playing the guitar.

Except for these joyful musical sessions, Mother seemed quite removed from everything. Even when Father died, she seemed far away in her thoughts. 'She certainly hasn't mourned very much for her husband,' the neighbours began to whisper. Of course she mourned, but I suspected she didn't want to show her pain. I did notice that she was hardly interested in family life any more, and would sit for hours by herself, sewing. Her greatest joy was the neighbourhood children. She was always making them little dresses or shirts, and during Carnival, she made costumes for the offspring of the entire area. It was as if she wanted to relive the time when she was a young mother and had all of us children around her.

'You have to watch out with all that generosity,' Father had said to her before he died, 'or else you might end up giving yourself away one day.' He was right. At one point Mother started giving away her jewellery. In her legendary dresser, she had hoarded the many gifts we had brought home with us from our tours all over the world, gifts from ex-boyfriends and admirers: rings, bracelets, expensive watches and necklaces. We had always given them to her for safekeeping. One day we noticed that the girl who played guitar in our band was wearing a new gold bracelet.

'Where did you get that?' Ondina shrieked.

'Your mother gave it to me.'

Ondina had given the gold bracelet with her name engraved on it to Mother a long time ago for safety, together with an expensive watch. The guitarist in question was barely out of the door before Ondina gave Mother a good talking-to. 'Did I ever give you permission to give that away? I entrusted you with it because I thought our valuables would be safest with you. And now look how well you're taking care of my things!' Ondina was quite beside herself. But Mother kept giving away our precious things. Stunned, we always found out a little too late that she was delighting friends and neighbours with our mementoes. It was apparently her personal interpretation of Communism. She often sat in the rocking chair on the covered veranda in front of our house. Any child could stroll by, stop and admire some ring that Mother was wearing, upon which she would instantly slip it off and give it away. Even a young brat who was doing sentry duty in the neighbourhood on behalf of the new 'Committee for the Defence of the Revolution' in order to legitimately stick her nose into everybody's business was given a silver bracelet. We were at a loss. We called a doctor to examine her and, finally, he gave us the verdict. 'Your mother is suffering from dementia.'

I sang romantic duets with Ada and we especially enjoyed it when friends and visitors were around. We would have an open house, visitors would lean back in the rocking chairs, and over canapés and cocktails they would listen to us sing of love in the manner of the Spanish noblemen – with a wink of the eye. As a young girl I thought the songs were terribly old-fashioned, but now it seemed their very age enriched them.

One day a newcomer joined us, a friend brought him along. He was a slim man with pale-brown skin, very serious and distinguished. Ezequiel Rodríguez was, like Ada, in his early fifties, and Ada and I enchanted him when we assumed the character of two lovers to sing 'Duda de Amor', 'The Doubt of Love':

[Duet]   *Don't ever doubt*
            that I was enraptured
            from the moment
            I met you

[Ada]   *But I swore to you . . .*
[Alicia]   *Certainly I have doubted it*
[Ada]   *. . . that I would be true to you*
           that I would adore you
[Alicia]   *I thought that was a lie*

[Duet]   *And that my love was yours*
           as long as I live

[Alicia]   *I doubt your love, I am unhappy*
[Ada]   *Why?*
[Alicia]   *I am yours alone until death*
[Ada]   *How horrible!*
[Alicia]   *Although your feelings are so unworthy . . .*
[Ada]   *Forgive me!*

[Duet]   *Forgive me, forgive me*

[Ada]   *The doubt…*

[Alicia]   *There will always be doubt in me*

[Ada]   *My love!*

[Alicia]   *I am yours alone until death*

[Ada]   *How horrible!*

[Alicia]   *You're wondering if I am right?*

[Ada]   *I'm thinking…*

[Alicia]   *Thinking is torture for me*

[Ada]   *Of me?*

[Alicia   *Of you*

[Ada]   *Why are you tormenting me?*

[Alicia]   *Because of your unfair behaviour*

[Duet]   *Forgive me, forgive me!*

Ezequiel became the biggest fan of our love songs. He just couldn't get enough – he called it a 'feast for the senses'. He kept thinking of new melodies that he would sing for us or teach us out of old songbooks. In this way he helped us build up an exquisite repertoire that was perfectly suited to our voices. And he knew his stuff, because he was an admirer of the *trova*, the romantic Cuban music with guitar accompaniment and spoken lyrics. He had educated himself as a musicologist, written several books and made something of a name for himself. He was eventually appointed director of the Casa de la Trova in Havana, the premier venue for performances by the *trovadores*, and insisted, 'Girls! You can't carry on like this. You have to get out of your dining room and share your songs with the world! Everyone should have the chance hear you.' He was so adamant that he promptly scheduled an appointment with the musical director of the National Culture Council in Havana, Angel Vázquez Millares. We played for him and were hired on the spot. This was November 1964.

We also included Colombian songs, *bambucos*, in our repertoire. They had come to Cuba by curious means. In 1909 the Colombian freighter *Cartagena* was towed into Havana harbour for repair after an accident of some kind. The crew members passed the time in bars and taverns. Some sailors sang in duos and trios, and their *bambucos* aroused great interest among the residents of the Regla district. The Colombian sailors in turn were fascinated by the Cuban women. When the *Cartagena* was ready to sail again, seven sailors jumped ship and stayed in Regla. The *bambucos* spread like wildfire and soon two very popular Cuban singers, Floro Zorilla and Miguel Zaballa, included them in their repertoire.

The duo Hermanas Castro

Ada and I immediately enjoyed great success, and we were invited to the big national events of the *trova*. Year after year we would travel to the festivals in Santiago, the home of many *trovadores*. There we stood on stage with our old friend María Teresa Vera and our great role models, the Hermanas Martí. It was such an honour to meet almost all the great composers and interpret-

Jazz concert at the Casa de Cultura Checa (Czech House of Culture) in Havana, 1966

At the piano: Frank Emilio Flynn

ers of the *trova* there – Elsa Valla, Eusebio Delfín, Rosendo Ruiz, Graciano Gómez and Sindo Garay, who was so old and shrivelled that his face looked like a raisin.

In Havana, the Palacio de los Capitanes Generales became a regular haunt of ours. The ornate building, the former seat of the Spanish colonial government, now housed the city museum and the director came up with the idea of us performing the dramatic spoken song while standing on the stone steps – near the statue of Columbus in the centre of the massive patio, surrounded by columns and arches. On special occasions we were asked to perform in the luxurious Hall of Mirrors, the Throne Room and the Golden Hall of the palace, amid the gilded furniture, oil paintings and the most precious pieces of porcelain.

Once again, we sisters were pushing boundaries through our music. We had always been innovative, picking up on and starting new trends. Not only did we initiate our *trova* duo and incorporate the *trova* into our performances with Anacaona, we also upheld the jazz style at a time when government officials at the state agencies were creating real obstacles against what they considered to be 'Yankee' music and, therefore, imperialistic. When the Czech embassy surprisingly arranged a jazz cycle in 1966, we girls from Anacaona were invited to play with our dear friend Frank Emilio, the best jazz pianist in Cuba.

Gradually the music scene underwent some fundamental changes. A system of fixed salaries was introduced for all musicians. As members of the orchestra we received thirty pesos per person per appearance. Four performances per month were prescribed as the quota for Anacaona, giving us a monthly salary of 120 pesos. A modest salary to be sure, but a steady one and I appreciated it, because the days of earning nothing were still fresh in my mind.

Odilio Urfé was another enthusiastic advocate of what was now called 'traditional music', which included not only *danzón*, but also *son*, jazz, rumba and mambo. He saw to it that the Septeto Nacional was reassembled, under Lázaro, and that numerous bands could continue to play – including us. But we were assigned to the state agency Ignacio Piñeiro, which was exclusively in charge of 'traditional music', while dance musicians were organized through a separate state agency. Like the Septeto Nacional, we were assigned gigs anywhere that was deemed to require 'culture'. At first we were just as disappointed by these shows as the audience must have been, as they had to remain sedately seated in long rows of chairs while we let rip; at most they could bounce along with us in their seats. At some events, the more spirited listeners might shove their chairs aside and dance, but that was very much the exception. We performed for schoolchildren, students and prisoners. We also played for pensioners! The revolutionaries had created day care centres for the elderly because, unlike in the old days, many women now had jobs and didn't know who would care for their parents. Now they took them to the 'House of the Grandparents' during the day, where they worked on crafts or went for walks. Musical activities were also part of the programme, because music is purely and simply a part of life, as essential to us Cubans as eating and drinking.

From now on I was kept very busy: I had to combine the obligations of my duo with Ada with my commitments to Anacaona, as well as playing double bass in the Orchestra for Opera and Ballet. Performances were mostly arranged in a way that avoided clashes, but whenever there was a problem I would ask Enemelio Jiménez, a friend who worked in the orchestra of Radio Progreso, to take my place in Anacaona. He bragged about being the only man in the world who played in an all-girl band.

In 1968 the word went out that they were introducing a new system of putting all musicians into categories, from A – the highest – to D. Everyone had to play to a committee, which then decided who went where. When it was our

Performing in the publishing house of El Mundo

turn, we were more nervous than when we had played for Mr Fischer in New York all those years ago, because this determined the level of our future salary. The committee was composed of twelve of the best musicians and music critics. After we performed, the chairman declared that they had found us worthy of category A. Now each of us earned 340 pesos. That was very good, because the minimum wage was 120 pesos, and a doctor made about 500. So I no longer had to do any more work on the side. Although our finances were in good shape for the first time since the revolution, we couldn't rest on our laurels. Everybody

was evaluated at regular intervals and sometimes colleagues were demoted to a lower rating.

The state agency also burdened us with a lot of bureaucracy. Ziomara took it upon herself to handle it all and had to go down to Ignacio Piñeiro as often as several times a week to take care of our paperwork, attend meetings or give interviews to the media. She did her best to represent our interests; for example, she learned that, as 'Category A' musicians, we were entitled to have assistants to carry our instruments. Ziomara pursued this repeatedly, but we never did get any help.

It wasn't enough that we performed with the band and the duo. Each year we also had to fulfil our obligations for so-called voluntary work. Everyone who worked in an office in the city was called upon to go to the country at harvest time for at least a few weeks a year. This was supposed to raise their awareness of the harsh living conditions of the rural population. The same applied to us. Emma, although now in her late fifties, insisted on being at the very front and swinging a machete during the sugar-cane harvest, at least for a few days. Later she switched to picking tomatoes. Nor did she shirk reserve training exercises at the Sports Palace. And she never missed a public demonstration, even joining in the '*Listos para Vencer*' ('Ready for Victory') campaign and a march supposed to demonstrate to the US government how ready we were to fight. In the early hours, employees poured out of the ministries. Emma marched from her workplace in the Old City to the beach of Jaimanitas, a good twenty kilometres. After that she marched with the crowd all the way back to the Old City.

Cachita and Cuchito, like most of the family, also volunteered for the tomato harvest. Or they would go to the sugar cane fields to provide the workers with refreshing beverages. Once, Cachita and Ondina discovered a more pleasant type of volunteer service: they joined a music brigade and together with actors gave free performances in the poorer districts of Havana and the countryside. Cachita played on a pianola, a portable piano. Even though there were strong young men in the brigade, none of them ever helped Cachita carry the instrument – apart from one, that is. He was the friend of Germán, the theatre director of the Ignacio Piñeiro state agency, a very elegant man. Ondina was angry that all the others paid such little heed to Cachita, and she quit the service in outrage. To this day she goes through the roof whenever we mention the volunteer services.

And where did I do my volunteer service?

~ **Anacaona** ~

In a rum factory!

I admit that I didn't seek out the hardest work, but then again I had a few health problems to deal with. An inflammation in my sinuses had become chronic and finally required surgery. I made a solemn vow to San Lázaro and prayed to him for my recovery, so that I would still be able to play clarinet and saxophone after the surgery. And he answered me. My complaints never went away completely, but I could still play.

A French colleague in the Orchestra for Opera and Ballet was the first to tell me that many opera singers were allowed to serve in the rum distillery, because the dust at harvest time was harmful to their voices. She urged me, 'Come on, Alicia! Let's go to there too. Then we can drink port every day.' We were accepted. In the factory near the Napoleonic Museum they assigned us the job of checking the rum and liqueur bottles, which stood on a long conveyor belt, and then packing them into boxes. For two weeks I made myself useful in the rum distillery from 8 a.m. to 1 p.m. It wasn't particularly strenuous work, and on top of that there really was free port for us volunteers.

Ada was very happy. Her son, Reinaldo, was twenty-five and happily married. She had a granddaughter, Ivonne, already two years old, a sunny, unusually pretty child. Reinaldo worked as a paymaster at the state hydraulic enterprise. However, shortly before a performance at the Casa de la Trova one time, we got a call: 'Reinaldo has had an accident. He's in the hospital in Campo Florido.' Ada rushed over there, but she wasn't allowed to see him. His best friend, Lázaro, told her what had happened. After work at Campo Florido, they had set off together in the official vehicle, a pickup, to Guanabo. Lázaro had suggested they go for a beer at the beach to celebrate the eve of his name day. After several drinks they

Reinaldo's wedding

drove back towards Havana. Normally Reinaldo sat in the passenger seat, but because there were many other colleagues who wanted a lift to the capital, he had climbed into the back with Lázaro. Neither of them noticed when the driver approached a roundabout much too fast. They grabbed hold of each other and together were flung from the truck and onto the pavement. Only then did they let each other go. Lázaro landed on the grass and was miraculously unharmed. He didn't have a scratch on him. But Reinaldo hit his head on the kerb and was severely injured. I don't know how many operations he had, but they were all in vain. Reinaldo died and Ada lost her only child.

I knew that I wouldn't be able to console her with words, so eventually I took Ada to Margarita, a good friend who lived a few blocks away. She was an experienced spiritualist and regularly held seances. I often consulted her about my respiratory problems. Each year Margarita celebrated, at great expense, the day of the Virgen de las Mercedes, 23 September. The Virgen de las Mercedes corresponds to the African saint Obatalá, who, as the supreme lord, created earth and humanity and is the possessor of dreams and thoughts. For this reason people also call him the 'Owner of All Heads'. Obatalá symbolizes peace, rest and justice. Margarita had set out many glasses with water and perfume on the altar in her cramped living room and had decorated it with all sorts of shiny white objects. There were silver plates, a champagne bucket and a soup tureen from the estate of Echarri's legendary brother-in-law López Serrano, who had left the country after the revolution. In among all this was a sea of white flowers such as lilies and arum. I noticed that the calm, peaceful atmosphere was doing Ada good. The visitors were all quite open with each other, and so we learned a lot about each other's troubles. It was comforting to know that many other people from the neighbourhood had also dealt with the heavy blows of fate.

Ada in her sixties

One day an elderly man, who was held in high regard by all because of his great spiritual powers and insight, brought his son along to Margarita's house. Andrés, a big, gangling man with dark, slightly wavy hair, was very pleasant company, but he looked downright despondent. This aroused my curiosity and during the course of the evening I drew him into conversation. He chatted away and told me about his divorce. His wife was making real problems, and the whole affair was proving messy and upsetting. His son in particular was bearing the brunt. I was full of sympathy for Andrés; I liked him right away. But I had come to the party with someone else, a cousin of Dalia's who played in our band, so I couldn't talk with Andrés as long as I would have liked. We made up for it later, though.

Andrés invited me on an excursion to Ernest Hemingway's house in La Vigía. After the Nobel Prize-winner moved to Idaho in 1960, his stylish Cuban

360
≈

~ **Anacaona** ~

residence was converted into a museum. Andrés had arranged for a car – no problem for him, because he worked in the administration of the state agency for rental cars. On the way to La Vigía he told me that he admired Hemingway more than anyone, because he saw Cuba with completely fresh eyes. When Andrés was studying literature, he had devoted himself extensively to the works of the great novelist. At La Vigía we entered the elegant white colonial building; while we were looking from the veranda into the room adorned with hunting trophies, Andrés told me that he planned to write scripts for television and radio. Writing was his passion, and he devoted as much free time to it as he could. We discovered that we both loved Alejo Carpentier, the great Cuban writer, whose work was inspired by the idea that Europe, America and Africa mutually influence each other and unite in classical music as well as in the popular *son* and rumba. We shared so much in common, the same interests and inspirations, that the time we spent together was a joy, pure and simple.

From then on we often took trips together to La Vigía, and my relationship with Andrés grew more intimate. When he proposed marriage to me, I seriously considered it. I was sure that we were compatible but I had reservations, especially since Andrés was more than ten years younger than me. Cachita tried to relieve me of any doubts. '*Niña!* Both my first and second husbands were much younger than me.' Well, *those* marriages weren't exactly happy, I thought to myself.

Ziomara was more convincing. 'I'm seven years older than Enrique!' The fulfilling partnership they shared encouraged me. And so, at the age of fifty-six, I decided to give marriage a go for the first time.

There was one more obstacle, though: Andrés' ex-wife. I went to a seance at Margarita's and sought advice. Margarita fell into a trance and a departed spirit warned me, 'Take care. That woman is a fireball. Make sure she doesn't find out that you're going to marry.' When Margarita awoke, she interpreted further

messages from the other side for me. She told me that Andrés's former wife knew witchcraft. No wonder, since she came from Oriente province in the far east of Cuba. Everyone knows that the Orientales are experts in matters of magic, and the women know very well how to steal a man. Margarita finally told me straight, 'You have to watch out and protect yourself, this woman will attack you.' Andrés agreed that we should make our wedding preparations in the utmost secrecy. He didn't even tell his son.

If there was going to be a wedding, I thought, then it should have all the trimmings, despite the circumstances. The state offered all sorts of privileges to those who got married and, because many things were in short supply, I took the opportunity to acquire a trousseau at a bargain price. I also bought a rose-patterned dinner service, and bedsheets and towels, to which a bride was entitled. I even conjured up shoes and some material for a wedding dress, because my sisters had managed to persuade me: 'So far none of us has exchanged rings in a long white wedding dress. So you're going to do it for all of us.' They wanted to live out a long-forgotten dream of their youth vicariously through me. Ada designed the gown, sitting day and night behind the sewing machine, while Ondina finished all the seams and hems masterfully with her fine, invisible stitches.

As with the previous weddings, we wanted to hold the celebration at home. For days we prepared croquettes, cooked chicken and shrimp, sliced the meat very thin and stirred béchamel sauce by the pot-full. We breaded three hundred croquettes and fried them in oil. For the dessert Ondina poured caramelized sugar into three square cake pans and made *tocino del cielo* – with twenty-four egg yolks, of course. I didn't invite my friends until the day before the wedding. My, were they surprised! But they all came to the party, even the pianist Frank

Prevoius page: Alicia and Andrés's wedding

~ **Anacaona** ~

Emilio and the guitarist Ñico Rojas. Andrés's ex-wife heard about it only at the last minute, so there was no way she could harm us with her magic.

Andrés and I moved into Cachita's house, only a block away from my parents' house. We agreed on everything, never quarrelled about anything important. At the same time I was still very close to my family. I was already spending a lot of time with my sisters because of our work in the band. In 1979 Anacaona celebrated its forty-seventh anniversary and a big award ceremony was organized at the América Theatre. To our joy the band for that occasion was almost complete. Millo was allowed to make her third visit home to Cuba since the victory of the revolution. It entailed great difficulties, of course, so she had to come by herself. Her husband and daughter were denied visas without explanation, but Millo was there and stood again on stage with her bongos and drums for the great event.

Professionally, things weren't going well for Andrés. His dream of making a living as a writer was receding into the distance. 'We liked your script very much, but it's not what we're looking for right now,' was the reply he got from television stations whom he approached. Many people told him that his work was outstanding, but no one would give him a job. All positions were filled.

It was 1980 and a turbulent time was dawning. Shortages of all kinds and a lack of housing were driving people crazy. Eventually, the Peruvian embassy was forcefully occupied by people who were eager to emigrate and didn't have the patience to wait any longer for their visas. Soon thousands more joined them, in the hope that their sheer number would persuade officials to let them leave the country. When the authorities eventually buckled under the pressure, there was a mass exodus. Many people, including some from our neighbourhood, went to the Peruvian embassy or even did something illegal in order to be deported. In that way they hoped to be able to arrange their emigration to the USA.

365
≈

Andrés and I had our first fight when, all of a sudden, he announced that he too wanted to go to the States. Two of his brothers were already living in Miami, and a short time ago they had invited their mother to come and visit. People over seventy were allowed to travel to see relatives in the US if all their expenses were paid in dollars. She had gone to Miami but when her visa expired and it was time to return to Cuba, her sons had prevented her, against her will. The brothers started pressuring Andrés to come to the States as well. That was the only way he would be able to see his mother.

Andrés was now seriously considering the idea of going to Miami to be with his family. I countered that I wanted to stay in Havana for the same reason. In addition, Cuchito was ill, and I was also thinking of the band. I just couldn't abandon my sisters. At another seance at Margarita's house I sought guidance. Andrés's father, whom I respected highly for his great spiritual insights, made a prophecy: 'If you go to the north, you will stay there and never come back.' That made my mind up once and for all.

Andrés, however, was ready to leave. His brother and sister-in-law visited him and said, 'So many people have managed it, leaving from the harbour at Mariel. You must try that too.' They organized everything, and when the opportunity came up – perhaps the only one he'd get – Andrés wanted to take advantage of it. He asked me one more time to come with him.

'I can't just leave Cuchito so abruptly. If I went with you to Miami, it would cause both of us great pain. You go first, then we'll see. I'll try to follow you later.' One night Andrés boarded a yacht that his brother had chartered as planned. He reached Miami in one piece, but fate was not kind to him. A few months after he arrived, his mother died. Then he wanted to return to Cuba, but that option was barred to him for ever.

I still hoped he would somehow be able to return, and I ran the household as if that would happen. Andrés, for his part, was convinced that I would eventually come to Miami, or so I gathered from his letters. But after a while I wrote to him, 'I have no idea when my situation might change and allow me to join you over there.'

Then he severed all contact.

He never answered my letters.

No doubt his brothers convinced him that I was to blame for our separation. He probably felt abandoned by me, but I felt free of any guilt – I too had a family.

Almost every family and quite a few musical bands were affected by the wave of emigration. It was heartbreaking, because we could understand people's motives for leaving and at the same time we loved our homeland. I had no idea that our band would also be affected by this dilemma. On the eve of the birthday of José Martí , our national author and hero, we gave a performance in the América Theatre. After the show we were called into the dressing room one by one. When it was my turn, a musician from the Barbarito Diez band sat down next to me and asked, 'Alicia, does one of you want to leave the country?'

I was stunned by the question. 'No. Why?'

'We've heard that someone is planning on leaving Cuba.'

'Not to my knowledge. What's going on?' I asked.

'Comrade Hilda has applied for an exit visa from the emigration authorities.'

Hilda played trumpet for us. Apparently she had officially applied to emigrate but had not said a word to us, not wishing to get us involved. The application was then forwarded to her place of employment. So now they knew.

'Didn't you get wind of this?' another man asked me.

'No. I'm hearing it from you for the first time.'

Hilda was then forbidden to play with us any more. Weeks later she left, choosing an illegal route. She, a nurse friend and a number of others made the journey in a small boat.

Both Cachita and Millo sadly died before reaching old age. Millo was living in Germany when she began having more and more trouble breathing. Her husband and daughter learned early on that she had lung cancer and her prospects were dim. In 1979 she came to Cuba several times by herself, because Karl and Ingrid could still not get visas. Each time she would feel so much better after a few weeks in the warmth – both the warmth of the climate and that of the people – that she felt rejuvenated and regained some of her strength. In January 1981 she visited us again. She had travelled alone and was already quite weak. Unforeseeable difficulties arose at customs. Millo had all her jewellery in her luggage – to this day no one knows why – everything from her gold earrings with rubies and diamonds, a gift from an admirer at the *aires libres*, to her wedding jewellery. The officers confiscated all of it, claiming she intended to sell her many mementoes on the black market. In despair, Millo defended herself, but the excitement was too much for her. She couldn't breathe and had to be taken to hospital. Three days later she died. The only consolation we had was that her final wish, to have her resting place in Havana with her parents and siblings, was fulfilled. Like all of our family, she was buried in the Colon cemetery, where the sunshine transforms the gravestones of brilliant white marble into a dazzling sea of light.

A year later a young woman suddenly appeared at our door whom I had last seen as a seven-year-old child and knew only from photos – Millo's daughter, Ingrid. I had just heated up a big pot of water and was about to pour it in the

Alicia and Ada, 1989

bathtub, when Ondina and Ada yelled something about Ingrid. I dropped the pot right on the floor in sheer surprise and joy! Ingrid told us that it was only after months of effort, by communicating through the Cuban embassy in Germany and by referring to her mother's death, that she had managed to obtain a visa to visit her relatives.

Cuchito, like Millo, also had a fragile constitution. We didn't tell her the truth when the doctor diagnosed a serious illness. It all started when we were practising in the living room one day. We had taken a break because our pianist Nereira had to go home. She also gave piano lessons on the side. 'Sure, go ahead, it's your work,' I told her. Then I said to Cuchito, 'It's already five o'clock,' thinking that she, as director, would declare the rehearsal over. But she merely opened her mouth and started shaking all over, unable to say a word. I ran to the telephone and called an ambulance. At the hospital they confirmed a thrombosis.

After Cuchito was discharged, her right hand was paralysed. But she exercised it every day with unbelievable tenacity, training herself to play guitar and saxophone again – and, incredibly, she succeeded. I let her get on with it, although I didn't know whether the exertion was really good for her. Oscar Pérez, the doctor from the neurological hospital, was astounded when he learned that she was playing music again. He offered to come to the house to examine Cuchito regularly. 'I'll gladly come over, I live nearby.' So Oscar came once a week and we became great friends.

When Cuchito suddenly grew weaker, Oscar said that her illness had developed into cancer, which was attacking her liver. No one told her anything about this, and Cuchito kept on practising every day as if things had to go on as before, no matter what. 'Relax,' I told her. 'You've made people happy with your music for so many years. Give yourself a rest until you have the strength to play again.' Eventually, exhausted, she did stop practising. Only then did the doctor manage to convince her that she shouldn't play any more.

A short time later Cuchito could no longer get out of bed. Every day she would sit up, look in the big mirror over the chest of drawers and ask, 'Alicia, do you think that I keep getting thinner?'

'No, my dear sister, no. You look just the same as before. Except for that period when you were heavier. You've often had times when you were even thinner than you are now.'

But finally she could feel that her days were numbered. She asked me to make sure she would be allowed to die at home. It was terrible; she was practically coughing her lungs up by the end. We helped her as best we could. Finally we all stood around her in silence, until she didn't move any more.

Nor did we.

Time stood still.

An eternity passed before we shook off the numbness.

And then I called Oscar.

Oscar had done so much for Cuchito. He was instantly taken by her extraordinary personality and had learned a lot about the story of our band during his visits. He liked to hear the anecdotes from the old days. Months later I invited him to dinner because of this. I took a nice rib roast out of the refrigerator. It's important to keep a fine piece of meat for special evenings, because having a good doctor for a friend is reassuring in old age, when you have to be prepared for anything. Oscar brought his wife and his colleague Adolfo along. After dinner we sat with our new friends on rocking chairs in the dining room – that tall, airy room with all the china plates on the walls – and we sisters tried to outdo each other telling stories from all the countries we'd visited over the years. After the second round of cocktails our visitors naturally started thinking of songs they would like to hear.

At that time I never would have dreamed that I myself would soon urgently need the medical assistance of our new friends, but later I had to go to the hospital because of intestinal troubles. Oscar and Adolfo worked at the newly opened Hermanos Almeijeiras hospital, an elegant skyscraper with twenty-five floors and twelve elevators which, before the revolution, had been the headquarters of the Chase Manhattan Bank. Fidel had ordered it to be remodelled into a first-class hospital; he equipped it with the latest technology and staffed it with all the best specialists. Oscar had me admitted there. The first examination brought bad news: I needed surgery and would have a temporary colostomy. I had hardly recovered before the second operation was arranged to reverse the first procedure and restore normal intestinal function. When I came out from under the anaesthetic, I was in terrible pain. A young doctor was looking after me in intensive care. I could hardly say a word and merely stammered, 'I'm in agony. On this side. And on this one too. And in my chest.' He smiled sympathetically but said nothing.

Two or three days passed before the young doctor, Dr Torres, told me what had happened. 'Forget about the pain, my dear. I had to work hard to bring you back to life. They had scarcely put you under the anaesthetic in the operating room when you stopped breathing. Your heart stopped beating.' They had to discontinue the operation.

I was very taken with Dr Torres, and he with me. He was tall, friendly and very handsome. On his second visit he told me that his parents had always been big fans of our band, from the jazz era and the time when we started at the *aires libres*. 'Soon after that I was born. And today I have you here as a patient. Now the circle is complete,' said Torres.

I felt that I was in good hands with him and the other specialists. They began subjecting me to all sorts of tests. But even these distinguished experts couldn't figure out why I had gone into cardiac arrest. The cardiologist only sighed, utterly baffled, 'It's not because of your heart; you have the heart of a fifteen-year-old girl!'

Finally Torres said in passing, 'My dear, you should go to Guanabacoa and visit a *babalao*.' Guanabacoa is the stronghold of the *babalaos*, the priests of *santería*. Lots of people go there seeking cures. 'Your illness is a hard nut to crack. Only a *babalao* can deal with it.'

I couldn't help laughing. Was this doctor and disciple of modern medicine a follower of *santería*? Gradually I noticed that there were quite a few *santeros* in the hospital, and they were among the care-givers. When a person dedicates himself as a son or daughter of a specific saint, he must wear all-white clothing from head to toe for a whole year. But party members disapproved of people openly displaying their belief in this 'superstition'. The only people who could risk going around dressed all in white from head to toe without drawing unwanted attention were hospital employees.

Two other doctors, on the other hand, Fonseca and Calderín, insisted that I have another operation. But I didn't forget Dr Torres's advice. I trusted him. Then I overheard Oscar Pérez saying to a colleague, 'If I were Alicia's relative, I'd advise her not to risk the operation.'

With that, my mind was made up. I told Fonseca and Calderín, 'No, thanks. I don't want to die on the operating table.' I was promptly released from the hospital.

Dr Torres wished me a hearty farewell. The young man gave me a big hug and said, 'I hope you'll plan a big party soon, so that you can invite me. Oscar has told me so much about your musical soirées. But don't forget to go to Guanabacoa first.'

Weeks later I had to go to the hospital to have lab tests on my blood. I was supposed to see all three doctors. After the consultation with Dr Fonseca I asked him where I could find Dr Torres. He looked at me for a moment, then said, 'He's dead, Alicia. He died of a heart attack at the Hotel Capri. He knew that he had a heart disease and took precautions. Still, death took him by surprise.'

I was speechless. It couldn't be true. I believed that at my age I was much closer to the hereafter than that vital young man. But who is able foretell his own fate?

Alicia on the clarinet, late 1970s

Chapter 16
Water for Obatalá

was discharged from hospital and was happy to have my dear friend Lázaro visit the house. We enjoyed a highball together and talked about the new developments shaking up Cuban music, and how they'd influence the entire Latin American scene. One was the advent of new romantic music, the *nueva trova*, with Silvio Rodríguez, Pablo Milanés and many other excellent singers, who had found an audience of all ages. Successful bands such as Los Van Van and Irakere had formed. They played *son*, but it was more stylized, faster, jazzier, even incorporating elements of rock. Lázaro spoke with great respect about these new interpreters, who had been educated at modern, prestigious music academies such as the Escuela Nacional de Arte. And yet he had some doubts. 'I admit that the graduates from there have achieved a very high level technically, higher than ours. But can you learn the *sabor*, the flavour of *son*, at a school? *Son* shouldn't be played with the head or intellectualized. *Sabor* is played from *inside*,' he added. 'When we're gone, there won't be any more real *son*.'

'That's true,' I agreed 'In the past we learned *son* by playing it with you and other experienced *soneros*, who would give us advice and little pointers. That way we could sense first-hand how the rhythms changed, how to give a song more spice, and how to move.' What a shame, I thought, that part of Cuba's musical heritage – the soft, harmonic *son* of our youth – was fast being forgotten.

Music rehearsal in the living room

After Cuchito's death in 1982 I had to take over leadership of the band. The job fell to me because she and I had always selected the arrangements together. Although there were only six of us sisters left, we decided to continue playing and started looking for replacements for the sadly missing instrumentalists. To our astonishment a whole string of young musicians started coming to us of their own accord. They were all very well trained but still felt that they lacked that certain something. They were looking for the capacity and inspiration to improvise, something that can only be learned through playing.

One of the youngsters who came, Dalia Rodríguez, I had already met at the Casa de la Trova. She had always showed up whenever Ada and I were playing as a duo. We taught her the fine points of conga drumming. Then a woman came to our house and introduced her two daughters, Georgia and Dorita Aguirre. They had studied at the conservatory, were good musicians and became a real asset to the band. Other new arrivals were Margarita Suárez, whom we had taught on percussion, Italian Raymat on saxophone and Mayling Selis on guitar. Together with these young colleagues we celebrated the fiftieth anniversary of Anacaona. Of course I was now over sixty-five and could easily have drawn my pension, but none of us were thinking about retiring. Many people were astonished by our energy, including the highly regarded American musicologist Peter Manuel. After his visit to Havana in 1986, he wrote:

'My friends and I – Latin music fans visiting from the United States – are trying to decide how to spend the day. The problem is that there is too much to choose from. The options are dizzying... Eventually I head off by bus for old Havana, the waterfront area dominated by colonial-era buildings, including the cathedral and the national museum, where free concerts take place. It's Saturday... The ensemble in front of the museum is performing a mixture of European light classics and Cuban nineteenth-

century salon dance pieces... As soon as they stop, I hear another band starting up in the courtyard, playing a fifties-style mambo. As I enter the courtyard, I am amazed to see that the performers consist of eight or nine rather ancient, matronly women. Several of them are wizened, stooped and bespectacled, but the music is hot, and a few couples are already dancing. "What the Fidel is going on here?" I wonder. I ask someone who the performers are, and it turns out that they are Orquesta Anacaona, the all-woman dance band formed in 1932, which is still going strong...'

I especially admired Ada's stamina, because not only was she seven years older than me, but she also had Echarri to worry about. Soon after he retired, the incorrigible carouser began to go downhill. A doctor diagnosed Parkinson's disease and soon he required constant nursing care. He spent his days in the big rocking chair on the veranda, receiving old friends and neighbours. At some

1984, tribute to the baseball legend Echarri

point Ada realized that his most frequent visitors were all Jehovah's Witnesses, and eventually Echarri revealed to us all that he had converted. At first we thought he was just pulling our leg, but then we noticed that he wasn't drinking any more. He became contemplative and we could tell from the things he said that he had distanced himself from his former ways. Had Echarri actually taken to religion? Or had the old fox merely thought: after such a self-indulgent life it can't hurt to have a few good friends in the hereafter? It doesn't really matter. He had indeed stopped drinking, but he didn't give up all his old passions. Ada caught him more than once flirting on the phone. Echarri was now merely a shadow of his former self, and older than the Devil, yet, ever the rogue, he was seducing the wife of a neighbour even shortly before he died, trying to get her to leave her husband for him.

We retired in 1989, though not entirely voluntarily. One day, at a gathering at the Ignacio Piñeiro state agency, they announced, 'Everyone over sixty has to make room for the younger generation.' We were being asked to take our final bows.

'If that's the way it is, then we'll just have to stop – and all at the same time,' we decided. I would have liked to carry on, but I didn't have any desire to argue with bureaucrats, and Ada thought that we had to call it quits sooner or later anyway. Almost immediately after she retired, she sold all her instruments except the guitar. Ondina still treasured her trumpet more than anything, but she no longer had the strength to play, she said. I'm the only one who still plays regularly, despite problems with my hearing. I play for relaxation.

A few years ago Ada and Ziomara were allowed to visit the United States for the first time since the revolution. Flora paid for the flight and the visas, which had to be purchased here in dollars. At the airport in New York, Flora and Albertico were not the only ones who came to meet them. Graciela Pérez and

With Mario Bauzá in New York, early 1990s

Mario Bauzá, the Mambo King, also showed up unexpectedly. They prepared a
moving welcome for my sisters, arranging so many parties and dinners that they
didn't have to go to a single restaurant during their entire visit. In memory of the
old days in Paris, Graciela served champagne, black beans and *boliche*, a roast
stuffed with chorizo, ham and olives. Celia Cruz was unable to make it, unfortunately, because she was filming in Hollywood at the time. But she has kept in
touch – only recently she sent greetings to us via Radio Martí. A neighbour tuned
in and came over to our house all excited. Celia had said, 'How are my friends
the Anacaonas doing?' We were quite touched.

I feel happy when former colleagues who now have a worldwide reputation
remember the years they spent with us. It's great that they are successful, that

Ada, 2000

they are able to enjoy their moment of glory. That's why we musicians practise for years, trying night after night to capture an audience. And when, without you really knowing how or why, fate is kind and you stand in a spotlight and receive applause from the crowd – it feels like justification for all the time and energy you've invested over the years. It's an incredible moment for any artist. Suddenly everyone thinks you're wonderful.

We experienced our moment of glory in New York and Paris. A few years ago, Ibrahim Ferrer, Ruben González and Omara Portuondo finally won the international recognition they had worked so many decades to achieve with the success of *The Buena Vista Social Club.* Sadly, not everyone who deserves it experiences this happiness. There are musical geniuses who never get the chance to compete with the best in the world or to show their talents. Many outstanding musicians have remained in obscurity.

Although things are quieter for us now and we live a secluded life, I don't have time to be sad. It's lovely that we still get regular visits from our niece, Ziomara and Enrique's daughter, along her two small daughters, and also from the daughter of Ada's deceased son, Reinaldo. Ivonne recently took us all by surprise. She announced that she wanted to introduce us to her great love and future husband. And who did she bring along? A superstar athlete, bristling with power and energy, somebody we all know from TV, one of the best baseball players in Cuba. He has two Olympic gold medals at home! And he's also very nice. Whether or not he'll turn out to be a hero like Echarri or not is of no concern to

Ondina, 2000

Ada. 'Why in heaven's name can't we defrost the chicken for dinner?' Those are the sort of issues that preoccupy her these days. I'd like to keep the chicken for a while. I'd rather play it safe. It's reassuring to have emergency provisions in the freezer. But Ada lobbies for eating it sooner rather than later. She is a child of the boom years, after all. 'Rice, a fried egg and the occasional deep-fried plantain is not enough for me,' she protests.

'It's up to you, Alicia. As the former bandleader you have the final say in this house. It's your responsibility to see to it that every day there's something decent to eat on the table!' Ondina exclaims, although she pretends she's not interested in food. But she wants to have her say. Fortunately she's become more amenable, partly because each day I put out a fresh glass of water for Obatalá.

'The chicken stays in the freezer. Ada will go and get some ice cubes from the house next door,' I decide. There, where she lived with Echarri right up until the end, she has a second refrigerator used just for making ice cubes. She busies herself there between errands, putting frozen cubes in plastic bags and pouring new water into the trays.

Just before noon, Ada goes to get the supplies. She packs the frozen bags in thick towels and comes strutting into the kitchen like a young mother with her first-born in her arms. I put lime juice with sugar and ice in the blender and pour the fruity slush into the glasses of rum. I feel the same sense of satisfaction and ease that we used to enjoy so much when, after a successful show at one of the cafés of the *aires libres*, everything seemed right with us and the world.

It's 12.30 p.m. on the dot. '*Salud!*' I say as I raise my glass.

'*Salud, dinero y amor,*' Ada replies – 'To health, money and love.'

Dámaso Pérez Prado and Anacaona at a party given in their honour in Mexico City, 1951.
Back row: Millo, Alicia and Nena Neyra. Middle row: Cuchito and Olga Duchesne.
Front row: Dámaso Pérez Prado.

Glossary

Aire Libre (literally: open air) Term used in Havana to refer to an open-air café on the stretch of the Paseo del Prado between the Hotel Saratoga and the Payret Theatre. The numerous cafés on this esplanade were called *Los aires libres del Prado*. Famous female orchestras such as Anacaona and Ensueño performed in these sidewalk cafés starting in the 1930s, contributing to the unique character of the place.

Areíto Musical and artistic expression of the Taíno Native Indians of Cuba, involving music (drumming in particular), dance and the ritual consumption of food, tobacco and alcoholic beverages.

Babalao Religious leaders of the Afro-Cuban religion of *santería*.

Barbudos (literally: the bearded ones) Epithet for Fidel Castro and his comrades-in-arms during the guerrilla war.

Bolero Cuban song form, a slow rhythmic ballad that combines Spanish and African elements and is often performed by vocal duos. It is different from the Spanish bolero, which reached Cuba in 1810.

China, chino Term often used as a form of endearment for a person with Asian features.

Clave An instrument consisting of two round, polished hardwood sticks and used to set the key or main rhythm of Afro-Cuban music.

Danzón Cuban instrumental music and dance form, developed in the late nineteenth century in the city of Matanzas, which was used as a vehicle for concert music. African influences in the *danzón* include the use of percussion instruments and polyrhythms. The *danzón* is danced by couples.

Guaracha Afro-Cuban genre of vocal music influenced by *son* but faster in tempo and incorporating bawdy or satirical lyrics.

Guarachera Shirt with ruffles on the sleeves, usually white, and worn with a neckerchief.

Hispaniola Name of the second largest island in the Caribbean, which is currently divided into the countries of Haiti and the Dominican Republic.

Jai alai Originally a Basque sport in which a hard rubber ball is hurled against a granite wall with great force and must be caught by the opponent with a long, curved wicker scoop strapped to one arm.

Jam session Free improvisation in jazz. Term also used in Cuba for informal get-togethers of musicians who experiment with new combinations and musical arrangements. Today in Cuba the term *descarga* (literally: 'unloading') is more commonly used.

Jitterbug Social dance which arose in the United States in the 1930s, in which couples execute acrobatic swings and lifts.

Macho (literally: man or male) Used in Cuba as a term for a son. The band-leader Frank Grillo, who became famous in the United States as 'Machito', owes his nickname to this usage. In a figurative sense *macho* means 'manly' and formerly had positive connotations. Only in recent decades has *macho* become a term for a man with an exaggerated masculine attitude.

Malecón Harbour promenade along the Havana Bay.

Maracas Hand-held rattles, usually a pair, consisting of a gourd or plastic shell filled with dried seeds.

Marímbula An instrument deriving from Africa that consists of a wooden box resonator with a hole cut in it and equipped with steel metal strips tuned to different pitches which the performer plays by plucking them with his fingers.

Orquestas típicas (literally: Folkloric orchestras) Ballroom dance ensembles that originally played *danzón* and in the nineteenth century included primarily European instruments such as the violin, acoustic bass, clarinet, trombone and the deep-keyed bugle. From the early twentieth century onwards, the *danzón* was played by bands called *charangas*. They included more violins, the flute, piano, double bass and the metal drum called timbal.

Polaco (literally: Pole or Polish person) General term for immigrants who came from any place in or near Europe like the Middle East.

Santería (literally: The way of the saints) Afro-Cuban religion that evolved from a combination of Catholic beliefs and West African religious traditions brought to the New World by African slaves.

Son The first musical genre created by Cuban performers. Today *son* is regarded in Cuba as a national symbol which blends African and Spanish traditions in a distinctive Cuban manner. Modern *son* originated in the rural eastern part of the island, in the Oriente province, and reached Havana around 1910. It was popularized in the late 1920s by septets consisting of a trumpet, guitar, tres, clave, maracas, bongos and double bass. *Son* combines different rhythmic figures (including those of the clave and the double bass) which are played within the same general tempo, thereby producing a uniquely powerful and at the same time fluid sound. It is fundamental to the creation of modern salsa dance music.

Sonero A performer of *son* music.

Tres A guitar-like Cuban instrument with strings arranged in three pairs of two, hence the name *tres* (three). A signature instrument of the Cuban *son*.

Trova Traditional popular song initially performed by street musicians (*trovadores*) that first became nationally popular at the end of the nineteenth century. It is stylistically influenced by the Italian opera and other classical genres.

Trovadores Performers of *trova* music.

Bibliography

Manuel, Peter. *Caribbean Currents: Caribbean Music from Rumba to Reggae.* Philadelphia, 1955, pp. 17—18

Secades, Elaido. *Estampas de la época.* Havana, 1941

—— *Estampas de la época. Cuentos y greguerias.* Habana, 1943

—— *Estampas de la época.* Havana, 1958

Vuillermoz, Emile. Carpentier, Alejo. *Temas de la lira y del bongó.* Edited by Emile Vuillermoz. Havana, 1994, pp. 273—8

Acknowledgements

We would like to thank Ada Castro, Ondina Castro, Ziomara Castro, Yolanda Castro, Flora González, Eduardo González, Berta Rodríguez, Pedrito Soroa, Enrique Ferreiro, Francisco 'Panchón' López, Lenin Castro, Nancy García, Karl Kummels, Frank Emilio Flynn, Lázaro Herrera, Ñico and Eva Rojas, Bert Hoffmann, Reinhard Kapfer, Günther Thönges, Christel Neumann and Cristóbal Díaz Ayala.

We recorded Alicia Castro's life history between the years 2000 and 2002. We would like to acknowledge that some of the musicians mentioned in the book – for example, Celia Cruz, who had accompanied Anacaona as a singer on a tour of Venezuela – were then still alive.

Ingrid Kummels and Manfred Schäfer

I would like to thank Sarah Castleton and Clara Farmer at Atlantic Books, and my good friend Joan Paxton, whose contributions to this edition of Anacaona were invaluable.

Ingrid Kummels

Additional information:
www.anacaona-info.de and www.anacaona-info.com
www.myspace.com/anacaonamusic